MODERN POETRY AND THE TRADITION

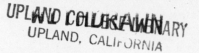
MODERN POETRY

AND

THE TRADITION

By

CLEANTH BROOKS

Chapel Hill

The University of North Carolina Press

1939

To

Allen Tate

PREFACE

EVERY POET that we read alters to some degree our total conception of poetry. Most poets, of course, modify it in only a minute degree, and we continually talk as if our conception were not modified at all. We assume that poetry is something quite fixed and absolute, a stable world in the light of which we can judge whatever particular poet is to be considered.

This is probably as it should be. If literature exists at all in any universal sense—if there are qualities shared by Homer and Webster, Keats and Auden, which allow us to compare all poetry, and rank it under a permanent standard —then it is proper that we should speak of poetry as we do. But even so, we are, as fallible human beings, constantly modifying our conception of poetry as we try to approximate the remote criterion. But most poems, as we have said, call for no major revisions. A reader brought up on Dryden may pass on to a reading of Pope with no drastic reordering of his basic conceptions. And a century ago, readers acquainted with the Romantic poets, did, as a matter of fact, see in the poetry of the Victorians something which was familiar and explicable. But from time to time poets appear, who, if they are accepted at all, demand a radical revision of the existing conception of poetry.

Of this sort are our modern poets, and herein lies the difficulty of accepting them, or, if they are accepted, the difficulty of accommodating them in the traditionally accepted

pattern. The critic whose habits were formed a generation
ago feels that they are obscure, difficult, and willfully per-
verse. His hostility toward them is based upon a perfectly
sound instinct. One cannot participate fully in the poetry
of John Crowe Ransom, for example, and continue to en-
joy Shelley on the old basis. This is not to try to enter an
act of conformity against the poets; but the matter at issue
cannot be settled by admirable tolerance and easy com-
promise. The harder-headed critic will see that he must
either condemn the modern poets in great part, or admit
them and modify his conception of poetry, and with it,
many judgments of the poetry of the past.

Critics have been faced with such a choice before in the
history of our literature. One could not participate fully
in Wordsworth's poetry while maintaining the conception
of poetry held by Pope; and one could not share Words-
worth's conception of poetry without modifying Pope's
view of the history of English poetry. To accept Words-
worth implied the acceptance of the folk ballad as poetry
on a higher level than Pope would have allowed. It im-
plied further, the appreciation of other qualities in Shake-
speare's poetry than those which Pope had found signifi-
cant. By the same token, Spenser rose in the scale along
with Thomson; Pope himself was lowered somewhat, and
with him Dryden.

The literary judgments recited are, of course, perfectly
familiar; and their familiarity testifies to the thoroughness
with which the revolutionists of the early nineteenth cen-
tury carried their point. The prevailing conception of
poetry is still primarily defined for us by the achievement
of the Romantic poets. Certainly every one-volume history
of English literature still conceives of the Romantic period
as the one, far-off, divine event toward which the whole
course of English poetry moves. The modern poetry of
our time is the first to call that view seriously in question.

The thesis frankly maintained in this study is that we are
witnessing (or perhaps have just witnessed) a critical rev-

olution of the order of the Romantic Revolt. It is only on this assumption that one can justify the space given in this study to the relation of the modern poets to the tradition. But if modern poetry does involve a critical revolution of the importance suggested, then any account of modern poetry which ignores its relation to traditional poetry will stress merely its accidental and superficial aspects. It will not succeed in making us aware of the full significance of modern poetry—probably will not succeed even in making modern poetry intelligible.

The treatment of traditional poetry in this work must obviously be sketchy and merely suggestive. No more is claimed for it; and with this statement, perhaps no further apologies for it are required. In an age when the professors of literature are largely technicians and specialists, there is all the more need for efforts at synthesis. And since the scholars, the appointed custodians of the tradition have, at least as a class, refused to attempt a new synthesis, preferring to labor at correcting the oversimplification of the last one, undoubtedly they may be depended upon to correct in good time the oversimplifications of the theory proposed here.

On the other hand, with regard to modern poetry, I can make no pretension to completeness either. The poets emphasized have been chosen because, in my mind, they provide the clearest and the most significant illustrations of our modern critical revolution. But there are others whose claim to inclusion in such a study might be powerfully urged. Ezra Pound, Wallace Stevens, Donald Davidson—to call particular names—represent only a few of the modern poets whose omission from this work is a matter of special regret. And there are still others whose claim to significance, whether or not they readily fall into the pattern argued for here, is obvious. Hart Crane, for example, possessed one of the most brilliant talents of his generation, and some of his poems are surely among the most important of our time. His omission from this study is based on

a general consideration of the clarity of the book as a whole
—not certainly on his lack of importance as a poet.

There is one further justification for limiting the list of
poets dealt with in detail. Most of the modern poets
treated herein are regarded as being excessively difficult.
This study provides, I hope, some sort of explanation for
that "difficulty." But the best defense against the charge
of unintelligibility is to submit detailed interpretations; and
detailed explanations of this sort allow for concentration on
relatively few poets.

Readers acquainted with modern criticism will find
obvious the extent to which I have borrowed from Eliot,
Tate, Empson, Yeats, Ransom, Blackmur, Richards, and
other critics. A special acknowledgement is, therefore,
hardly called for here; and such credit as I may legitimately
claim, I must claim primarily on the grounds of having pos-
sibly made a successful synthesis of other men's ideas rather
than on the originality of my own. By the same token, I
must take responsibility for what are perhaps unjustified ex-
tensions and applications of their ideas.

Some further acknowledgement, however, remains to be
made to a number of friends whose help is not indicated
specifically in the text, and who, save for mention here,
would be otherwise unacknowledged. I mention particu-
larly Robert Penn Warren and Albert Erskine, friends and
colleagues; and I should add to these the names of three
of my students, Leonard Unger, Leslie McKenzie, and
Morgan Blum.

CONTENTS

I too think of famous works where synthesis has been carried to the utmost limit possible. . . . I think of recent mathematical research, and even my ignorance can compare it with that of Newton . . . with its objective world intelligible to intellect; and I recognize that the limit itself has become a new dimension. . . . *Having bruised their hands upon that limit men, for the first time since the seventeenth century, see the world as an object of contemplation, not as something to be remade.* . . .

(William Butler Yeats, *A Vision*)

I

METAPHOR

AND THE TRADITION

MANY READERS find modern poetry difficult, and difficult in a special sense. I am thinking not so much of the person who has read little poetry of any kind as of the man who has some acquaintance with the English classics. He is apt to find the modern English and American poets bewildering, and his knowledge of nineteenth-century poetry not only does not aid him but actually seems to constitute a positive handicap. What, for example, is he to make of a poem like the following?

> Sir, no man's enemy, forgiving all
> But will his negative inversion, be prodigal:
> Send to us power and light, a sovereign touch
> Curing the intolerable neural itch,
> The exhaustion of weaning, the liar's quinsy,
> And the distortions of ingrown virginity.
> Prohibit sharply the rehearsed response
> And gradually correct the coward's stance;
> Cover in time with beams those in retreat
> That, spotted, they return though the reverse were great;
> Publish each healer that in city lives
> Or country houses at the end of drives;
> Harrow the house of the dead; look shining at
> New styles of architecture, a change of heart.*
> —W. H. Auden

If he recognizes in the phrase "a sovereign touch" a reference to the custom of the sovereign's touching for the king's

* Reprinted by permission of Random House, Inc., New York.

1

evil, he still may wonder at the poet's motive in using the phrase. To compare contemporary neuroses to a disease cured by a sovereign touch may seem overingenious, and perhaps unpleasant. Is poetry not to be sublime and elevating? Moreover, "sovereign" as used seems to come perilously near to a pun. But the pun, he knows, is the lowest form of humor; and yet, the poem is apparently a serious poem. The last line clearly demands a serious tone.

"The liar's quinsy" may also be puzzling. Why should a liar be described as a person suffering from quinsy? And why should the coward have a stance to be corrected? Is the coward being compared to an awkward athlete, and if so, why?

Moreover, the reader may feel some shock at the use of the word "spotted" in the sense of "located," "caught in the glare of the searchlight." Does not this use of "spotted" border on slang? What place does slang have in a serious poem? And what of the figure of the retreaters caught in the beam of the flashlight before they have got too far away and coaxed into coming back? Has the poet sufficiently prepared for it? Is it fair to expect the reader to grasp it at all? Or, if he does grasp it, are not the associations of such a figure out of tone in a poem which subsequent readings indicate is a prayer?

The reader brought up on nineteenth-century poetry may quite understandably conclude that the poet is writing with his tongue in his cheek, indulging in a private joke at the expense of the reader. For such a reader, the only apparent alternative is to conclude that the poet is incompetent, his own dupe.

In recent years several books have appeared which state the "common reader's" view, notably Eastman's *The Literary Mind*, Sparrow's *Sense and Poetry*, and Lucas' *The Decline and Fall of the Romantic Ideal*. Mr. Eastman is inclined, in most cases, to view the modern poet as being the dupe of his own theories; Messrs. Sparrow and Lucas, to regard him as somewhat more knowing and cynical.

But they agree in finding much modern poetry to be unintelligible and in general unaccountable under any reasonable canons of the art.

The questions raised by Auden's poem, it is interesting to notice, are primarily questions of imagery. The poet uses comparisons which the reader feels are unpleasant or difficult or both. Some readers may feel that there are more important objections, but any reader who finds the poem unsatisfactory will almost certainly question the use of imagery, and perhaps begin by questioning the imagery. Moreover, he will recognize in such imagery a characteristic trait of much of the modernist poetry which bewilders him:

> We are the eyelids of defeated caves.
> —Allen Tate

> . . . the evening is spread out against the sky
> Like a patient etherized upon a table . . .
> —T. S. Eliot

> And that a slight companionable ghost
> Wild with divinity,
> Had so lit up the whole
> Immense miraculous house,
> The Bible promised us,
> It seemed a gold-fish swimming in a bowl.
> —W. B. Yeats

What, in each case, is the poet trying to do? Such comparisons point to a mode of organization characteristic of modern poetry which to the common reader must seem illogical and puzzling. Our best point of entry into the problems raised by modern poetry would seem to lie here, in a consideration of the imagery.

If the reader objects to use of the unpleasant and the obscure in poetry, an introduction of them by way of a figure must seem doubly offensive because gratuitous. The poet is *obviously* being willfully perverse, for surely he might have chosen another metaphor. This last proposition is firmly grounded in the uncritical reader's mind. If challenged on it, he would be able to appeal to Mr. Eastman or Mr. Lucas. Or, to take a more impressive name, he might find his position stated almost as a matter of course in A. E. Housman's *The Name and Nature of Poetry*. Housman frankly says that metaphor and simile are "things inessential to poetry." Housman's account of their function will indicate why. They are frankly "accessories," for they are employed by the poet "to be helpful, to make his sense clearer or his conception more vivid"; or, they are used by the poet "for ornament"—used because the image contained possesses an "independent power to please."

It is this view of the function of metaphorical language which causes the difficulty with the comparisons in the poetry of Auden, Tate, Eliot, and Yeats which we have examined. As ornament, they demean rather than adorn. The patient etherized upon the table, for example, may be thought to have little or none of the "independent power to please," whereas Wordsworth's

> The holy time is quiet as a Nun
> Breathless with adoration

makes use of an object which has this power, an object which is exalting and "poetic." As illustration, they darken rather than illuminate. At any rate, they are too difficult— demand too much intellectual effort. Even if the emotion in Eliot's comparison were a pleasant one, the pleasant emotion would be lost in developing the parallels between the evening and the etherized patient.

If we grant these premises, then hostile critics and readers are quite right in condemning such figures. The hostile critic (who usually prides himself on being traditional) is inclined to stop discussion at this point with his appeal to the premises. But it is with the premises that we must concern ourselves if we are to understand the phenomenon of modern poetry.

Those premises are firmly embedded in the poetry of the Romantic Revolt. If we examine that poetry we shall find a rationale of the premises as well as instances of what Housman meant by "illustration" and "ornament."

The lines quoted from Wordsworth's "Beauteous Evening" are a typical instance of Romantic metaphor, and Wordsworth's prose will furnish quite explicit justifications of such metaphor. Perhaps the most explicit account of these principles is to be found in Wordsworth's famous distinction between the "fancy" and the "imagination." Modern comparisons like those of Eliot, Tate, and Yeats would have been felt by Wordsworth to be merely fanciful. The function of fancy is merely to "beguile the temporal part of our natures." The fancy trifles; the imagination is about serious business, for its function is to "incite and to support the eternal."

Notice what kind of materials Wordsworth assigns to the fancy: "Fancy does not require that the materials which she makes use of should be susceptible of change in their constitution, from her touch; and, where they admit of modification, it is enough for her purpose if it be slight, limited, and evanescent. Directly the reverse of these, are the desires and demands of the Imagination. She recoils from everything but the plastic, the pliant, and the indefinite." Wordsworth's terms are vague, but there need not be much doubt as to what Wordsworth means—particularly with the example of his own poetry to guide us. Materials which are technical, sharply realistic, definite in their details are materials to be shunned in serious poetry. They have too much stubborn angularity to be absorbed easily into the fabric of the poem. Significantly, Wordsworth avoids in his own poetry the recalcitrancy of such figures as the etherized patient and the goldfish swimming in a bowl.

How does the fancy manage to "get by" with such figures at all? By a sort of sleight of hand, Wordsworth says in effect: the quickness of the hand deceives the eye. "Fancy depends upon the rapidity . . . with which she scatters her thoughts and images; trusting that their number, and the felicity with which they are linked together, will make amends for *the want of individual value* [italics mine]." Wordsworth also offers an alternative explanation; the fancy hopes to fob off on us an intellectual interest in place of a poetic: ". . . she prides herself upon the curious subtilty and the successful elaboration with which she can detect their lurking affinities."

As Wordsworth puts it in his general summary: "In the higher poetry, an enlightened Critic chiefly looks for a reflection of the wisdom of the heart and the grandeur of the imagination. Wherever these appear, simplicity accompanies them; Magnificence herself, when legitimate, depending upon a simplicity of her own, to regulate her ornaments."

The implied antithesis to "wisdom of the heart and the grandeur of the imagination" is "subtlety of the mind and the ingenuity of the fancy." One finds, thus, in Wordsworth, warrant for the view that the play of the intellect is inimical to deep emotion. And Wordsworth also obviously supports the view that certain words and objects are intrinsically poetic—even if he did try to reincorporate in poetry "the language of men."

Coleridge condemns the ingenious and exact figure, and for the same reasons. For example, he states that certain "rhetorical caprices" of style (with reference to one of Cowley's figures) consist in "the excitement of surprise by the juxtaposition and *apparent* reconciliation of widely different or incompatible things. As when, for instance, the hills are made to reflect the image of a *voice*." Cowley's comparison, it is true, is rather trivial, but the terms which Coleridge uses show that Coleridge agrees with Wordsworth in being suspicious of the intellect. This interpretation is supported by what Coleridge goes on to say in the same passage: "Surely, no unusual taste is requisite to see clearly, that this compulsory juxtaposition is not produced by the presentation of impressive or delightful forms to the inward vision, nor by any sympathy with the modifying powers with which the genius of the poet had united and inspirited all objects of his thought; that it is therefore a species of *wit*, a pure work of the *will*, and implies a leisure and self-possession, both of thought and of feeling, incompatible with the steady fervor of a mind possessed and filled with the grandeur of its subject."

Coleridge is a much greater critic than Wordsworth, and he saw fit to correct Wordsworth on a number of points including the precise nature of the fancy and the imagination. But on the points at issue here, Coleridge and Wordsworth are in substantial agreement. Coleridge not only distrusts the ingenious or difficult figure; he seems also to concur with Wordsworth in believing that certain words and objects are intrinsically poetic, as his phrase "presentation of impressive and delightful forms" seems to imply. Certainly his "grandeur of its subject" and Wordsworth's "grandeur of the imagination" are members of the same critical family.

We think of the Romantic Revolt as being radically opposed to the whole neoclassic conception of poetry. But, in fact, the line of reasoning used by Wordsworth and Coleridge can be traced back into eighteenth-century criticism. Dr. Johnson, we may be sure, differed widely with the Romantic critics in his judgment of particular figures. But the principles which he uses to attack the figures which he does not like are precisely those which they themselves used. Housman's judgment of the function of metaphor and simile is his judgment: it must "both illustrate and ennoble the subject." A good comparison is one which is "natural and new, that which, though not obvious, is, upon its first production, acknowledged to be just." It must not be too difficult. (Apparently it would not be enough for it to prove "just" on a second or third reading.)

In further agreement, Johnson censures the too particular or too detailed figure. For Wordsworth's term "indefinite" he doubtless preferred the word "general"; but the objection is the same. "Great thoughts," he insists, "are always general, and consist in positions not limited by exceptions and in descriptions not descending to minuteness." The poet who pursues "his thoughts to the last ramification . . . loses the grandeur of generality. . . . what is little can be but pretty, and by claiming dignity becomes ridiculous. Thus all the power of description is destroyed by a scrupulous enumeration, and the force of metaphors is lost, when the mind, by the mention of particulars is turned more upon . . . that from which the illustration is drawn than that to which it is applied."

The utterance is characteristically Johnsonian. But the key phrase, "the grandeur of generality," tells us with what basic conception of metaphor we are dealing. Johnson, no less than his Romantic successors, is anxious to preserve a certain sublimity which he feels is injured by too much show of ingenuity or the use of undignified and prosaic diction.

We can trace this process of reasoning still further back into the neoclassic period. At the beginning of the century, Addison, for example, thoroughly corroborates Johnson and Wordsworth. And Addison can be made to serve a useful purpose here; for Addison can be depended upon to present the issues with a completely naked and unashamed naïveté.

The aesthetic pleasures, or, as Addison calls them in some of the *Spectator* papers, "The Pleasures of the Imagination," fall into two categories. Those of the first type "proceed from the sight of what is *Great, Uncommon,* or *Beautiful*." They are the emotions which spring from the contemplation of actual, objective experience.

The second type (and here we shall find the pleasure to be derived from poetry) "proceeds from that Action of the Mind, which compares the Ideas arising from the Original Objects, with the Ideas we receive from the Statue, Picture, Description, or Sound that represents them." Addison goes on to point out that "any Thing that is Disagreeable when look'd upon, pleases us in an apt Description. Here, there-

fore, we must inquire a new Principle of Pleasure, which is
nothing else but the Action of the Mind, which *compares*
the Ideas that arise from Words, with the Ideas that arise
from the Objects themselves. . . . For this Reason, there-
fore, the Description of a Dunghill is pleasing to the Imagi-
nation, if the Image be represented to our Minds by suitable
Expressions; tho', perhaps, this may be more properly called
the Pleasure of the Understanding than of the Fancy [i.e.,
the Imagination], because we are not so much delighted
with the Image that is contained in the Description, as with
the Aptness of the Description to excite the Image." To
put the matter briefly, Addison reasons as follows: If the
poet gives us a good description of a beautiful woman, his
reader will have a double enjoyment, participating as he
does in both the primary and the secondary pleasures of the
imagination; whereas if the poet elects to describe the
dunghill, the reader will enjoy only one, the secondary. A
mere knowledge of mathematics is sufficient to dictate the
choice. The wise poet will obviously confine himself to
objects which are "Great, Surprising, or Beautiful . . . be-
cause here we are not only delighted with *comparing* the
Representation with the Original, but are highly pleased
with the Original itself."

For Addison, the poetry obviously resides in the *poetic
quality of the materials themselves.* The good poet can do
little more than reflect these undiminished. If the poet
perversely uses unpoetic materials, there is, of course, a
pleasure to be derived from a comparison of his representa-
tion with the objects themselves; but Addison, with his
cautious gentility, hardly allows this to be an imaginative
pleasure at all: "This may be more properly called the
pleasure of the Understanding than of the Fancy." We do
not have to wrench "understanding" from its usual meaning
to hold that Addison is one of the first to damn such poetry
as being too "intellectual." Indeed, it is just this pleasure
of the understanding, says Addison, "that raises the little
Satisfaction we find in the different Sorts of false Wit." In

the greatest poetry, even "true wit" finds little place: "The Similitudes in Heroick Poets, who endeavor rather to fill the Mind with great Conceptions, than to divert it with such as are *new and surprising,* have seldom anything in them that can be called Wit [italics mine]." Addison points out that "Mr. Dryden is very sparing in it. Milton had a Genius much above it."

The "false wit" against which Addison invokes the examples of Milton and Dryden is, of course, the wit of the metaphysical poets of the early seventeenth century. Addison is summing up the indictment passed upon them in the critical revolution of some seventy years before. Poets like Dryden had purged English poetry of its conceits. The false wit of abrupt, daring imagery had been excluded in favor of a true wit which later critics tended more and more to identify with mere propriety—"What oft was thought, but ne'er so well expressed."

However jejune Addison's critical summary may seem to be, one observes that he has anticipated the two main points which his successors were to insist upon: (1) the assumption that some things are intrinsically poetic and (2) that the intellectual faculty is somehow opposed to the emotional (the poetic).

What the Augustan and Romantic critics would agree in saying about the figures of some of our moderns is easy to surmise. Addison would obviously term Hart Crane's

> The window goes blonde slowly

a prime example of false wit. Ransom's statement concerning a "painted head," that it

> Is nameless and has authored for the evil
> Historian headhunters neither book
> Nor state

would have been cited by Wordsworth as the product of the fancy, the poet priding himself on the "curious subtilty and the successful elaboration" with which he has detected the "lurking affinities" between headhunters and historians.

But such figures *would presumably have been accepted* by the poets of the early seventeenth century—by Donne, Marvell, Carew, Herbert, or by Shakespeare, Webster, and Tourneur, for that matter. Their own practice would sanction such comparisons. At the least, their practice would indicate that they did not fear being censured as too prosaic, or difficult, or daring, or fanciful, or "unpoetic." Whatever their positive standards, they were free from the negative inhibitions carefully cultivated from Dryden's time onward and now long established in the traditional account as orthodox criteria.

The significant relationship between the modernist poets and the seventeenth-century poets of wit lies here—in their common conception of the use of metaphor. Ultimately, it is not Donne's personality which has fascinated the moderns—his tortured doubts, his "monstrous ingenuities," his modern "sensous cynicism." Such descriptions make very pretty reading; and doubtless this picture of a romanticized Donne furnishes the superficial critic with the most plausible rationalization of the tremendous resurgence of interest in Donne. It does not touch the real reason for Donne's renewed importance for poets. The significant relationship is indicated by the fact that the metaphysical poets and the modernists stand opposed to both the neoclassic and Romantic poets on the issue of metaphor.

And what can be said in defense of the moderns of our day and of the metaphysical poets of the seventeenth century? First, that things are not poetic per se, and conversely, that nothing can be said to be intrinsically unpoetic. Addison's attempt to derive an intrinsic poetic quality from the materials which the poet uses, represents a retreat of the imagination—a retreat which may be traced ultimately to Hobbes. Hobbes reduced the poet from the status of *maker* to that of *copyist* by making the imagination merely the file-clerk of the memory. He would have the poet take literally the phrase "to hold the mirror up to nature." A mirror can only reflect the poetic object placed before it. But if we are to use the term mirror at all, it is rather a distortion mirror which the poet carries, or better still, a lens with which he gives a focus to experience. At all events, the emphasis must be placed on the poet's *making*. In Donne's famous comparison of the lovers to a pair of compasses, the compasses are poetic in the only sense in which objects can ever be legitimately poetic—they function integrally in a poem.

The matter of importance is not whether or not a pair of compasses possesses an "independent power to please" the reader. Presumably, a pair of compasses is about as prosaic as any object can be. But the pair of compasses in "The Valediction: Forbidding Mourning" is necessary and integral to the total effect of the poem. For those who feel that the poem is successful, the pair of compasses is sufficiently "poetic." Indeed, in this context and for the effect aimed at, a more "pleasing" object might be weakening, and thus "unpoetic."

To take another illustration, consider Andrew Marvell's "Definition of Love." Marvell, in developing the idea that the very perfection of his love for his mistress is the reason for the impossibility of their being united, compares himself and his mistress to parallel lines:

> As Lines so Loves *oblique* may well
> Themselves in every Angle greet:
> But ours so truly *Parallel,*
> Though infinite can never meet.

It is possible to argue, with the Romantics, that in this case, even if we allow that the poet has succeeded in finding a figure which will state his rather complex idea with a certain accuracy, yet he has lost his grasp on the connotations in question; that if the connotations of the figure do not actually make a ludicrous contrast with the associations appropriate to a love poem, at least they support the tone of the poem hardly at all, being dry, logical, and precise, whereas the poem ostensibly sets out to give an intensely passionate experience. This argument would then go on to question, quite logically, whether the poet had not won a Pyrrhic victory if accuracy of complex statement had been gained only at the sacrifice of every other quality demanded of a simile.

Such criticism is shortsighted, however. It neglects to consider the figure in relation to the total context, and fails to consider that a figure may be used for *contrast* as well as for comparison. In Marvell's comparison, the associations are not neglected. They are extremely important. The geometrical figure gives a sense of logical inevitability and finality to a relationship which is usually considered irrational—a sense of even mathematical order to a relationship usually considered chaotic. The diverse associations of lovers and mathematics enforce the paradox. Moreover, the contrast in associations serves a further function: throughout the poem the lover has been making the most extreme assertions about his love. He might easily be felt to protest too much—in particular if he excludes all material which may seem to contradict his hyperbole. Marvell, far from making such an exclusion here, insists on the literal rationality of his figure. He consciously faces the connotations of mathematics and does not flinch from them. The obvious clash between the associations of lovers and of mathematics is, therefore, calculated and justified.

In the second place, the play of the intellect is not necessarily hostile to depth of emotion. Wordsworth and Coleridge * are quite justified in pointing out that a light, fantastic playfulness is often served by the methods which the fancy employs. Addison shared this view. He con-

---

* In his *Use of Poetry*, Eliot says, "When it came to Donne—and Cowley—you will find that Wordsworth and Coleridge were led by the nose by Samuel Johnson; they were just as eighteenth century as anybody." Richards disagrees and reminds Eliot that Coleridge did appreciate Donne. So he did, but there is no recognizable influence of Donne on Coleridge's own poetry, nor can he be said to have led English poetry back to Donne's influence.

fines the legitimate use of mixed wit to "Epigram, or those little occasional Poems that in their own nature are nothing else but a Tissue of Epigrams [i.e., *vers de société*]." In other words, if the poet is frankly light, he may be licensed to be ingenious. This prejudice was still strong enough in our own times to cause Eliot's witty poetry to be labeled *vers de société*. But Wordsworth and Coleridge go too far in implying that only playfulness is served by the methods and materials which they assign to fancy. There are complex attitudes in which there is an interplay—even a swift interplay—of intellect and emotion; and these Romantic critics neglect the possibility that levity itself may sometimes be used to *intensify* seriousness.

One may sum up by saying that the methods and materials which Wordsworth and Coleridge confined to the fancy may sometimes be employed to attain heights of *imaginative* power. This is evidently the meaning of Eliot's comment that "the difference between imagination and fancy, in view of this poetry of wit [the poetry of Donne and his followers], is a narrow one." (I interpret Richards' remark that "Donne most often builds, in the mode of Fancy, with imaginative units formed in 'meaning's press and screw,'" as indicating that he is in substantial agreement with Eliot here.)

If the eighteenth- and nineteenth-century principles for testing the goodness of metaphor are too narrow, what is to be the test? When is a figure justified? One must not hope for a neat formulation which can be applied a priori. Indeed, it is just this a priori application of the conventional tests of simplicity and decoration which does most damage at the present time. Each figure must be dealt with separately and individually. But some of the values and functions of the radical comparison may be suggested.

Coleridge, in a passage in which he states matters in more elastic terms than in the passages previously quoted from him, says that the true poet will know intuitively "what differences of style it [the imagination] at once inspires and justifies; what intermixture of conscious volition is natural to that state." And so he will. But the modern poet will probably feel that a larger "intermixture of conscious volition" is natural than Coleridge felt was natural, and will probably regard as truly imaginative the figures which Coleridge and his nineteenth-century followers would dismiss as "mere works of the will." Moreover, with the modern poet, the value of the figure must in all cases be referred to its function in the context in which it occurs, with the recognition that the range of possible functions is wide; the figure may have a negative function as well as a positive—may serve irony as well as ennoblement. Our only test for the validity of any figure must be an appeal to the whole context in which it occurs: Does it contribute to the total effect, or not?

Most clearly of all, the metaphysical poets reveal the essentially functional character of all metaphor. We cannot remove the comparisons from their poems, as we might remove ornaments or illustrations attached to a statement, without demolishing the poems. The comparison *is* the poem in a structural sense.

And now one may consider the fundamental fallacy which underlies the Romantic and neoclassical account of the functions of figurative language. In that account, metaphor is merely subsidiary. For "to illustrate" is to illustrate something, and the illustration of a proposition implies that the proposition could be made without recourse to the illustration. Obviously, the phrase "to decorate" assumes for the decoration merely a subsidiary function. Housman, as we have seen, gives the show away by frankly regarding metaphor and simile as "accessories."

Metaphor is not to be considered, then, as the alternative of the poet, which he may elect to use or not, since he may state the matter directly and straightforwardly if he chooses. It is frequently the only means available if he is to write at all. Consider the example quoted from Marvell. If we count as part of his statement, not only the proposi-

tion in its logical paraphrase, but the qualifications which
it receives from the poet's emphasis and the poet's attitude
—obviously the "what" that is stated is stated by the meta-
phor, *and only by the metaphor.*

One need not rest upon an illustration drawn from one
of the metaphysical poets, however. Keats will easily yield
examples:

> Thou, silent form! dost tease us out of thought
> As doth eternity; . . .

What do the lines say? If we are content with a logical
paraphrase they may be summarized as follows: The urn,
though it cannot speak, prompts in us the same thought
(or lack of thought) which a meditation upon eternity may
prompt. But obviously to assume that this is all that the
lines say, or even exactly what they say, is to go very wide
of the mark. The word "tease" is tremendously important.
The metaphorical sense is complex. The poet uses the
word "tease" to imply an attitude of mischievous mockery
on the part of the urn, though he immediately qualifies the
quality of this mockery by suggesting that it is of a kind
which may be shared by eternity itself; and he qualifies it
further by reminding us that it is the kind of mockery which
is conveyed not by words but by silence. Keats here, like
all other poets, is really building a more precise sort of
language than the dictionaries contain, by playing off the
connotations and denotations of words against each other
so as to make a total statement of a great deal more ac-
curacy than is ordinarily attained.

The general point is obvious enough. We continually
remark that poets are always remaking language. But the
point is often forgotten, and it is forgetfulness that allows
us to fall into misapprehensions when we consider a vigor-
ous and even violent use of metaphor such as the meta-
physical poets or some of the modern poets furnish us.
Mere vigor of metaphor is not enough to insure success.
Many of the so-called "conceits" of the metaphysical poets

and of the moderns remain unsuccessful no matter what terms we use to describe the function of metaphor. But it is highly important to understand the fundamental function of figurative language if we are to do justice to poetry which insists upon the imaginative process, as opposed to that poetry which merely makes agreeable, high-sounding propositions, or which merely mentions "beautiful" objects.

2

WIT AND HIGH SERIOUSNESS

CRITICS LIKE Johnson and Wordsworth are inclined, as we have seen, to suspect the good faith of poets who indulge in witty comparisons. Wordsworth, thinking of poetry as a spontaneous overflow of powerful emotions, naturally distrusted the lack of spontaneity in the poets of wit. There seemed to be no overflow at all—merely an ingenious ladling out. The witty poets impressed him as lacking what Arnold was later to term "high seriousness." The phrase has become prescriptive. As the authors of a recent textbook put it: "There is plenty of room in verse for frivolity, light humor, the tongue-in-cheek attitude, but great poetry, absolute poetry, will tolerate none of these insincerities."

The necessity for high seriousness is the principle usually appealed to in order to discredit the radical poetry of the moderns, and it has a particular convenience. The critic is allowed to compliment the poets on their cleverness while at the same time denying that they are true poets at all.

Arnold's position, of course, represents no real advance over that of the Romantic critics. Arnold too believed in a poetic subject matter—that it was "an advantage to a poet to deal with a beautiful world." He dealt with such in his own poetry. He believed in poetic diction; indeed, he makes the diction of a poem one of the most important elements by which the poet's high seriousness is revealed.

But even in his making the violation of this special subject matter and diction a mark of insincerity, Arnold is fore-

shadowed by earlier critics. If Arnold states that high
seriousness "comes from absolute sincerity," one remembers
Coleridge's objection to the play of wit because it implied
"a leisure and self-possession . . . incompatible with the
steady fervor of a mind possessed and filled with the
grandeur of its subject." Arnold's high seriousness amounts
to little more than this "steady fervor."

Leisure and self-possession are attributes of the critical
intellect, and the poet for both Coleridge and Arnold is
possessed.* The divine madman must not testify against
the reality of his frenzy.

There is a sense, of course, in which Arnold and his pred-
ecessors are right. Trifling may indicate a lack of deep
feeling; and where the poet enters into a compact with his
reader to be direct, and to mean literally what he says, such
trifling is best disposed of by saying that the poet is insin-
cere. For Arnold, the poet necessarily enters into such a
compact. But the play of the intellect and the play of wit
are not incompatible with the poet's seriousness, nor with
his sincerity in implying to the reader that he means to be
taken seriously. To see this, one need only consider the
poets themselves. But one must ask a reader brought up
in the tradition of the last century to lay aside his prejudices
for the moment in considering them.

The Elizabethan and Jacobean poets will be instructive.
The Elizabethans wrote a great deal of witty verse, par-
ticularly in their sonnet sequences, some of it good, some
bad, but in any case, verse which was meant to be read as
a sort of courtly *vers de société*. John Lyly's "Cupid and
Campaspe Played" will represent very well this sort of
verse at its best.

---

* This idea probably derives ultimately from Plato. See the long
passage in the *Ion* which begins: "For all good poets . . . compose
their beautiful poems not as works of art, but because they are in-
spired and possessed. And as the Corybantian revellers when they
dance are not in their right mind, so the lyric poets are not in their
right mind when they are composing their beautiful strains. . . ."

Cupid and my Campaspe played
At cards for kisses, Cupid paid;
He stakes his quiver, bow, and arrows,
His mother's doves, and team of sparrows;
Loses them too; then, down he throws
The coral of his lip, the rose
Growing on's cheek (but none knows how);
With these, the crystal of his brow,
And then the dimple of his chin:
All these did my Campaspe win.
At last, he set her both his eyes;
She won, and Cupid blind did rise.
    O Love! has she done this to thee?
    What shall (alas!) become of me?

This is not love poetry of the type of Burns's "O my luve is like a red, red rose," and critics like Sir Sidney Lee have badly confounded matters by judging this kind of verse as an attempt at such poetry. At its best this witty poetry is arch, adroit, and graceful. The figures which it employs are often enough instruments of fancy, merely in Coleridge's use of the term "fancy." But we shall find among the Elizabethans, and to a greater extent among the poets of the seventeenth century who followed them, witty poets who use the effect of frivolous ingenuity as a means to a serious intensity. It is important to distinguish between mere *vers de société* and this other poetry with its more profound repercussions. The line of division between the two types is vague, and the poets of the period are continually crossing over it with confidence that their readers are on the alert to follow them. There are many poems, for instance, which begin frankly with a tone of *vers de société* only to deepen into something more serious. It is most important to notice that the increasing seriousness, when it occurs, is *not* accompanied by a correspondent lessening of the play of wit. Habington's "To Roses in the Bosom of Castara" begins, as the title would suggest, by striking the note of conscious and artful gallantry appropriate to an occasional poem of exaggerated compliment:

> Yee blushing Virgins happy are
> In the chaste Nunn'ry of her brests,
> For hee'd prophane so chaste a faire,
> Who ere should call them *Cupids* nests.
>
> Transplanted thus how bright yee grow;
> How rich a perfume doe yee yeeld?
> In some close garden, Cowslips so
> Are sweeter than i' th' open field.
>
> In those white cloysters live secure
> From the rude blasts of wanton breath,
> Each houre more innocent and pure,
> Till you shall wither into death.

But with the last stanza the poem has surely modulated into something else:

> Then that which living gave you roome,
> Your glorious sepulcher shall be,
> There wants no marble for a tombe,
> Whose brest hath marble beene to me.

A still more serious tone is achieved in Carew's "Ask Me No More":

> Ask me no more where *Jove* bestowes,
> When *June* is past, the fading rose:
> For in your beauties orient deep,
> These Flowers as in their causes sleep.
>
> Ask me no more whither doe stray
> The golden Atomes of the day:
> For in pure love heaven did prepare
> Those powders to inrich your hair.
>
> Ask me no more whither doth hast
> The Nightingale, when *May* is past:
> For in your sweet dividing throat
> She winters, and keeps warm her note.

Ask me no more where those starres light,
That downwards fall in dead of night:
For in your eyes they sit, and there,
Fixed, become as in their sphere.

Ask me no more if East or West,
The Phenix builds her spicy nest:
For unto you at last she flyes,
And in your fragrant bosome dies.

Here, certainly, are all the appurtenances of wit. There is
the clever ingenuity (e.g., the falling stars find in the
spheres of her eyes their proper spheres, and thus become
fixed stars with a permanent place in the universe, etc.);
there is the exaggerated compliment; there is the witty
verbal ingenuity ("orient" is used to suggest the gorgeous
splendor of the east, and the east associated with the day-
spring, and the orient where the phoenix was fabled to
live); there is even the tag of scholastic philosophy "These
Flowers as in their causes sleep." Yet the poem does give
a definite effect of seriousness—not in spite of the wit, but
by means of the wit. Without the calculated, yet grace-
ful ingenuity, the poem would be merely a trifle of glib
hyperbole. The poet's sincerity is not to be measured by
whether he believes that the nightingale really inhabits
his mistress's throat any more than it is to be measured by
his literal belief in the existence of the phoenix. The test
of his sincerity is to be measured by the integrity of tone
which the poem achieves, and this in turn, as the poem
indicates, may be achieved by ingenuity as well as sim-
plicity—by a sense of consciously artificial statement as well
as by a sense of natural statement.

The case of John Hoskins' "Absence" is somewhat more
complex. The poem begins with the lover's statement that
absence cannot estrange him from his mistress:

Absence heare my protestation
    Against thy strengthe
    Distance and lengthe,

Doe what thou canst for alteration:
    For harts of truest mettall
    Absence doth joyne, and time doth settle.

Who loves a Mistris of right quality,
    His mind hath founde
    Affections grounde
Beyond time, place, and all mortality:
    To harts that cannot vary
    Absence is present, time doth tary:

My Sences want their outward motion
    Which now within
    Reason doth win,
Redoubled by her secret notion:
    Like rich men that take pleasure
    In hidinge more than handling treasure.

But in the course of the poem, the simple defiance of the
power of absence is ingeniously developed into an argu-
ment for the positive advantages of being absent:

By absence this good means I gaine
    That I can catch her
    Where none can watch her
In some close corner of my braine:
    There I embrace and kiss her,
    And so enjoye her, and so misse her.

A superficial view might dismiss the poem as merely a
pleasant sophistry. But closer reading will show that the
development of the wit has succeeded in endowing the
poem with a sense of personal tenderness and sincerity
lacking in the more abstract opening stanzas. The ability
to be tender and, at the same time, alert and aware intel-
lectually is a complex attitude, a mature attitude, but not
necessarily a self-contradictory attitude. Only a senti-
mentalist will feel it to be so. Moreover, the tenderness is
achieved, not in spite of the wit, but through it. One has
only to remember that with later poets "close corner of my

braine" would probably have become vulgarized to "depth of my heart" in order to appreciate its importance here in dictating the particular delicacy of tone achieved.

That the use of wit to intensify seriousness was frequently conscious on the poet's part is very clearly illustrated in Donne's "Valediction: of My Name, in the Window." After arguing that his name engraved in the glass of his mistress's window will serve to remind her of him during his absence, and after a series of brilliant analogies developed from the image of the engraved name, the poet in the last stanza apparently dismisses all that he has said as merely idle speculation:

> But glasse, and lines must bee,
> No meanes our firme substantiall love to keepe;
> Neere death inflicts this lethargie,
> And this I murmure in my sleep;

The fancies in which he has indulged are merely the images of a sort of delirium—they are a mere babbling induced by approaching death. He now seems to be on the point of repudiating them in favor of a completely final word. But with the last lines

> Impute this idle talke, to that I goe,
> For dying men talke often so—

we are suddenly back on the same level with the material of the earlier stanzas. The "death" is the parting which he must endure, and far from making a retraction of the play of wit, the retraction is itself caught up into the pattern of wit.

But the effect of the repudiation-of-the-repudiation, is not to end the poem on a note of mere flippancy. On the contrary, the effect is to justify the poet's use of wit here as an adequate—and in this experience, at least, an inevitable —instrument. We may describe the effect somewhat clumsily as follows: the poet is conscious of the fantastic nature of his development of the original conceit, but having indicated his awareness of this, can only brazen out the fantasy; or, he would tell his mistress what he wishes to tell her in sober statement, not in "idle talk," if he could, but, having considered the possibility, he can, after all, make use of no better instrument than his original metaphorical language. The poem, then, may be said to carry within itself an ironical justification of the method which it employs.

Here one may pause to reflect that all the examples so far considered represent poems in which there is a considerable development of the poet's attitude, and definite, even violent, shifts in the tone of the poem.   To cite one more instance of this, Marvell's "To his Coy Mistress" represents at least two powerful shifts of tone, and a development of the poet's attitude from the frank playfulness of the opening lines into a passionately serious, though controlled, apprehension of the meaning of death.   We have said that Arnold's high seriousness is little more than Coleridge's "steady fervor of a mind . . . filled with the grandeur of its subject."   The damaging bias of this view ought now to be thoroughly apparent.   Identification of depth of sincerity with a steady fervor leaves out of account the possibility of dramatic *development* of the fervor.   It is significant that Arnold attempts to realize in his own poetry a sort of magnificent monotone.   Granting that it is one of the ways to write poetry, it does not exhaust the ways, nor does it indicate necessarily the best way.

Thus far we have considered only love poems.   The same considerations, however, apply to the religious poetry of the metaphysical poets.   This poetry will present an even more striking indictment of the belief that wit and sincerity are antithetical, for surely religious poetry imposes the most stringent requirements of sincerity.   Indeed, on the assumption that wit is inevitably bound up with an attitude of levity, we should expect the metaphysical poets to lay aside their witty devices when they undertake religious poetry.   But this is precisely what they do not do.   Unless we are prepared to count the pious rector of Bemerton and the Dean of St. Paul's, cynics, we must allow that they at least felt that wit might be employed appropriately in their most solemn poems.

To grant this is not to prove, of course, that their witty religious poems are successful in transmitting a sense of their seriousness to us as readers. Here again, one must ultimately rest his judgment on the poems themselves. To take a rather well-known example, consider Donne's "Batter My Heart, Three-Personned God," which, after a series of bold figures, ends as follows:

> . . . for I
> Except you' enthrall mee, never shall be free,
> Nor ever chaste, except you ravish me.

The application of the sexual figure to the idea of spiritual chastity is audacious, but most unprejudiced readers will experience here the charm and surprise of great poetry. Notice also that in this case the question of the poet's seriousness—whatever else may be questioned—does not arise. The same generalization may be made with regard to Herbert and Crashaw. Their failures are many and notorious. The reader who knows nothing else of metaphysical poetry, is familiar with the absurdity of Crashaw's "walking baths" and his pillow "stuffed with down of angel's wing." But even cases of admitted failure do not call in question the poet's personal sincerity; and the successes, it is important to notice, are not achieved by the poet's abandoning his characteristic method in favor of unintellectual simplicity.

Most destructive of all to the proposition that wit can never be united with seriousness is the case of poetry in which the pun, that most frivolous of the instruments of wit, contributes to serious effects. Donne's poem, "To Christ," has been much admired by critics of all schools, largely, one suggests, because of its supposed simplicity and freedom from conceits. But many critics have failed to notice the puns in the third and fifth lines of the following stanza:

> I have a sinne of feare, that when I have spunne
> My last thred, I shall perish on the shore;
> But sweare by thy selfe, that at my death, thy Sonne
> Shall shine as he shines now, and heretofore;
> And, having done that, Thou haste done,
> I feare noe more.

The second of the two is quite startling; but "Thou haste done" would have been recognized as a play on the poet's name by an age which recognized a similar play in Shakespeare's one hundred and thirty-fifth sonnet. The pun does not disfigure the poem; and it allows the poet to say "Thou hast finished" and "Thou hast me" in what is literally the same breath.

F. C. Prescott has pointed out an even more striking example of the pun in *Romeo and Juliet*. He shows that the verb "to die" was used in the seventeenth century with the meaning "to experience the consummation of the sexual act," and suggests that there is a shade of this meaning latent in

> *Juliet.* Yea, noise?—then I'll be brief. —O happy
> dagger! *[Snatching Romeo's dagger]*
> This is thy sheath; *[Stabs herself]* there rust, and let me
> die. *[Falls on Romeo's body and dies.]*

Prescott points out that the mature and thoughtful reader "will remember Shakespeare's constant word-play—sometimes coarse, sometimes poetical—in this tragedy and throughout. He will note that Romeo puns in his dying speech ('Oh, here will I set up my everlasting rest') and indeed falls with this same word 'die' as his last ('Thus with a kiss I die'). The wordplay here ceases to be mere pun or witticism and becomes highly poetical, adding greatly to the dramatic effect, though it is perhaps a little more in the Elizabethan taste than ours. Indeed the whole tragedy of love and death is summed up in this last word and corresponding last action of each of the two lovers." Prescott's observation that Shakespeare's pun "is perhaps a little more in the Elizabethan taste than ours" deserves a further comment, for it raises the whole problem with which the present book concerns itself. The historical considerations which Prescott introduces are really irrelevant here. If the wordplay is once effective and justified, then it is always justified—regardless of the period in which the play was produced. To justify it by saying that it is "in the Elizabethan taste" is gratuitous and misleading.

Some of the functions performed by devices of wit have already been indicated by the examples cited above: we have noticed the use of wit for precision (as in Donne's compass conceit or in Marvell's comparison of the lovers to parallel lines), and for concentration (as in Shakespeare's pun just referred to). One might make out a very good case for breaking over the conventional boundaries of the "poetic" for the sake of an increased psychological subtlety or for dramatic concentration of effect. But the most general and most important function of wit is that which must be termed—for want of a more accurate phrase—the ironical function.

This function too has already been dealt with by implication. It may well bear some elaboration. As long as figurative language is regarded as inessential to poetic communication—as long as one's test for good metaphor is the fact that it "both illustrates and ennobles" the subject—the immensely important function of metaphor in qualifying the poet's attitude will be slighted. To repeat what was said in the previous chapter: To "illustrate and ennoble" implies that what the poet says may be said without benefit of metaphor and that the real excuse for using metaphor is that the metaphor decorates the idea and states it more clearly. But we have argued that the poet's attitude is a highly important element of *what* is communicated; and figurative language is continually used to indicate shadings of attitude. The phrase, "to illustrate and ennoble," itself indicates some sort of realization of this function. But it allows room only for the attitude of approbation. There is no recognition of the need on occasion for an ironical function—for imagery which will do other than ennoble. It may be argued that the orthodox criticism does, however, allow room for derogatory imagery *in its proper place*—in lampoon, satire, and comedy—and that none would be quicker than Dr. Johnson himself to allow for such use of figurative language. The point is well taken. But lampoon, satire, and comedy are by implication less serious forms. Orthodox criticism hardly allows a place in *serious* poetry for ironical imagery. Most important of all, by rigorously segregating the approbative and satirical attitudes it has obscured the fact that very many, and, indeed, nearly all mature attitudes represent some sort of mingling of the approbative and the satirical. Frequently, the more complex attitudes are expressed, and necessarily expressed, in varying degrees of irony: bitter, playful, whimsical, tragic, self-inclusive, etc. To illustrate what is meant, consider the following stanzas from Yeats's "All Souls' Night":

> Horton's the first I call. He loved strange thought
> And knew that sweet extremity of pride
> That's called platonic love,
> And that to such a pitch of passion wrought
> Nothing could bring him, when his lady died,
> Anodyne for his love.
> Words were but wasted breath;
> One dear hope had he:
> The inclemency
> Of that or the next winter would be death.
>
> Two thoughts were so mixed up I could not tell
> Whether of her or God he thought the most,
> But think that his mind's eye,
> When upward turned, on one sole image fell;
> And that a slight companionable ghost
> Wild with divinity,
> Had so lit up the whole
> Immense miraculous house,
> The Bible promised us,
> It seemed a gold-fish swimming in a bowl.

The final comparison comes as a shock in this particular context. It is hardly a decorative image. But most readers who feel the shock will also sense the rightness of the figure in the total context of the poem.

It may be difficult to give specific reasons for the rightness, but speculation on the matter may touch upon such observations as these: The poet has a deep respect for his friend and means to stress his friend's passionate belief. At the same time, he does not identify himself with the belief. Horton's platonic love is after all a "sweet extremity of pride," partaking of fantastic exaggeration, though magnificent in its exaggeration. The primary shock in the comparison rests in the clash between "Immense miraculous house,/The Bible promised us" and the matter-of-fact domesticity of the goldfish bowl. But the comparison, shock and all, does justice to the various factors of the situation. If it is whimsical with a trace of irony, the whimsy grows legitimately out of what is, after all, only an accurate description of the friend's belief. The poet is aware of the element of magnificence in the belief, if at the same time aware of the fantastic element; and he has found means of letting the two elements work together in his picture of the crystal sphere of the heavens holding one golden and magnified image, "wild with divinity."

If this attempt to indicate how the poet uses his figure to qualify, to make reservations, to notice by implication "the other side" of the matter, seems too crude—if we have distorted Yeats's irony into an attitude of satire which is not intended—the commentary has at least this virtue: It indicates by its literal crudity that figurative language is the indispensable tool of the poet. There are nuances of attitude that can be given in no other way than by the aid of the qualification which the metaphor or simile produces.

The effect produced by Marvell's figure of the parallel lines may be cited here as another instance of this function. But one is not forced to rely on the metaphysical poets or on the moderns for illustration. One may find, to cite an instance from the Romantic poets, a very brilliant case of qualifying irony as used by Keats. Consider the transition from the seventh to the eighth stanzas of "The Ode to a Nightingale":

> The same that oft-times hath
> Charmed magic casements, opening on the foam
> Of perilous seas, in faery lands forlorn.
>
> Forlorn! the very word is like a bell
> To toll me back from thee to my sole self—

In the first instance, "forlorn" is being used primarily in its archaic sense of "utterly lost." The faery lands are those of a past which is remote and far away. But the meaning of "forlorn" is definitely shifted as the poet repeats the word. In its meaning, "pitiable; left desolate," "forlorn" describes the poet's own state, and applies, as he suddenly realizes in the poem, to his own case. The very adjective which is used to describe the world of the imagination which the bird symbolizes, ironically enough can be used to describe his own situation. The psychological effect is that of a man in a reverie suddenly stumbling, and being wrenched out of the reverie. The real world makes its demands; no matter how beautiful the realm of the imagination, one cannot free himself from actuality and live in the imagination permanently. Indeed, the general theme of the poem may be described as that of the following paradox: the world of the imagination offers a release from the painful world of actuality, yet at the same time it renders the world of actuality more painful by contrast. Keats's repetition of "forlorn" is thus a concentrated instance of the theme of the whole poem. Recognition of the irony makes the poem not less, but more, serious.

The foregoing account of the various uses of wit will allow us to understand more clearly the real significance of the change in taste which occurred in the middle of the seventeenth century. For the really important effect of the change was to play down the importance of qualifying irony. That this is true we shall see by re-examining the critical revolution of this period. It was an aspect of the general codifying process of the mid-century, a process carried on with the best of intentions under the auspices of rationalism and the new science, and backed by the authority of Hobbes with his simplified picture of the mind. Primary emphasis was placed upon analysis and classification. There was a tendency to departmentalize the mind, separating into neat categories the emotional and the intellectual, the serious and the frivolous, the dignified and the mean, the "poetic" and the "nonpoetic." Moreover, not only was there a tendency toward distinction and separation but toward segregation as well. The tendency of the period toward "order" had, in literature, far more important effects than that of making the closed heroic couplet *de rigueur*. It tended to remove the conflict of opposites which is the very life of metaphysical poetry.

The effect was pervasive, but it expresses itself most clearly in the treatment of metaphor. Hobbes is willing, of course, to allow metaphor a place in poetry (as he is willing, indeed, to allow a place to poetry itself). But the function of metaphor is conceived of as unimportant. Metaphor is essentially linked with absurdity, even in common expressions: "For though it be lawful to say, for example, in common speech, *the way goeth, or leadeth hither, or thither, the proverb says this or that,* whereas ways cannot go, nor proverbs speak; Yet in reckoning, and seeking of truth, such speeches are not to be admitted." It is Hobbes's constant concern in the *Leviathan* to point out that in "all rigorous search of truth, judgment does all, except sometimes the understanding have need to be opened by some apt similitude . . . [Hobbes's own metaphor here is obscure; presumably he means that metaphor may be used to stimulate the mind to come to serious grips with the problem.] But for metaphors, they are in this case utterly excluded. For seeing they openly profess deceit: to admit them into counsel, or reasoning, were manifest folly."

No one will object to Hobbes's attempt to remove the poetry from scientific discourse. But if metaphor is not to be used in such discourse, where is it properly used, and what function is it to perform? Hobbes makes a fourfold division of the uses of speech. One and two deal with scientific aspects, three with practical. Plainly poetry falls under the fourth use which is "to please and delight ourselves and others, by *playing with our words,* for *pleasure or ornament, innocently* [italics mine]." The function allowed metaphor is all too plain.

If we inspect Hobbes's literary criticism we shall find that metaphor never loses this taint of extravagance and unreliability. The extravagance must be curbed by judgment, particularly in more serious poetry.

What was apparently the Jacobean and Elizabethan view of the problem has received a powerful restatement in our own day in the view that the poet, the imaginative man, has his particular value in his superior power to reconcile the irrelevant or apparently warring elements of experience. As Eliot has put it, "When a poet's mind is perfectly equipped for its work, it is constantly amalgamating disparate experience; the ordinary man's experience is chaotic, irregular, fragmentary. The latter falls in love, or reads Spinoza, and these two experiences have nothing to do with each other, or with the noise of the typewriter or the smell of cooking; in the mind of the poet these experiences are always forming new wholes." Or to quote from another modern critic, Richards has contrasted the poet with the ordinary man thus: ". . . the ordinary man suppresses ninetenths of his impulses, because he is incapable of managing them without confusion. He goes about in blinkers because what he would otherwise see would upset him."

The neoclassic poets were apparently far more modest in their ambitions than the Elizabethans. The weight of

Hobbes, their foremost aesthetician, was definitely in favor of the ordinary man. For the imaginative act of fusing what in ordinary experience is inharmonious, the Hobbesian poet tended to substitute the rational act of sorting out the discordant and removing it from the context.

The critics of the period talk as if they were the first in English to insist on decorum. But obviously the Elizabethan and Jacobean poets had a decorum too; theirs, however, was an imaginative decorum as opposed to the essentially *logical* decorum of the Restoration. Hobbes and the members of the Royal Society were thinking primarily of expository prose, of course, when they thundered against the general unreliability of metaphor, for even the tamest metaphor involves some violation of science. But it is not easy for a writer to keep his right hand from knowing what his left hand is doing. In squeezing the poetry out of science, some of the poetry was squeezed out of poetry itself.

Confusion on the point was made all the easier by the didactic theory of poetry which the critics of the period had inherited from the Renaissance. A poem was conceived of as essentially a statement; the test of the statement's value, its truth; and the success of the poet, his success as an expositor. The poet of course differed from the scientist or moralist in that the truths which he had to impart were less sublunary, less urgently practical, and in that he might decorate his information with pleasing imagery and harmonious sound. But the implication was clear that the imagery and the metrics were to give an absolute pleasure in themselves. They do bear a relation to what is said in the poem: they may render it more agreeable to the reader by their capacity to give pleasure. But this is a very different conception of the function of imagery and meter from that which holds that they actually determine what is said by the poem. It is no accident that the neoclassic poets reprehend Donne, not only for his difficult imagery, but also for his rough verse.

When we conceive of the poet as primarily the expositor, the character of the imagery is predetermined. And here we come—to indicate how little the Romantic Revolt altered the essentially Hobbesian conception—upon the basis of Matthew Arnold's high seriousness. A serious expositor, one who endeavors to state "high poetic truth," will use clear illustrations and illustrations which dignify and heighten; he will not indulge in fanciful playfulness; he will not leave the reader in doubt as to what he means; his attitude will be relatively simple. Quite naturally, Arnold's high seriousness is a function of the poet's sincerity—for the poet is a teacher.

The first critical revolution in modern English poetry, then, may be described as a *simplification* of poetry—a simplification, not primarily of the ideas expressed, but rather a simplification of the poet's attitude toward his material. Dryden's famous stricture on Donne will illustrate. Dryden objected to Donne's love poems because he "perplexes the minds of the fair sex with nice speculations of philosophy, when he should engage their hearts, and entertain them with the softnesses of love." This is to state the fault as that of an inappropriate intellectual difficulty. But there is further the clear implication that, whereas there might be legitimate difficulty in a theological or political poem, there is surely no conceivable justification for difficulty in a love poem. Moreover, Dryden goes on to imply that if you persist with the difficulty, using it not ignorantly but with full consciousness, the fair sex might properly doubt whether you were serious about the love after all.

It is this same objection, basically, that is raised by such a poem as, to cite a modern example, John Crowe Ransom's brilliant "Captain Carpenter." Captain Carpenter resolutely engages in combat with the forces of hell, only to be regularly defeated, and to lose in combat various pieces of his anatomy until there is left only the tongue to shout defiance. The irony in the poem is anything but a matter of simple contrasts and adjustments. To notice specifically only two or three facets of the poet's attitude: there is abundant sense of the Captain's bluster:

> Captain Carpenter mounted up one day
> And rode straightway into a stranger rogue
> That looked unchristian but be that as it may
> The Captain did not wait upon prologue.

But there is also definitely the sense that Captain Carpenter has been betrayed. According to all the stories the Captain should win, but his enemies perversely refuse to abide by the conventional formulae:

> Their strokes and counters whistled in the wind
> I wish he had delivered half his blows
> But where she should have made off like a hind
> The bitch bit off his arms at the elbows.

The poet does not conceal Captain Carpenter's ridiculous bravado:

> I heard him asking in the grimmest tone
> If any enemy yet there was to fight?

Yet Captain Carpenter is allowed to have at least a suggestion of self-irony: he chivalrously warns his enemies that he is a dangerous man, but he is willing to entertain the possibility that they may win. In that case the victor

> has a pretty choice
> From an anatomy with little to lose
> Whether he cut my tongue and take my voice
> Or whether it be my round red heart he choose.

The irony of the poem as a whole is a rich and complex blending of pity and laughter in which the attitude of the reader, far from being simplified, is developed and complicated. It is important to notice that irony functions here not only to give precision to the poet's attitude, but also to give another dimension to the symbol. But the plain reader

(as Laura Riding and Robert Graves put it) "wants to know
definitely whether he is to laugh or cry over Captain Car-
penter's story, and if he is not given a satisfactory clue he
naturally doubts the sincerity of the poet, he becomes sus-
picious of his seriousness and leaves him alone."

This statement puts forcibly the contrast between the
sincerity on which Arnold's high seriousness is based and
the concept of sincerity which emerges from our discussion
of irony. The two conceptions are almost diametrically op-
posed. Arnold's sincerity expresses itself as a vigilance
which keeps out of the poem all those extraneous and dis-
tracting elements which might seem to contradict what the
poet wishes to communicate to his audience. It is the
sincerity of the conscientious expositor who makes his
point, even at the price of suppressions and exclusions.
Poetry which embodies such a conception of sincerity, when
it is unsuccessful, has as its characteristic vice, sentimental-
ity. For sentimentality nearly always involves an over-
simplification of the experience in question. The senti-
mentalist takes a short cut to intensity by removing all the
elements of the experience which might conceivably mili-
tate against the intensity. Every poet, of course, makes a
selection, but the sentimentalist, we feel, selects on too nar-
row a basis. To put the matter in terms of the poet's ac-
curacy and fidelity to experience, the sentimental poet
makes us feel that he is sacrificing the totality of his vision
in favor of a particular interpretation. Hence the feeling
on reading a sentimental poem that the intensity is the re-
sult of a trick.

The second conception of sincerity, on the other hand,
reveals itself as an unwillingness to ignore the complexity
of experience. The poet attempts to fuse the conflicting
elements in a harmonious whole. And here one may sug-
gest a definition of wit. Wit is not merely an acute percep-
tion of analogies; it is a lively awareness of the fact that the
obvious attitude toward a given situation is not the only
possible attitude. Because wit, for us, is still associated

with levity, it may be well to state it in its most serious terms. The witty poet's glancing at other attitudes is not necessarily merely "play"—an attempt to puzzle us or to show off his acuteness of perception; it is possible to describe it as merely his refusal to blind himself to a multiplicity which exists.

One is even tempted to indulge in the following paradox: namely, that wit, far from being a playful aspect of the mind, is the most serious aspect, and that the only poetry which possesses high seriousness in the deepest sense is the poetry of wit. But some obvious reservations are to be made and some misapprehensions anticipated. We have defined wit in its most general terms. The wit of a Donne or of a Marvell is after all only one form, and an extreme form, which wit may take. There are obviously many fine poems, including some of Arnold's, which are not "witty" in the superficial sense at all. But if we are to understand the poetry of the Elizabethan and Jacobean periods we must discard the view that wit is to be associated with barren and shallow ingenuity.

3

METAPHYSICAL POETRY

AND PROPAGANDA ART

WITH THE definition of wit suggested in the last chapter we come very close to a definition of metaphysical poetry. One might, indeed, let the matter rest on the definition of wit: viz., metaphysical poetry (whatever the term metaphysical may mean or may have meant) is witty poetry. But the matter of definition is important enough to deserve some further exploration, even if one admits that further exploration will probably merely clarify rather than add anything of importance to what has been already implied.

Before attempting a definition, however, it may be well to point out that we shall hardly be able to avoid giving a definition of *poetry* rather than merely a definition of metaphysical poetry. It will not be enough to describe those features which set off the school of Donne from other schools, or to summarize those mannerisms and particular adjectives which an Edna Millay or an Elinor Wylie can take over into her poetry without altering its basic principle. If we are interested in getting at the core of metaphysical poetry, we should not be surprised if we find that we are dealing with something basic in all poetry, poetry being essentially one. Our definition of metaphysical poetry, then, will have to treat the difference between metaphysical poetry and other poetry as a difference of degree, not of kind. As has been implied in the earlier chapters, we require a reshaping of our conception of poetry to allow room for the inclusion of the school of Donne rather than the addition of one more conception which may be counted on to exist in amicable tolerance side by side with other conceptions. Our radical poets compel us to be *radical*, not merely liberal.

In beginning this exploration, we may well take our start from Dr. Johnson's famous phrase, "heterogeneous ideas yoked by violence together." Johnson has here seized upon the core of the method. It was a method, needless to say, of which he heartily disapproved—hence the "yoked by violence." But his criticism is relieved of much of its reprehension if we go on to qualify it with Coleridge's statement that the imagination is able to achieve "the balance or reconcilement of opposite or discordant qualities." The statement occurs in the famous passage in which Coleridge describes the kind of unity which the poet achieves: "[The poet] diffuses a tone and spirit of unity, that blends, and (as it were) fuses, each into each, by that synthetic and magical power, to which I would exclusively appropriate the name of imagination. This power . . . reveals itself in the balance or reconcilement of opposite or discordant qualities: of sameness, with difference; of the general, with the concrete; the idea, with the image; the individual, with the representative; the sense of novelty and freshness, with old and familiar objects; a more than usual state of emotion, with more than usual order; judgment ever awake and steady self-possession, with enthusiasm and feeling profound or vehement. . . ." Coleridge, as the passage shows, was prepared to believe that the uniting of the opposite and the discordant was one of the legitimate functions of the imagination, and further, that more than a mere yoking—a reconciliation—might be accomplished.

I. A. Richards seems to have derived much of his critical theory—certainly the most important part of his critical theory—from this passage. His development of Coleridge's conception of the imagination as a synthetic (i.e., as a synthesizing) power has been too much neglected by

other critics in their interest in his theories of the use of
poetry. It deserves more notice, and it comes pat to our
purpose here. In the all-important chapter of his *Principles
of Literary Criticism,* that which treats "The Imagination,"
Richards distinguishes between two general types of poetry:
first, poetry which leaves out the opposite and discordant
qualities of an experience, excluding them from the poem;
and second, poetry in which the imagination includes them,
resolving the apparent discords, and thus gaining a larger
unity. He goes on to state: "The structures of these two
kinds of experiences are different, and the difference is not
one of subject but of the relations *inter se* of the several
impulses active in the experience. A poem of the first group
is built out of sets of impulses which run parallel, which
have the same direction. In a poem of the second group
the most obvious feature is the extraordinary heterogeneity
of the distinguishable impulses. But they are more than
heterogeneous, they are opposed. They are such that in or-
dinary, nonpoetic, nonimaginative experience, one or other
set would be suppressed to give as it might appear freer
development to the others.

"The difference comes out clearly if we consider how
comparatively unstable poems of the first kind are. They
will not bear an ironical contemplation. We have only to
read *The War Song of Dinas Vawr* in close conjunction with
the *Coronach,* or to remember that unfortunate phrase
'Those lips, O slippery blisses!' from *Endymion,* while read-
ing *Love's Philosophy,* to notice this. Irony in this sense
consists in the bringing in of the opposite, the complemen-
tary impulses; that is why poetry which is exposed to it is
not of the highest order, and why irony itself is so constantly
a characteristic of poetry which is."

The distinction between the two types of poetry is, as
Richards points out, not an absolute one; but this basis of
distinction seems valid, and more than that, very fruitful.
Metaphysical poetry obviously belongs on principle to the
second class. Its failures belong to the second class quite

as apparently as its successes, for the failures, when they occur, are failures to reconcile discordant materials—not failures based on a too precious exclusion of discordant materials. Richards' description of the poetry of synthesis may be used, therefore, to throw special illumination on metaphysical poetry, particularly on its constant recourse to wit and irony and on its possession of a certain tough-minded integrity.

That this use of Richards' classification of poetry is not a forced one may be demonstrated emphatically by comparing Richards' description with Eliot's comments on the school of Donne. The two critics are certainly far enough apart in general attitudes, sympathies, and terminologies. Their agreement is therefore all the more forceful. Eliot has suggested the general nature of metaphysical poetry in pointing out some of the characteristics of seventeenth-century wit: it appears in metaphysical poetry as "a tough reasonableness beneath the slight lyric grace." It is characterized by an "alliance of levity and seriousness (by which the seriousness is intensified)." It is a function of the poet's ability to synthesize diverse materials. The poets who employed it possessed "a mechanism of sensibility which could devour any kind of experience."

These qualities, one observes, are just the qualities possessed by Richards' poetry of synthesis. Compare the "tough reasonableness" of Eliot's poetry of wit with the invulnerability to irony of Richards' poetry of synthesis; the "alliance of levity and seriousness" with Richards' unification of opposed impulses; Eliot's "sensibility which could devour any kind of experience" with Richards' statement that "tragedy [he holds tragedy to be the poetry of synthesis at its highest level] is perhaps the most general, all-accepting, all-ordering experience known. It can take anything into its organization." One may suggest one more definition of metaphysical poetry, a definition based on Richards' terms: it is a poetry in which the opposition of the impulses which are united is extreme. Or, to base oneself directly on

Coleridge: it is a poetry in which the poet attempts the reconciliation of qualities which are opposite or discordant in the extreme.

Such a definition of poetry places the emphasis directly on the poet as a *maker*. It is his making, his imagination that gives the poem its poetic quality, not some intrinsic quality (beauty or truth) of the materials with which he builds his poem. The metaphysical poet has confidence in the power of the imagination. He is constantly remaking his world by relating into an organic whole the amorphous and heterogeneous and contradictory. Insisting on imaginative unity, he refuses to depend upon nonimaginative classifications, those of logic or science. He is not content, therefore, merely to call attention to likeness with like. Refusing to compromise with the easier kinds of unity, he gambles on an all-or-nothing basis: his failures are as egregious as his successes. (One must never forget, however, that the roads which lead to absurdity are many and various: if Crashaw's description of the Magdelene's eyes as "walking baths" is absurd, so is Wordsworth's "Idiot Boy.")

The principle on which the poet risks his gamble can be justified, however, and justified out of Dr. Johnson himself. In one of his finest critical passages, Johnson likens a successful comparison to the intersection of two lines, pointing out that the *comparison is better in proportion as the lines converge from greater distances*. The observation is a sound one, and will bear a little elaboration, even in the metaphysical manner. We may say that the metaphysical poet (though Johnson was not prepared to agree that Donne often made the lines really intersect) converges his lines from the farthest possible distances. The parallelism of the lines—too close a resemblance between the objects compared, a matter which Johnson illustrated by Addison's angel simile—results, as Dr. Johnson rightly insists, in no true comparison at all. The net result of the refinement of English poetry in the seventeenth century was toward a parallelism in comparisons. In order to have convergence one must have divergence. Yet great divergence was frowned upon.

The definition of metaphysical poetry proposed above will allow us to connect the increasing regard for metaphysical poetry in our day with intensification of our dislike for sentimentality. The two phenomena are related, whether consciously or not. For wit, as we have defined it in the previous chapter, is incompatible with the sentimental. As Richards has pointed out, "Irony [in one sense at least] consists in the bringing in of the opposite, the complementary impulses." His "poetry of exclusion" is incapable of enduring an ironical contemplation because in such poetry the complementary impulses have been excluded from the poem. The accidental introduction of the poem into a context where they occur means the destruction of the poem; for the poet has not in this case come to terms with these correlative aspects of the experience. The sentimental experience, as we have seen, always has to be viewed in the "right" perspective—else it crumbles. Richards' poetry of synthesis, on the other hand, is impervious to irony for the very reason that it carries within its own structure the destructive elements—the poet has reconciled it to them. We may go further and say that the poet has included enough of the context in his experience so that the poem can never be thrown, raw and naked, into a new context in which it may appear foolish and ridiculous. In other words, the poet has been just to the complexity of experience, and has not given us an abstraction in the guise of experience.

It will be easy to illustrate this general principle of metaphysical poetry from its use of metaphor. Any comparison has in it an essential incongruity, even the most trite comparison. Eyes are not really very much like stars, nor love like a red, red, rose. The poet who is at the mercy of a narrow decorum, logical or scientific, is apt to depend too much on the likeness existing between the objects which he compares. He lets no recognition of these disparities ap-

pear in the poem. Consequently, the fault of timid meta-
phor is that it does not wear well. On a first reading it may
seem plausible. Closer acquaintance, however, reveals the
disparities, and a shift of the poem into an ironic context
reveals them cruelly. The metaphysical conceit represents
a complete reversal of this situation. The disparities are
recognized and deliberately exploited by the poet; they
are gathered up into the context of the poem. Since the
destructive elements are contained within the comparison,
the conceit, if unsuccessful, rather than wearing out, ex-
plodes from within. If it does not explode with a first
reading, it is extremely durable. There are no further
ludicrous disparities to be revealed on later readings.
The metaphysical poet, with his constant awareness of in-
congruities and disparities, does not run the risk of taking
his poem for science. He does not deal in eternal like-
nesses and approximations. His unity is a perilous one,
wrested by his own effort from a world of incongruities.
Marvell, for example, in his "Definition of Love" is never
allowed to forget that he deals with fictions. He and his
mistress are obviously not parallel lines, nor is he likely to
forget that Fate's "iron wedges" are of nonferrous material.
That this is an important asset becomes apparent when we
come to observe the general nature of poetic symbols, and
the relation of the poem to truth.

For poetic symbols are not *true*. The statement that
they are true is in itself a metaphor. The didactic view
of poetry, with its emphasis on the illustrative function of
metaphor, assumes that poetic symbols are to stand for
ideas, and naturally true ideas are to be preferred to false.
Under such a theory the goodness of a poem is to a great
extent determined by its truth. This, however, is to bring
poetry into a competition with science, which falsifies their
real relationship. As John Crowe Ransom has well put it,
"Not now are the poets so brave, not for a long time have
they been so brave, as to dispute the scientists on what they
call their 'truth'; though it is a pity that the statement can-

not be turned round. Poets will concede that every act of science is legitimate, and has its efficacy."

A didactic poetry which takes its didacticism seriously, Ransom calls "Platonic" poetry. The Platonic poet discourses in *terms* of "things, but on the understanding that they are translatable at every point into ideas," or he elaborates "ideas as such, but in proceeding introduces for ornament some physical properties." He is unwilling to let his metaphors, unscientific at best, become too daring and violate science too flagrantly; he is gingerly in his identification of image with idea. He is cautious in these matters, because he is a scientist; he is interested primarily in the general and the abstract. The metaphysical poet, on the other hand, is under no illusion that he is a scientist. And unhampered by this illusion, he is free to assert boldly his unscientific and miraculous predications. Moreover, his predications, though consciously unscientific, are not necessarily to be dismissed as idle fancies. They constitute *myth,* and myth is "true in the pragmatic sense in which some of the generalizations of science are true: it accomplishes precisely the sort of representation that it means to. It suggests to us that the object [considered in the poem] is perceptually or physically remarkable, and we had better attend to it." (We shall have occasion to recur to the matter of what sort of truth is contained in myth later in examining the poetry of W. B. Yeats.)

Allen Tate makes a similar distinction between a "Platonic" or "allegorical" poetry and the poetry of the imagination. Platonic poetry is essentially a recipe for action as contrasted with imaginative poetry which sets up an object for contemplation. As such, Platonic poetry is to be regarded as an expression of the will. In this Platonic poetry Tate distinguishes two sub-varieties, a positive and a negative phase. The first is "a positive Platonism, a cheerful confidence in the limitless power of man to impose practical abstractions upon his experience. Romantic irony is a negative Platonism, a self-pitying disillusionment with the positive optimism of the other program: the romantic tries to build up a set of fictitious 'explanations,' by means of rhetoric, more congenial to his unscientific temper."

There is some danger that the reader will confuse this negatively Platonic poetry with the poetry of the imagination. The difference is profound. The Romantic ironist defiantly, or in disillusion, revolts against Science. The non-Platonic poet knows that he is not competing with it— is, as a matter of fact, dealing with another order of description from that in which science indulges.

All this is directly applicable to the problem of propaganda art, for in insisting on art as propaganda, some of the Marxist critics (though not all) have merely revived and restated the didactic heresy. For them, the end of poetry is to instruct and convert. The truth of the poet's doctrine has, thus, everything to do with the value of his poetry, and the truth, needless to say, is Marxism.

Whether stated baldly and naïvely as above, or accorded a more sophisticated treatment, the ultimate fallacy in the position remains the same. It is the confusion about the truth which poetry gives which we have seen to inhere in the old didactic conception of the function of literature. As long as one conceives the end of poetry to be that of instruction, it seems plausible to say that a poem must either be true or false, and that a poet who refuses to speak in these terms is forced into the isolation of the Ivory Tower.

Ransom's account, or Tate's account of the relation of poetry to science will indicate why the dilemma between propaganda art on the one hand and that of the Ivory Tower on the other is a false one. The point does not need laboring, but since it is Marxist tactics to attack their opponents for relying on an old-fashioned, "unscientific" psychology— Tate, for example, has been reprehended for using the phrase "poetry of the will"—it is amusing to compare their position on the matter with that of I. A. Richards.

Richards, no more than Tate or Ransom, would accept the dilemma which the Marxist critic offers: that of propaganda art on the one hand and the Ivory Tower on the other. For him, a poem is not a more or less true statement in metrical garb, but an organization of experience, and it is in terms of what may be called its psychological structure —"the resolution, inter-animation, and balancing of impulses—that all the more valuable effects of poetry must be described." He has expressed this more simply and emphatically elsewhere in the statement that "it is never what a poem says that matters, but what it is."

T. S. Eliot quotes this statement with approval. Even earlier he has indicated in his *Dante* (though with careful qualifications) that his theory of poetic belief is similar to that of Richards. In his *Use of Poetry* he advances his position a further stage. After saying that if literature exists at all, we must allow that "one may share the essential beliefs of Dante and yet enjoy Lucretius to the full," Eliot points out that Shelley's beliefs do get in the way of his enjoyment of Shelley's poetry. He accounts for the apparent inconsistency in this way: "I suggest that the position is somewhat as follows. When the doctrine, theory, belief, or 'view of life' presented in a poem is one which the mind of the reader can accept as coherent, mature, and founded on the facts of experience, it interposes no obstacle to the reader's enjoyment, whether it be one that he accept or deny, approve or deprecate. When it is one which the reader rejects as childish or feeble, it may, for a reader of well-developed mind, set up an almost complete check."

What Eliot has done, however, in making his point, is to shift the matter at issue from a consideration of the truth of the poem's doctrine to the poem's structure—from what the poem says to what it is. It is easy to throw his last development into Richards' terms. The poetry of synthesis with its union of opposed impulses and its invulnerability to irony is obviously a poetry, the doctrine of which impresses the reader as being "coherent" and "mature." The phrase, "founded on the facts of experience"—however Richards might choose to restate it—clinches the matter. And it is this toughness and maturity which is salient in the poetry of the metaphysicals.

Richards, furthermore, makes explicit provision for Eliot's "complete check" in the following terms: "The question of belief or disbelief never arises when we are reading well. If unfortunately it does arise, either through the poet's fault or our own, we have for the moment ceased to be readers and have become astronomers, theologians, or moralists [and one may add "or economists"], persons engaged in a quite different type of activity."

It is the type of activity, I take it, which Tate scores in what he calls "Platonic poetry" in which "the will asserts a rhetorical proposition about the whole of life, where the imagination is incapable of seizing that whole implicitly. If the lines [Life like a dome of many-colored glass/ Stains the white radiance of eternity] were an integral part of a genuine poem, *the question of their specific merit as truth or falsehood would not arise* [italics mine]."

We may summarize the position on the question of poetic belief as follows: First, the scientific truth of the doctrine enunciated will not save the poem just as its scientific falsity will not damn it. The poet then must not place an illegitimate dependence in the possible scientific truth of his doctrine. As Tate puts it, the assertions made by the poet must be "a quality of the whole poem"—not "willfully asserted for the purpose of heightening a subject the poet has not implicitly imagined." Second, the doctrine must be one suitable to a poem which is to stand up under "an ironical contemplation."

But if the truth of the doctrine enunciated in a poem cannot in itself make the poem good, there are, in addition, special and positive risks which the propagandist-poet incurs. Because he is intent on the truth of his statement and preoccupied with the inculcation of a particular message, his poetry may easily take the form of a poetry of exclusion, leaving out of account the elements of experience not favorable to the matter in hand, and thus oversimplifying experience. In this sense, at least, the distinction between Tate's Platonic poetry and his poetry of the imagination, or the distinction between Ransom's Platonic poetry and metaphysical poetry, parallels the distinction existing between Richards' poetry of exclusion and his poetry of synthesis. Tate's reprehension of such poetry is perfectly just: it is an "over-simplification of life" which is undertaken "in the face of the immense complication of life as a whole." It is therefore imitative of science (which legitimately and as a consequence of its method makes use of systematic oversimplification); and it lacks the inner poise and stability, the constant self-criticism of poetry of the highest type. (I do not wish to force resemblances among the theories of Eliot, Tate, Ransom and Richards. Least of all do I mean to intimate that any one is derived from the others. But the very fact that these four critics, employing diverse terminologies and approaches, should corroborate each other so emphatically, in itself is a commentary on the importance of the present critical revolution.)

Here perhaps we have an answer for Horace Gregory's defense of propaganda art in which he states that "Shelley's failures *are not traceable to his use of propaganda.*" One could hardly choose a more apt case. The characteristic fault of Shelley's poetry is that it excludes on principle all but the primary impulses—that it cannot bear an ironical contemplation. What Shelley's regenerated world of *Prometheus Unbound* really has to fear is not the possible resurrection of Jupiter but the resurrection of John Donne. Grant that, and chaos comes again.

If one prefers modern examples, one may find them in abundance in the recently published anthology, *Proletarian Literature.* The characteristic fault of the type of poetry exhibited is *sentimentality.* The term is used advisedly. These poems demand a sympathetic audience upon which they may rely for a sympathetic context. At their worst, even the more obvious aspects of sentimentality appear. It requires no special definition of the term to convict the poems of Genevieve Taggard, Langston Hughes, and others in the collection of just this vice. The experience established involves illegitimate exclusions and a special posing in a special light.

To take an extreme example, consider the following stanzas from Don West's "Southern Lullaby":

> Eat, little baby, eat well,
> A Bolshevik you'll be,
> And hate this bosses' hell—
> Sucking it in from me . . .
>
> Hate, little baby, hate deep,
> You mustn't know my fears,
> Mother is watching your sleep,
> But you don't see her tears.

Propaganda has apparently blinded the editors of the anthology in this instance, as well as the poet.

I suggest that the terminology used above is not unrelated to Kenneth Burke's recent warning to the first American Writers' Congress against *propaganda by exclusion.* He would prefer to substitute for this, *propaganda by inclusion,* stating that "the imaginative writer seeks to propagandize his cause by surrounding it with as full a cultural texture as he can manage, thus thinking of propaganda not as an over-simplified, literal, explicit writing of lawyer's briefs, but as a process of broadly and generally associating his political alignment with cultural awareness in the large." The warning, on the basis of the poetry exhibited in *Proletarian Literature,* has not come any too early.

The error made by some of the more naïve Marxists, ironically enough, arises from a clumsy and inadequate account of poetry. However revolutionary their economics, the aesthetic theory of such critics is not revolutionary at all. It represents little advance over the Victorians with their "message-hunting" and their Browning societies.

The foregoing discussion of the structure of poetry and

its relation to science should make somewhat clearer what has been said earlier about the influence on poetry of the scientific movement in the middle of the seventeenth century, and the magnitude of the change in taste which it effected. One may perhaps be permitted to summarize thus: We have abundant evidence of the esteem in which such poets as Cowley, D'Avenant, and Dryden held Thomas Hobbes, and as Ransom has admirably put it: "What Bacon with his disparagement of poetry had begun, in the cause of science and protestantism, Hobbes completed. . . . The name [of Hobbes] stood for common sense and naturalism, and the monopoly of the scientific spirit over the mind." The weakening of metaphor, the development of a specifically "poetic" subject matter and diction, the emphasis on simplicity and clarity, the simplification of the poet's attitude, the segregation of the witty and the ironical from the serious, the stricter separation of the various genres—all these items testify to the monopoly of the scientific spirit. This process of clarification involved the *exclusion* of certain elements from poetry—the prosaic, the unrefined, and the obscure. The imagination was weakened from a "magic and synthetic" power to Hobbes's conception of it as the file-clerk of the memory. It was obviously the antirationalistic magic that Hobbes was anxious to eliminate.

This change in taste constitutes the first great critical revolution that has occurred in the history of modern English poetry. The second major critical revolution, the Romantic Revolt, had as its ostensible objective, the liberation of the imagination. Unfortunately it failed to be revolutionary enough. As we have seen, the Romantic poets, in attacking the neoclassic conception of the poetic, tended to offer new poetic objects rather than to discard altogether the conception of a special poetic material. Even Coleridge himself, with all his critical acumen, did not completely free himself from the didactic conception. The didactic function, clad in irridescent colors as a revelation of the Divine, remained to confuse his critical theory.

The importance of the third critical revolution lies in the fact that it attempts a complete liberation of the imagination.* The successful use of prosaic or unpleasant materials and the union of the intellectual with the emotional are symptoms of imaginative power—not, as Mr. F. L. Lucas would interpret them, symptoms of the death of poetry. Moreover, the important resemblance between the modern poet and the poets of the sixteenth and seventeenth centuries lies not in the borrowing of a few "metaphysical" adjectives or images, or the cultivation of a few clever "conceits." That is why the "metaphysical" quality of the best of the moderns is not the result of a revival, or the aping of a period style. The fundamental resemblance is in the attitude which the poets of both periods take toward their materials and in the method which both, at their best, employ.

* I suppose that Richards must have meant something of this sort in his much-discussed remark that Eliot in *The Waste Land* had effected a complete severance with all beliefs. If so, he has stated negatively and ambiguously what he might more happily have stated positively. The point is not whether or not the poet "believes" in something, but that, though dealing with beliefs, he has not depended illegitimately on our emotional allegiance to them as beliefs. But the accomplishment is not "modern"; in this sense, Dante's *Divine Comedy* effects such a severance.

4

SYMBOLIST POETRY

AND THE IVORY TOWER

IN DISCUSSING the influence of the seventeenth-century metaphysical poets on modern poetry, we have considered metaphysical poetry as primarily an assimilation of the diverse and discordant. There remains the problem of relating to this influence on modern poetry the influence of the French Symbolist poets of the nineteenth century. A discussion of symbolism offers an opportunity to explore more thoroughly one further aspect of figurative language: subtlety of statement. Two problems, already raised, however, reappear in slightly different form when one begins to discuss symbolism. The first is that of obscurity (we have discussed it thus far primarily in terms of the author's attitude); the second, that of escapism.

Obscurity and escapism appear as functions of each other in Edmund Wilson's *Axel's Castle*. The poet, withdrawing from the objective world outside him in order to communicate "unique personal feelings," is, because he is expressing his private world, obscure and difficult. Indeed, for Wilson, symbolism is frankly "a second flood" of romanticism; and since he agrees with Eliot in finding a close similarity between the French Symbolists and the English metaphysicals, presumably Wilson considers metaphysical poetry also a "romantic" poetry.

Edmund Wilson has, however, taken care to show that there are branches of symbolism, the "serious-aesthetic" typified by Verlaine, and the "conversational-ironic" typified by Jules Laforgue and Tristan Corbière. Wilson's terms are interesting in the light of the previous chapter. One should not perhaps insist on his grouping. But his placing of "serious" in opposition to "ironic" may have some significance. It is from the antiromantic branch, the "conversational-ironic," that Wilson indicates that Eliot derives. But having made this division, Wilson does not seem to me to maintain it sufficiently, and consequently the romantic traits of the serious-aesthetic tradition get themselves attributed to symbolism in general. Eliot, for example, is clearly connected by Wilson with romantic escapism.

It will be necessary to follow rather closely Wilson's account of the beginnings of symbolism in France in order to make out a fair criticism of his position. After pointing out Poe's influence on the French Symbolists, and after quoting Poe's statement "that indefiniteness is an element of the true music [of poetry] . . . a suggestive indefiniteness of vague and therefore of spiritual effect," Wilson observes that "to approximate the indefiniteness of music was to become one of the principal aims of Symbolism."

One must pause over the term "indefiniteness" for special comment. Just what is meant by the term here? It is possible to sort out several possible meanings. It may mean: (1) not limited as prose (considered as a mode, not as a "fine art") is limited, in the direction of a single uncomplicated meaning; (2) richly connotative as opposed to sparely denotative; (3) aiming at the generation of shadowy, imprecise moods as opposed to more sharply realized "meanings"; and (4) characterized by the use of the vague and the blurred as opposed to the sharp and detailed. All poetry tends to be subsumed under meanings (1) and (2). As for meanings (3) and (4), they may well apply to a great deal of romantic poetry as well as to some symbolist poetry. But (3) and (4) do not apply to the symbolist poetry with which we are specifically concerned in this chapter, and they are hostile on principle to the genius of metaphysical poetry. Most important of all, there is no reason why they should apply in the least to poetry which is thoroughly "indefinite" in senses (1) and (2). (We have earlier in this book argued that Wordsworth's proposition that the imagination "recoils from everything but the plastic, the pliant, and the indefinite" springs from a *limited* conception of the imagination.)

The next characteristic of symbolism mentioned by Wilson is of a very different nature, and is a characteristic which it shares with metaphysical poetry. "This effect of indefiniteness was produced not merely by the confusion I have mentioned between the imaginary world and the real; but also by means of a further confusion between the perceptions of the different senses.

> Comme de longs échos qui de loin se confondent . . .
> Les parfums, les couleurs et les sons se répondent,

wrote Baudelaire. And we find Poe, in one of his poems, *hearing* the approach of darkness."

Now this confusion "between the perceptions of the different senses" is susceptible of quite a different account. It was never a characteristic of the Romantic poets. It represents a movement in the direction of metaphysical poetry. For example, we remember that Coleridge reprimands as a "species of *wit*, a pure work of the *will*" such "rhetorical caprices" as that of making, for example, hills "reflect the image of a *voice*." Although Poe's juxtapositions would hardly have offended Coleridge so violently, they are of the same nature.

Wilson continues: "This notation of super-rational sensations was a novelty in the forties of the last century—as was the dreamlike irrational musical poetry of 'Annabel Lee' and 'Ulalume'; and they helped to effect a revolution in France." One pauses here to comment: what other sorts of sensation are there? Surely, there are no *rational* sensations. The notation of sensations is always that of irrational sensations. The slip is worth noting only because it betrays a Hobbesian

bias which Wilson himself may not be aware of, but one
which is highly important in gaining conviction for the
thesis on which *Axel's Castle* is based. The important
question is not the increased irrationality of the sensations
which the Symbolists attempted to convey, but the attempt
to gain an increased subtlety in the notation. So long as
the notation is to be superficial and crude, the language
may very well be what Wilson has termed "the conventional
and universal language of ordinary literature." (A *com-
pletely* conventional and universal language, takes us, of
course, out of literature altogether and over into science.)

Wilson goes on to observe that: "For an English-speaking
reader of today, Poe's influence may be hard to understand;
and even when such a reader comes to examine the produc-
tions of French symbolism, it may surprise him that they
should have caused amazement. The medley of images;
the deliberately mixed metaphors; the combination of pas-
sion and wit—of the grand and the prosaic manners; the
bold amalgamation of material with spiritual—all these may
seem to him quite proper and familiar. He has always
known them in the English poetry of the sixteenth and
seventeenth centuries—Shakespeare and the other Eliza-
bethans did all these things without theorizing about them.
Is this not the natural language of poetry? Is it not the
norm against which, in English literature, the eighteenth
century was a heresy and to which the Romantics did their
best to return?" Except for the last sentence one can readily
agree, though one may question whether the average
"English-speaking reader of today" would consider this the
natural language of poetry. Certainly it is a view of poetry
against which the eighteenth century was a heresy. But did
the Romantic poets do their best to return to it? One must
answer: to some of its traits, yes, but toned down; and to
others not at all. In particular, the Romantics were careful
not to mix their metaphors too much, and not to be too bold
in their "amalgamation of material with spiritual"; as for the

"combination of passion and wit—of the grand and the prosaic manners" we shall find very little indeed.

Such figures as Eliot's

> Midnight shakes the memory
> As a madman shakes a dead geranium

or Allen Tate's

> The singular screech-owl's bright
> Invisible lyric seeds the mind

are simply not to be found in the poetry of the early nineteenth century. The presence of wit, as a matter of fact, would destroy a great deal of the "romantic" quality, and in so far as the Symbolists have succeeded in bringing wit into their poetry, they have usually precluded the charges of escapism, sentimentality, and the other pejorative associations of "romantic."

Wilson draws nearer to his final definition of symbolism by stating that "to intimate things rather than state them plainly was thus one of the primary aims of the Symbolists." This, taken with his statement that "the symbols of the Symbolist school are usually chosen arbitrarily by the poet to stand for special ideas of his own—they are a sort of disguise for these ideas," may give the impression that the poet is striving to baffle the reader. And of course, there is some warrant for this assumption in the statements made by the Symbolists themselves. But one must remember the special material with which the poet works. The phrase "to intimate things rather than state them plainly" suggests that the poet might state them plainly if only he chose to. It corresponds to Housman's conception of metaphor and simile as "accessories." Certainly, there is much to be said for calling a spade a spade, but suppose that the object to be called does not have any name. The "things" that the symbolist poet has to "state" have to be intimated if they are to be given at all.

There is a further consideration: The poet does not have the relatively simple task (as the more naïve adherents of the doctrine of communication imply) of noting down a certain state of mind. The experience which he "communicates" is itself created by the organization of the symbols which he uses. The total poem is therefore the communication, and indistinguishable from it.

The imagery of these poets is thus an integral part of the communication just as, for that matter, the rhythm of the poem is an integral part of the communication. We are not tempted, as a rule, to consider the rhythm as used for the illustration of "something else," but the rhythm of a poem is one of the conditioning factors modifying the tone, supplying emphasis, corroborating and underlining the play of the thought. It is hardly more absurd to say that the poet "intimates" with a subtle rhythm rather than "stating plainly" with an emphatic rhythm, than to criticize a poet's metaphor as being merely an intimation. The subtlety of the figurative language of the symbolist poets is analogous to that of the metaphysicals—and for the same reasons.

It is possible, consequently, to restate Wilson's final definition of symbolism in language far less prejudicial. "Symbolism," Wilson sums up, "may be defined as an attempt by carefully studied means—a complicated association of ideas represented by a medley of metaphors—to communicate unique personal feelings." The phraseology implies that the symbolist poet is deliberately trying to exclude the mass of people from participation in his poetry—the view which Max Eastman plumps for in his account of the symbolist poets as members of a "Cult of Unintelligibility." But a more accurate statement would be this: The symbolist poet refuses to sacrifice the subtlety and complexity of his total vision of reality. Such a poetry will undoubtedly result in a limitation of the audience, but the limitation will be an unfortunate necessity conditioned by the nature of the poetry, not the effect of the poet's personal snobbery.

In general, Wilson's attempt to connect classicism with

science, opposing to these the "poetic-romantic," is gratui-
tous and confusing. There is nothing inherently romantic
in unscientific poetry just as there is nothing inherently
scientific in classical poetry. And we must not allow our-
selves to be confused by the critical terminology of the
"Age of Reason." The so-called "reason" of eighteenth-
century poetry is not more rational than any other code of
conventions is rational. Lack of dependence on logical
structure distinguishes symbolist poetry from simple ex-
pository prose; but this is also true of poetry in general.

In this sense, then, all poetry is *symbolist* poetry, for all
poetry characteristically seeks its symbols—its "objective
correlatives"—for the experience to be communicated. Since
more than a mere intellectual concept is involved, the poetic
symbol must always be more "private" than the scientific
symbol. By the same token, it will also always be more
"obscure." This proposition holds true for a poet even so
simple as Wordsworth. Consider his "Resolution and Inde-
pendence": An aged leech-gatherer in principle is a more
private and obscure symbol for the resolution and inde-
pendence for which it stands than is the term "triangle" for
the concept for which it stands.

More is involved here than the statement of a truism.
We shall not be able to judge fairly the more extreme in-
stances of symbolist method unless we are perfectly clear
on this point: that privacy and obscurity, to some degree,
are inevitable in all poetry.

The symbolist poets, then, are akin to the metaphysicals
in the subtlety of their descriptions of feelings, and in the
subsequent limitation of their audience. With the "con-
versational-ironic" branch, the approach to metaphysical
poetry becomes much closer. The serious-aesthetic tradi-
tion, as the name implies, has held somewhat to tradition-
ally poetic subject matter and poetic diction, increasing the
subtlety but hardly going so far as to develop apparent dis-
cords. Such poets as Laforgue and Corbière, on the other
hand, broke radically with the traditional concepts of the

poetic. They attempted to integrate all sorts of materials, and accordingly we find in their work the recurrence of all the various phenomena of metaphysical poetry: verbal conceits such as Corbière's *"O Venus dans ta vénérie!"*; violent comparisons such as that which makes the rain the soup of the dogs in heaven; and the play of wit such as

> *Prends pitié de la fille-mère,*
> *Du petit au bord du chemin. . . .*
> *Si quelqu'un leur jette la pierre,*
> *Que la pierre se change en pain!*

With the acquisition of these qualities—irony, realistic diction, wit—symbolist poetry coalesces with metaphysical. The faults to be censured may be many: lack of taste, strained images, and the like. What is important to observe, however, is that they will not be the faults characteristic of romanticism: sentimentality, vulnerability to irony, and escapism.

The development of William Butler Yeats will furnish in itself an excellent illustration of the relation of symbolist to metaphysical poetry; for if Yeats's early poetry lies in what Wilson calls the serious-aesthetic tradition of symbolism, his later poetry approaches the conversational-ironic —and approaching it, comes very close to the school of Donne. The mistiness, the "Celtic twilight," have cleared away, and there is, though with no loss of subtlety, an increased hardness and wit.

Edmund Wilson has cited "On a Picture of a Black Centaur by Edmond Dulac" as an especially clear example of the influence of the French Symbolists upon Yeats. So it is, but it may be taken also as an especially clear example of metaphysical poetry.

The centaur symbolizes, obviously, the animal side of man as opposed to the intellectual side. The poet formerly, he tells us in the poem, did not give the life of the body its due: "I knew that horse play, knew it for a murderous thing." Now, however, he recognizes his error:

Stretch out your limbs and sleep a long Saturnian sleep;
I have loved you better than my soul for all my words,
And there is none so fit to keep a watch and keep
Unwearied eyes upon those horrible green birds.

The "horse play" is literally the play of the centaur—of
the concrete, physical man. But "horse play" has very
definite associations with boisterous, rowdy, mischievous
activity; and the poet consciously makes use of these. They
make vivid his former conception of the physical; but they
have a more significant function. They preserve the poet's
realism. In coming to celebrate the body rather than to
deprecate it, he does not propose to strike an attitude. The
black centaur, with its classic and heroic associations, is a
fitting symbol for the physical, but the poet does not mean,
by using this symbol, to romanticize it. He refuses to leave
the boisterous and rowdy aspects out of account. "Horse
play" and all, it is superior to mere intellectual abstractions.
Moreover, the fact that the phrase has two different signifi-
cances, and that it means them simultaneously—this verbal
compression in itself prepares for the fusion of the two ap-
parently opposed meanings into a larger and richer mean-
ing. The device amounts to the serious pun such as occurs
in Donne or Shakespeare.

Yeats's symbols are, after all, nothing but concrete and
meaningful images in terms of which the play of the mind
may exhibit itself—that play being, not rigidly conceptual
and bare, but enriched with all sorts of associations.
Yeats's later poetry, like the poetry of Donne, reveals the
"mind at the finger-tips."

Consider, for example, his "Sailing to Byzantium." If
we follow the poem carefully, we shall be able to detect
even the syllogistic framework which characterizes so much
of metaphysical poetry. The poet reasons as follows: His
country is a land of natural beauty, beauty of the body.
But his own body is old. The soul must, therefore, sing
the louder to compensate for the old and dying flesh.

An aged man is but a paltry thing,
A tattered coat upon a stick, unless
Soul clap its hands and sing, and louder sing
For every tatter in its mortal dress.

But there is no singing school for the soul except in studying
the works of the soul. "And therefore" he has sailed to
Byzantium, for the artists of Byzantium do not follow the
forms of nature but intellectual forms, ideal patterns. He
appeals to them to

Consume my heart away; sick with desire
And fastened to a dying animal

and by severing him from the dying world of the body, to
gather him into what is at least "the artifice of eternity."

Once out of nature I shall never take
My bodily form from any natural thing,
But such a form as Grecian goldsmiths make
Of hammered gold and gold enamelling
To keep a drowsy Emperor awake;
Or set upon a golden bough to sing
To lords and ladies of Byzantium
Of what is past, or passing, or to come.

A comparison of this paraphrase with the poem in its
entirety illustrates better than anything else why the poet
must write as he does—how much we lose by substituting
abstract statements for his richer "symbols." Byzantium
is, for instance, a very rich symbol. It may be thought a
very indefinite one. But richness and complexity are not
vagueness, and it will be easy to show that the symbol has
its precision. It means many things, but if one misses the
connection with intellectual art, one has missed the poem.
(Some of the further things which it means may be best
deferred to Chapter VIII, where we shall consider Yeats's
poetry in relation to his system of esoteric beliefs.)

The images, for the most part, are not especially unpoetic.
The average reader will balk, not so much at the images as

at the amount of intellectual exercise demanded of him. And yet one observes that the poet has the soul perform in a more unconventional manner ("clap hands and sing") than most Victorians would have permitted; and that Yeats has brought a scarecrow and the "lords and ladies of Byzantium" into close and successful fusion. There is irony and wit—serious wit—in a phrase like "the artifice of eternity." Indeed, the fantasy and extravagance of the poem would cause one to call it, in Wordsworth's terms, a poem of the fancy as opposed to the imagination, except that it has a tragic seriousness which has nothing to do with the playful fancy of Wordsworth. And this is perhaps the surest mark of all that here we have a case of symbolist poetry becoming metaphysical.

The ultimate identity of metaphysical and symbolist poetry can be abundantly demonstrated in Yeats's later poetry. But we can go further and find Yeats testifying explicitly to the fact. In his "The Tragic Generation," for example, he writes of Donne as follows: "Donne could be as metaphysical as he pleased, and yet never seemed unhuman and hysterical as Shelley often does, because he could be as physical as he pleased. . . . I have felt in certain early works of my own which I have long abandoned . . . a slight, sentimental sensuality which is disagreeable, and does not exist in the work of Donne. . . ." To paraphrase Yeats's statement, Yeats, in his "Sailing to Byzantium," can deal with the unnatural and the artificial as much as he pleases without seeming hysterical or sentimental, because he can be thoroughly unliterary and natural. "Sailing to Byzantium" is a metaphysical poem quite as much as it is a symbolist poem. We may prefer to use the former term when we are thinking primarily of the assimilation of diverse materials which it accomplishes; the latter term, when we are thinking primarily of the mode of its statement as opposed to that of "scientific" prose— the use of image rather than abstract concept. But such a distinction (I have no enthusiasm for it) is merely one of convenience and points to two different aspects of a poetry which are not mutually exclusive, and which are both basic to the poetic method. They are not only not mutually exclusive—they tend to occur together.

The attempt has been made, however, to erect this distinction into a matter of permanent difference of method. John Sparrow in his *Sense and Poetry* sees a great difference between the obscurity of metaphysical poetry and that of symbolist poetry. The first he can understand and even approve: "Certain qualities make a process of thought difficult to follow—abstractness, for instance, and elusiveness in the component ideas, intricacy and incongruity in their connection. . . . 'Metaphysical' poetry is difficult just in this way. . . ." But there is another kind of obscurity which Sparrow deplores: it is that which arises from the poet's deserting a logical structure altogether. ". . . it is when Mr. Eliot and his contemporaries abandon a logical for a psychological structure, and when they make play with the associative magic of ideas, that difficulty ceases and, for better or for worse, impossibility begins." The symbols in these cases, according to Sparrow, represent little more than the personal associations which the images have for the poet. They are therefore private and hopelessly obscure. (Sparrow, however, holds legitimate the use of a set of consistent or conventional symbols, for then the reader need only be provided with the key. Symbolist poetry thus is confined to allegory!)

To see how much Sparrow builds upon this supposed distinction between logical and psychological organization one has only to quote the following sentence: "Yet even in lyrical poetry, if it is of the orthodox kind, the intelligible skeleton is there, and from the finished work it is possible to abstract a meaning." Sparrow has to go on to admit, rather lamely, however: "This meaning may be a poor thing, in itself not worth seeking and not worth expressing, but it is there, it can be abstracted, it might have been otherwise expressed. The poet might have chosen different words to express it, or he might have used a different set of ideas to express his theme—his 'meaning' in a wider sense."

Quite! But this should cause us to wonder just how important the "intelligible skeleton" is for the poem, if it is no more than a certificate which can be produced at a pinch to testify to the poem's virtue. As a matter of fact, does Sparrow's statement come to anything more than that he feels that he can give a logical paraphrase of the poems he understands (even if they are not organized logically on the surface) and that he cannot give a logical paraphrase of the poems which he does not understand? Is not "the meaning in a wider sense" the only meaning which ultimately concerns the reader of poetry? And has not Sparrow himself testified in the passage quoted above that this "meaning in a wider sense" is to be found even in that lyrical poetry which does not make use of a logical structure? And if here, why not in other poetry? There are various strategies which the poet may employ, but we shall only confuse matters if we try to make more than a distinction of strategy between the characteristic methods of the metaphysical poet and the symbolist poet.

Sparrow's theory is based, finally, on the didactic heresy, as his insistence on a logical frame or skeleton indicates. The only unity which matters in poetry is an imaginative unity. Logical unity when it occurs in a poem is valued, not in itself, but only as an element which may be brought into the larger imaginative unity—that is, it is not valued in itself unless we value the poem as science or as exhortation to a practical purpose. Logic may be used as a powerful instrument by the poet, as for example by Donne, but the logical unity does not organize the poem. Donne may argue as in "The Nocturnal on St. Lucy's Day" that he is nothing, and "prove" it for us by logical arguments:

But I am by her death, (which word wrongs her)
Of the first nothing, the Elixer grown;

> Were I a man, that I were one,
>   I needs must know; I should preferre,
>   If I were any beast,
> Some ends, some means; Yea plants, yea stones detest,
> And love; All, all some properties invest;
>   If I an ordinary nothing were,
>   As shadow, a light, and body must be here.

But the logic, though brilliant, is bad logic if we are to judge the poem on its value as a logical exercise. The show of logic, it is true, is justified; but it is justified in imaginative terms—not in logical terms. The logic is used to dictate a particular tone. It is really employed as a kind of metaphor. Nonlogical relationships are treated here as if they were logical.

Since Sparrow speaks approvingly of Yeats and feels the obscurity of his poetry is justified, it may be well to turn to Yeats's essay on "The Symbolism of Poetry" for a final word. If one accepts the theory that poetry moves us because of its symbolism, Yeats says, it would not "be any longer possible for anybody to deny the importance of form, in all its kinds, for although you can expound an opinion, or describe a thing when your words are not quite well chosen, you cannot give a body to something that moves beyond the senses, unless your words are as subtle, as complex, as full of mysterious life, as the body of a flower or of a woman. The form of *sincere poetry, unlike the form of the popular poetry,* may indeed be sometimes obscure, or ungrammatical as in some of the best of the Songs of Innocence and Experience, but it must have the perfections that escape analysis, the subtleties that have a new meaning every day . . . [italics mine]."

The terms of the antithesis, "sincere" and "popular," are calculated. It is one of our contemporary ironies that some of our finest modern poetry which is accompanied by a necessary complexity and obscurity should be labelled by some critics as "escapist." It is possible, of course, to prove that certain modern poets inhabit the Ivory Tower by measuring the size of the reading public which appreciates them. Surely a fairer test, however, is to measure the scope and breadth of experience which their poetry assimilates. And if we apply this test to both poets and reading public, we shall come to a strange and perhaps illuminating conclusion, namely, that it is the public which inhabits the Ivory Tower, separating its emotional life—at least that which it is willing to contemplate in poetry—from the actual world, and most of all from its intellectual activities; and that the poetry which it does appreciate presents certain conventional emotional responses, uncontaminated by the actual world and untroubled by the play of the mind.

5

THE MODERN POET

AND THE TRADITION

MODERN POETRY is still regarded by the overwhelming majority as on principle antitraditional—not only by its adverse critics but by its proponents. The history of modern American poetry as written by the Untermeyers and Monroes tends to take something of the following form: The modern American poet has rid himself of clichés, worn-out literary materials, and the other stereotypes of Victorianism. Having sloughed off these dead conventions, he has proceeded (with the critic's hearty approval) to write of American scenes, American things, and the American people.

In so far as the tradition is to be understood as meaning "Victorianism," the approval given is just. There is obviously no value in adhering to lifeless conventions. But a healthy tradition is capable of continual modification, and the English tradition includes much more than the nineteenth century. The tendency to identify the tradition with Victorianism is in itself a vivid testimony to the thinness of the tradition in America. The new poets tended to make the simplest sort of readjustment, that of flat rejection. The net result of the revolt was probably healthy. At the same time, one must now see more and more clearly that much of the poetry of this revolt was negative in effect; and one must realize that a number of poets were then hailed as geniuses, not so much for what they wrote as for what they refused to write. Too often the American poet, after discarding the rags of Victorianism, was to be found walking in a barrel.

One effect of the revolt was to set a higher premium on originality in itself. The insistence on originality, too, was healthy. But as Eliot has pointed out: "The most individual parts of [the poet's] work may be those in which the dead poets, his ancestors, assert their immortality most vigorously." This sort of originality the poets of the revolt did not possess: their most individual passages are those in which they are most strongly merely themselves; their most imitative, those in which they lean hardest, consciously or unconsciously, on the poets of the past.

This is strikingly true of Vachel Lindsay, for example. His Victorian passages represent him uniformly at his worst: see, for example, his "Galahad, Knight Who Perished" or "The Litany of the Heroes." To be still more specific, his "General Booth Enters Heaven" is good in proportion as the poet has violated Victorian conventionality—the conception of heaven as an American small town with the court house in the square, and the audacious introduction of the Salvation Army band and parade into heaven itself. The poem is weak in proportion as the lines are padded with "literary" phrases—American bums described as

> Lurching *bravos* from the ditches dank

or, after their regeneration, more startlingly "literary" still, as

> *Sages* and *sybils* now, and athletes clean,
> Rulers of empires, and of forests green!

Edgar Lee Masters will also furnish some extreme examples. His *Spoon River Anthology,* clearly his best and healthiest work, shows Masters again and again, when he wishes to rise to a point of sublimity, returning as a matter of necessity to Victorian diction, rhythms, and sentiment. After a number of sordid, sociological epitaphs, Masters will give us this sort of thing, as in his "Anne Rutledge":

Wedded to him, not through union,
But through separation.
Bloom forever, O Republic,
From the dust of my bosom!

One sympathizes with the intention of the poet here. Presumably, the poet wants his vision of a beautiful life to seem to arise out of a total view of society—a view which does not blink at the ugliness that is there. But the portrait of Lincoln's sweetheart stands on a different level of perception from those of her fellow-townsmen. The poet refuses to consider her in terms of the total view—as the diction, imagery, and rhythms of her epitaph indicate. We get an anomalous Victorian patch in the prevailingly frank and "modern" examination.

This healthy animus against second-hand, "literary" subject matter tended, moreover, in practice, to confine the poet to realistic, "American" materials—on the surface at least. And the concomitant reaction against Victorian "messages" and statements tended to make the poet content merely with the presentation of a surface. Sandburg, for example, often displays a crust of modern American materials thrown over statements which are as vague, and sometimes as sentimental, as those of Whitman.

In general, the revulsion from Victorianism manifested itself in a preoccupation with the materials of poetry as such. This preoccupation revealed itself in two forms. In the first place, it revealed itself in a tendency to rest in the mere objective description of things (the kind of poetry which John Crowe Ransom has defined as *physical* poetry, a poetry of things without ideas).

In the second place, the preoccupation with subject matter expressed itself in a tendency to substitute new and unworked material for old. Here is to be placed Whitman's appeal to the Muse to migrate from the European scene to the poetic exploitation of a virgin continent. The tendency merges with self-conscious nationalism, or more lately, with certain kinds of regionalism, to produce a poetry of local color. To take recent examples, Paul Engle's "American Song" will illustrate the first case; Jesse Stuart's "Man with a Bull-Tongue Plow," the second.

But whether, as with the Imagists, the poet was primarily cosmopolitan, or whether he was the native local colorist like Sandburg, in neither case was he able to make much more than superficial changes in the organization of his poetry. The Imagist Manifesto is symptomatic; it proclaimed the legitimacy of experiment and innovation in subject matter and in versification. But it did not strike at the heart of the problem by redefining the structure of poetry. For example, the Manifesto attempted to liberalize the Victorian restrictions which hedged about the "poetic." Steam engines, said the Imagists, were also to be regarded as poetic—that is, as possible material for poetry. But the Manifesto did not indicate what use was to be made of them in the new poetry. Most of all, it did nothing to determine the relationship of these new materials to the older "poetic" materials. And this relationship is a matter of basic importance.

The Manifesto was obviously sound, in so far as it went. But one can now point out (making use of a justified hindsight) how limited it was. Its function was fundamentally negative—its real importance, that of cutting away dead wood.

If we have been led to consider imagist poetry as essentially symbolist poetry *manqué*, we must consider the poetry which attempted to resolve violent discords as metaphysical poetry *manqué*. It is true that Sandburg in his "Definitions of Poetry" proposes that poetry is a "synthesis of hyacinths and biscuits"; but neither his own poetry nor that of the other poets of the revolt succeeds in making so daring or interesting a fusion. The synthesis is as thin and oversimple as are the Imagists' "symbols." If this statement seems ungracious, one need only remind the reader that credit for helping clear the ground of dead materials (here freely given) is another thing than credit for positive achievement. The positive achievement is there, but usually on the simplest of levels. Sandburg's poem, "Washington Monument by Night," presents a sort of epitome of the characteristic strength and weakness of these poets— if not as a typical specimen, at least as a sort of fable. The poem begins auspiciously enough with a description of the physical object:

I

The stone goes straight.
A lean swimmer dives into night sky. . . .

But as the poet moves away from the monument as an object to the monument as a symbol, the poem weakens. The psychology of Washington, the man, is far less sharply realized. We get the most general and indefinite aspects— a sort of common denominator of all situations in which strong men battle with fate.

VI

Tongues wrangled dark at a man.
He buttoned his overcoat and stood alone.

And finally, with the attempt to concentrate the meaning, the poem peters out completely:

VIII

The name of an iron man goes over the world.
It takes a long time to forget an iron man.

IX

[The lines of this stanza are thus in the poem.]

. . . .
. . . .

The lack of psychological subtlety, the lack of complexity in the poet's attitude, the weak dramatic sense, the general crudity of "form"—all these are aspects of a violent repudiation of the poetic tradition. The poets attempt to do in one generation what it requires generations of poets to do. The result is a retreat toward the elementary, undifferentiated "stuff of poetry." Indeed, there is a great deal of primitivism to be found in the poetry of the revolt. With the rejection of formal verse systems there is a reversion to loose chant lines and repetition (Sandburg's "Chicago"); complex structure, logical or symbolical, gives way to the simple method of development by cumulative accretion— poems develop by the poet's piling up detail on detail (H. D.'s "Sea Gods"); raw "content" overrides and determines form (Masters' *Spoon River Anthology*).

Granting his circumstances, each of these poets is to be congratulated on having chosen as he did. If the traditional forms were stifling, then the poet did best to write without conscious form; if the poet's poetic ancestors were not an aid but a burden, he did best to dispense with their help, and start again from scratch. But the choice is a hard one: it certainly enforces tremendous limitations on the poet's flexibility and range.

One can see the importance of this effect by comparing the poets of the revolt with those of the Romantic period. When Wordsworth and Coleridge rejected Pope and Dr. Johnson, they did not expatriate themselves; they found in the tradition elements previously neglected which were apt to their purpose; among other things, the romantic Shakespeare and the folk ballad. Carl Sandburg, on the other hand, in rejecting Keats and Tennyson, cuts himself off from the English tradition altogether.

Victorian poetry was, as we have seen, a poetry of sharp exclusions. What was required in our own time was a poetry based upon a principle of inclusion. The rediscovery of the school of Donne becomes, thus, an event of capital importance. It is a discovery particularly associated with Eliot, but one which other poets, the Nashville group, for example, made for themselves. The poetry of Allen Tate, John Crowe Ransom, and Robert Penn Warren will furnish some very clear instances of the third revolution in poetry.

These poets make a good choice here to illustrate the point, not only because of the intrinsic goodness of their poetry and because their criticism helped accomplish the revolution, but also because their achievement is closely associated with the vexed questions of regionalism and traditionalism—questions raised in acute form by all American poetry. The two questions are, obviously, intimately bound up with the technique of inclusion. We have suggested that the problem posed for poets like Masters and Sandburg was this: a choice between the raw, unqualified present, and the dead past. The poets who have been able to avoid the dilemma have succeeded in avoiding it because they could weld past with present. Indeed, every past is dead which is unconnected with the present—the past of the literary vacuum. Conversely, a present which is nothing but the immediate present of sensation—the present unrelated to history—is not even the present. It is apt to be merely a collection of sensations, or at best, unrelated images.

The problem presented by an attempt to hold on to a tradition is, thus, ultimately a problem of sincerity or integrity. To take a specific case, and, since the poets chosen for discussion here are Southern poets, one relevant to Southern poets: the Old South cannot exist in the mind of the modern Southerner apart from its nonexistence in the present. The sentimentalist can, of course, dwell upon the Old South exclusively, giving a romantic construct which has no connection with the present and therefore no real connection with the actual South of the past. (It is not even a paradox to say that we cannot know the past without knowing the present.) Consequently, the Southern poet who is unwilling to sentimentalize the past or to limit himself to objective descriptions of the local color of the present, must of necessity mediate his account of the Old South through a consciousness of the present; that is, of its present nonexistence. (This general principle applies, of course, to whatever other subject matter he may use.) To sum up, his experience will include both positive and negative elements, and his real test as a poet will be his ability to bring the two sorts into unity.

In the same way the relation of the poet to his particular region is subsumed under the problem of integrity. Nineteenth-century poets like Stedman or Taylor felt that they could detach themselves from America and strike directly at the universal. But their poems seem too empty and thin —literary in the worst sense. The converse belief—that poetry should merely express the local color of a region— is false also.* The depth of our confusion on the point is to be seen in the tendency—still active—to associate tradition with dead conventionality and regionalism with mere local color. With the poets whom we are to consider, the structure of inclusion is the basic structure. For example, in John Crowe Ransom's or Allen Tate's verse, for all their interest in regionalism, a description of the Southern scene never becomes the *raison d'être* of the poem. The following lines from Ransom are thoroughly Southern:

> Autumn days in our section
> Are the most used-up thing on earth . . .
> Having no more colour nor predilection
> Than cornstalks too wet for the fire

but the figure serves the poem—is not served by it. The distinction is most important.

---

* Whitman may be thought to have resolved the contradiction by finding a new unity; and certainly he struggled to achieve this. But the diverse elements in all but his best poetry tend to stay apart: there is, on the one hand, the particularity of the long "catalogue" passages, and on the other, the too frequent, vague, and windy generality about democracy and progress. Emily Dickinson, on the other hand, does achieve very often a unity which is thoroughly faithful to her New England environment and yet is not limited to local color. Her best poetry obviously manifests a structure of inclusion, and significantly enough, displays the vigorous, sometimes audacious metaphor, which we have seen to be a characteristic of the other types of poetry which we have examined.

In Robert Penn Warren's sequence of poems, "Kentucky Mountain Farm," the reader might expect to find an exploitation of Southern rural life, and there is enough accurate description to validate the poet's localizing of his scene. Consider for instance, the third poem of the sequence, "History among the Rocks." The poet recounts the various ways of dying in the country of the rocks—freezing, drowning, the bite of the copperhead in the wheat:

> By flat limestone, will coil the copperhead,
> Fanged as the sunlight, hearing the reaper's feet.

But the items of local color are absorbed in the poem as adjuncts of the larger theme. These ways of dying are all "natural," and the poet, by making them seem to inhere in the landscape, makes them seem easy, effortless, appropriate. "But," the poet goes on to say,

> there are other ways, the lean men said:
> In these autumn orchards once young men lay dead . . .
> Grey coats, blue coats. Young men on the mountain-
> side
> Clambered, fought. Heels muddied the rocky spring.
> Their reason is hard to guess, remembering
> Blood on their black mustaches in moonlight.

This sort of death—death sought for—cuts in sharply and puzzlingly across the other kinds of death. The poet does not, however, allow his poem to fall into an easy resolution with a comment on the meaninglessness of war in general. The young men's death is "unnatural" but that quality allows of more than one interpretation: it may signify that all war is meaningless, but it may also suggest that their choice was not an easy one and therefore meaningful and heroic for them. The poet himself abjures explicit commentary:

> Their reason is hard to guess and a long time past:
> The apple falls, falling in the quiet night.

The last figure not only recapitulates the earlier examples of "natural" death, it comes with an ambiguity to accentuate the ironic contrast. Man is not merely natural; his capacity for defying nature is the typically *human* trait. But the poet does not elaborate on the young men's act, or try to justify it explicitly. Their reason is "hard to guess," and it happened a long time ago. The poet is willing to let the matter rest in calling attention to the contrast of the apple's effortless fall.

The poem is typical of the general structure of Warren's poems, a structure which may be described as follows: There is a rich and detailed examination of the particular experience with the conclusion, which may be drawn from the experience, coming as a quietly ironical statement or as modest and guarded understatement. It is as though the poet felt that only the minimum of commentary was allowable if he was not to do violence to the integrity of the experience. This general method is frequently used in order to state a theme closely related to that of the poem just discussed: the relation of the rational to the irrational, of the experience as experience to the interpretation or commentary on the experience.

This is the theme, for example, of "Aged Man Surveys the Past Time." The old man weeps, and perhaps

> Grief's smarting condiment may satisfy
> His heart to lard the wry and blasphemous theme.

The blasphemous theme is that regret is linked to the stuff of experience—whatever the commentary on experience and whatever the true account of experience may be.

> Truth, not truth. The heart, how regular
> And sure! How ambidextrous is regret!
> Time has no mathematic.

Man's regret is a handle which will fit either tool—either a knowable universe or an unknowable.

> By fruitful grove, unfruited now by winter,
> The well-adapted and secular catbird
> Whimpers its enmity and invitation.
> Light fails beyond the barn and blasted oak.

Man is not "secular." He is cut off from nature, and consequently can take the bird's call as "enmity" or "invitation," for it is both and neither. Nature is indifferent and goes on with its regular processes. Evening is falling; spring has come, and "godless summer" will follow.

So much for the theme. But the poem "works" in somewhat more intricate fashion. The inflections of tone are managed largely by the rhythm and imagery. For example, the man's grief springs from the fact that he is not "well-adapted," not "natural" like the bird. But his sorrow—the imagery suggests ironically—is thoroughly "natural":

> And aged eyes, like twilit rain, their effort
> Spill gentlier than herb-issue on a hill.

The bird "whimpers" in company with the weeping man; but the "whimper," one realizes in a moment, is only ironically appropriate to the scene. The bird is not "weeping" with the man, or indeed weeping at all. The word "whimper" merely describes accurately the bird's song.

Ironical shifts of tone are used far more violently in "The Return: an Elegy." The poem has for its subject the experience of the son returning home at the death of his mother, and in the poem occur elements of memory and of grief, scenes from the landscape flashing through the train window on the homeward journey, memories of childhood, and the various associations—both serious and frivolous—that death and dying have. The discordant elements appear as the casual, irrelevant, and even bawdy associations which flicker through the consciousness when the mind is held in the grip of a deep grief. For example, after such a passage as

> The wheels hum hum
> The wheels: I come I come
> Whirl out of space through time O wheels
> Pursue down backward time the ghostly parallels

> Pursue past culvert cut fill embankment semaphore
> Pursue down gleaming hours that are no more.
> The pines, black, snore

follows

> turn backward turn backward o time in your flight
> and make me a child again just for tonight
> good lord he's wet the bed come bring a light

> What grief hath the heart distilled?
> The heart is unfulfilled
> The hoarse pine stilled

The shock of these discordant associations could be justified
on the basis of honesty. But one need not rest the case
for them with this. Their general function is to accommo-
date the poem to reality, toughening it against the senti-
mental. They guarantee the intensity of the positive pas-
sages, and particularly, the climax of the poem. The poem
ends as follows:

> If I could pluck
> Out of the dark that whirled
> Over the hoarse pine over the rock
> Out of the mist that furled
> Could I stretch forth like God the hand and gather
> For you my mother
> If I could pluck
> Against the dry essential of tomorrow
> To lay upon the breast that gave me suck
> Out of the dark the dark and swollen orchid of this
>   sorrow.

The last image, when we reach it, is so heavily charged
with the tension that it comes with sharp impact. But in
another context the image might easily become soft and
spurious. The poem, written in terms of conventional ex-
clusions, would have had to forego intensity in order to
avoid sentimentality.

The use of contrasts may be less violent, however, as in
the fine "Bearded Oaks," where the surface of the poem is
smooth, and even suave, though the internal structure is a
pattern of contrasts and resolutions. The poem has for its
subject the contemplation of a moment which, in its ideality,
seems to lie out of time altogether and to partake of the na-
ture of eternity. The quality of the experience is built up
carefully; the atmosphere is one of almost preternatural
relaxation and quiet. But the smoothness of the poem is not
devised merely to harmonize with the quiet and perfection
of the hour under the oaks. The unity which it represents
is achieved by the resolution of complexities, and thus the
structure of the poem reflects what the poem is saying:

> And violence, forgot now, lent
> The present stillness all its power.

In like manner, the tone of effortless intuition—direct and
unclouded illumination—is played off against the rather
intricate logical relations which it overlays. The effect is
much like that which Marvell achieves in many of his
poems.

The sharpness of the imagery and its ordination parallel
Marvell again. The poet begins by comparing the scene
under the oaks to the bed of the sea. And with the second
stanza, far from abandoning the image, the poet continues
to develop it:

> The grasses, kelp-like, satisfy
> The nameless motions of the air . . .

The qualities of the experience receive their development
in terms of this dominant image. The lovers in their un-
troubled stillness at the bottom of the sea of time rest, as if
made of coral. And, like coral, ages have gone into their
making. Now they lie far below the storms of the troubled
surface, and

> Passion and slaughter, ruth, decay
> Descended, whispered grain by grain,
> Silted down swaying streams, to lay
> Foundation for our voicelessness.

> All our debate is voiceless here,
> As all our rage is rage of stone;

The resolution of the experience and the exit from it is made in terms—not so much of irony as—of understatement.

> So little time we live in Time,
> And we learn all so painfully,
> That we may spare this hour's term
> To practice for Eternity.

The experience is rare and precious, but the emphasis on that fact is made obliquely. The poet does not exult in the sense of revelation which the hour has given, or proclaim that the meaning of life has been revealed to him in the experience. Rather, he makes what amounts to a covert apology for his indulgence in the experience. The hour may be "spared"; and the reason given adds a new development to the thought. The hour seems out of time and like eternity, but since life "in Time" is short, the lovers may well use it "to practice for Eternity." The development here is especially rich. If the hour under the oaks is associated with "Eternity," that eternity is also associated with death. If death—in its resemblance to the passive quiet of the hour—is made more acceptable, the process also works the other way; the hour is qualified by being associated with death. The effect is to make the tone of the last stanza seem modest and restrained. The poet has not in his experience of the hour lost his hold on reality.

The "Letter from a Coward to a Hero" will illustrate another delicate handling of tone. The poem begins frankly enough as a letter. The hero's day (any man's day) with its confusion and disappointment, is suggested; and the poet, after reviewing it, says,

> I think you deserved better;
> Therefore I am writing you this letter.

The letter is personal, and deals with the springs of the hero's courage. The broken shards of the hero's day recall the confused, "plural" experience of childhood:

> The scenes of childhood were splendid,
> And the light that there attended,
> But is rescinded:
> The cedar,
> The lichened rocks,
> The thicket where I saw the fox,
> And where I swam, the river.

The plurality of the child's world does not require "heroism." But the plurality of the world in which the "coward" lives is not attended by a splendid light, nor is it a succession of fairy-tale wonders.

> Guns blaze in autumn and
> The quail falls and
> Empires collide with a bang
> That shakes the pictures where they hang . . .
> But a good pointer holds the point
> And is not gun-shy;
> But I
> Am gun-shy.

The violence, the abrupt transitions, are functional. They indicate the reasons for gun-shyness—"the sudden backfire," which causes the coward to break his point. But the image of the pointer, one notices, is being used to qualify and define the coward's attitude toward the hero. The virtues of the pointer are solid virtues—but they are hardly the virtues of the imagination. The coward cannot propose to claim them, though he admires the good pointer.

The poem does not veer off into a mockery of the hero, however. The poet is sincere in his admiration and even tender.

You have been strong in love and hate. . . .
Rarely, you've been unmanned;
I have not seen your courage put to pawn.

But disaster won't play according to the rules. There comes
another image from the boyhood scene which opens the
poem. Even if disaster is outstripped in the race,

. . . he will cut across the back lot
To lurk and lie in wait.

And then another image, also from the boyhood scene,
which goes further to define the poet's attitude:

Admired of children, gathered for their games,
Disaster, like the dandelion, blooms,
And the delicate film is fanned
To seed the shaven lawn.

The ironic shock resides primarily in the comparison of dis-
aster to the familiar, commonplace flower. But the irony
goes on to inform the deeper relations: the figure implies
that the hero, like a child, is playing with disaster; the
quality of disaster, it is suggested, is its ability to propagate
itself innocently in the most "shaven lawn." The coward is
really standing in the role of Tiresias; but the tone of the
utterance is that of a boyhood friend; and the example is
one drawn from a childish game.

The last section of the poem states indirectly the reasons
for the speaker's "cowardice," and, by implication, his
criticism of the hero's "heroism." The criticism takes the
form of a question:

At the blind hour of unaimed grief,
Of addition and subtraction,
Of compromise,
Of the smoky lecher, the thief,
Of regretted action,
At the hour to close the eyes,
At the hour when lights go out in the houses . . .
Then wind rouses

The kildees from their sodden ground:
Their commentary is part of the wind's sound.
What is that other sound,
Surf or distant cannonade?

But the hero at such hours is apparently not troubled by
intimations of fear. He is beset by no such questions.
And the speaker can finally resolve his mixture of admira-
tion and criticism only by a piece of whimsy.

No doubt, when corridors are dumb
And the bed is made,
It is your custom to recline,
Clutching between the forefinger and thumb
Honor, for death shy valentine.

The note of real admiration is guaranteed by the tone of
the banter. The admiration is genuine. But one observes
that the whimsical compliment, *though* compliment, at the
same time reduces the hero to a small boy, and, ironically,
a shy young boy.

A number of Warren's poems, we have said, concern
themselves with explorations of the problem of knowledge:
What is the relation of actor to the act—of the thing done to
the interpretations which are placed upon it, the "meanings"
that it bears. His most ambitious treatment of this occurs
in the brilliant "History." Here the theme is dramatized by
the poet's making the speaker of the poem a member of
some band of invaders on the point of descending upon the
land which they are to conquer. The imagery of the poem
suggests that the invaders are the Israelites preparing to
take the Promised Land, but they are any invaders, or more
largely still, any men entering upon any decisive act.

The speaker recalls the hardships, the dangers, the hun-
ger now past. He sees before him

The delicate landscape unfurled:
A world
Of ripeness blent, and green:

> The fruited earth,
> Fire on the good hearth,
> The fireside scene.

This is the land which they are to seize and possess. But the speaker goes on to survey the future:

> In the new land
> Our seed shall prosper, and
> In those unsifted times
> Our sons shall cultivate
> Peculiar crimes,
> Having not love, nor hate,
> Nor memory.

But some, in that distant future, world-weary and "defective of desire," will ponder on what their ancestors have done, will strive, vainly, to assess the motives of their ancestors' action, and will

> In dim pools peer
> To see, of some grandsire,
> The long and toothéd jawbone greening there.

The situation is peculiarly the modern situation: we are obsessed with a consciousness of the past which drives us back upon history in a search for meanings. The absolutes are gone—are dissolved, indeed, by our consciousness of the past—by our consciousness of a plurality of histories and meanings. For us, the moderns, as for the descendants of the invaders of the poem, time is

> . . . the aimless bitch
> —Purblind, field-worn,
> Slack dugs by the dry thorn torn—
> Forever quartering the ground in which
> The blank and fanged
> Rough certainty lies hid.

The fall of night stirs him out of his reverie. It is time for the attack. And why are they to attack? He tries to frame an answer, and by the very act of searching for an answer, indicates what he is to say in the lines that follow:

> We seek what end?
> The slow dynastic ease,
> Travail's cease?
> Not pleasure, sure:
> Alloy of fact?
> The act
> Alone is pure.

The act is the only absolute, the irreducible item which begets the explanations rather than that which is explained by them.

The poem levels out to an end with another glance at the time of the future:

> We shall essay
> The rugged ritual, but not of anger.
> Let us go down before
> Our thews are latched in the myth's languor,
> Our hearts with fable grey.

The poem, for all its use of the Israelites, is a modern poem. Its focus lies in the "unsifted times" where men have "not love, nor hate, / Nor memory." Its integrity rests in the fact that it does not flinch from the modern problem. The Israelites do not become merely decorative figures. All men are Jews—wanderers, rootless, seeking a promised land. America, in especial, is the latest promised land, and the Israelites constitute an especially apt symbol for ourselves.

The poem, thus, deals with the poet's own environment, with America, and, indeed, with the South. The problem raised in terms of the Israelites is a variation of that raised by the young men whose heels "muddied the rocky spring." In the poem, the items of past and present are unified by an act of the imagination which, if it transcends the region, remains rooted in it and derives its vitality from it.

These general points may all be illustrated from the poetry of John Crowe Ransom; but it may be valuable to take a more special approach to his work. Ransom's characteristic instrument is that of irony. But the irony remains always an instrument—it never becomes a mere attitude adopted by the poet for its own sake.

In its simplest form it is to be found in poems like "Amphibious Crocodile," where it lies very close to mere good-humored self-deprecation. Mr. Robert Crocodile undertakes the Grand Tour and tries successively the various expected careers before giving up and settling down in the family creek. But even here the attitude is not quite so simple nor so light as we have stated it. It is only a step further to the quality of self-irony to be found in "Tom, Tom, the Piper's Son," where the speaker's whimsy is playful in only the more serious senses of the word.

Certainly Ransom's more typical irony is to be found in his commentaries on the human predicament, commentaries which he usually finds occasion for by throwing aspects of that predicament into the form of a little fable. But the commentary is not stated as a conclusion to the fable—it is, rather, diffused throughout the fable as the qualifying tone with which the poet relates it. For this reason, it is difficult to isolate the commentary in each instance. Indeed, tone is so important in Ransom's poetry and so intimately related to the effect of each poem as a whole that quotation of fragments from his poetry does Ransom an especial injustice.

One cannot hope, therefore, to give a full sense of the power of his poems short of quoting them in their entirety, but it will be possible to indicate something of their structure and something of the basic attitude from which the poet's irony springs.

To an astonishing degree, the problems which engage Ransom's attention turn out to be aspects of one situation: that of man's divided sensibility.

There is the ironical commentary on Ralph ("Morning") whose vision of loveliness as he lies half-awake—

>   . . . such a meadow
> Of wings and light and clover,
> He would propose to Jane then to go walking—

is dismissed by the return of his "manliness":

> Suddenly he remembered about himself,
> His manliness returned entire to Ralph;
> The dutiful mills of the brain
> Began to whir with their smooth-grinding wheels—

so that he is left with

> Simply another morning, and simply Jane.

Or there is the case of the "poor bookish hind" of the "Miller's Daughter" with "too much pudding" in his head "of learned characters and scraps of love" and tongue-tied before the fabulous daughter of the mill, whose eyes "are a blue stillwater," and can only

>   . . . stare—
> A learned eye of our most Christian nation
> And foremost philosophical generation—
> At primary chrome of hair. . . .

In the form most familiar to us, the division reveals itself in the contrast between the broken and confused life of the mature man and the innocent and total world of childhood which he has grown out of. The characters of "Eclogue" comment on the change from the time when

> . . . precious little innocents were we.
> Said a boy, "Now shall we let her be the fox?"
> Or a girl, "Now which of you will climb the tree?"
> We were quick-foot the deer, strong-heart the ox,
> Business-man the bee. . . .
>
> We were spendthrifts of joy when we were young,
> But we became usurious, and in fright
> Conceived that such a waste of days was wrong
> For marchers unto night . . .

> . . . And every day since then
> We are mortals teasing for immortal spoils,
> Desperate women and men.

The poem has its focus in the plight of the lovers, but not romantically or exclusively. Even here the lovers are moderns, and their predicament, though universally human, is a symbol of the predicament of a scientific civilization.

The desperation of Ransom's characters springs finally from the fact that they cannot attain unity of being. Childhood—the childhood of a race or of a culture—gives a suggestion of what such unity can be, but development into maturity, and specialization, break up the harmony of faculties and leave intellect at war with emotion, the practical life with the life of sentiment, science with poetry.

In Ransom's poetry it is this conflict which receives most attention. It is the theme, for example, of "Persistent Explorer," whose fable is that of the poet himself thrown up upon the neutralized world of modern science. The explorer hears a waterfall, and then climbs to a height from which to look at it. It teases his ears and eyes with the suggestion that it is something more than mere water falling.

> But listen as he might, look fast or slow,
> It was water, only water, tons of it
> Dropping into the gorge, and every bit
> Was water—the insipid chemical H_2O.

The thunder of the cataract is appropriately loud enough to be the voice of a god; the mist that rises from it, beautiful enough to be that from which a goddess appears. But no god speaks to him, no goddess appears. Moreover, the poet has too much integrity to resolve his theme with an easy pathos. He must confess that he does not even know what he would have the cataract "mean" to him.

> What would he have it spell? He scarcely knew;
> Only that water and nothing but water filled
> His eyes and ears, nothing but water that spilled;
> And if the smoke and rattle of water drew

From the deep thickets of his mind the train,
The fierce fauns and the timid tenants there,
That burst their bonds and rushed upon the air,
Why, he must turn and beat them down again.

But the poet also rejects the resolution of his dilemma
afforded by "romantic irony"—the self-pitying disillusion-
ment with science:

So be it. And no unreasonable outcry
The pilgrim made; only a rueful grin
Spread over his lips until he drew them in;
He did not sit upon a rock and die.

There were many ways of dying. . . .

But there were many ways of living too,
And let his enemies gibe, but let them say
That he would throw this continent away
And seek another country,—as he would do.

The protagonist of the poem refuses anything less than the
complete experience. He is not retreating before the ad-
vance of science. He is significantly an "explorer," not a
refugee.

The relation of science to poetry has been treated by
Ransom in his discussion of religion, *God Without Thunder.*
Science gives always an abstract description, and because
abstract, powerful; whereas poetry attempts a complete, a
total description of the object, including not only those
elements which make the knowledge "useful," but other
"useless" elements as well. And religion differs from phi-
losophy, which abstracts at least to the level of principles, by
clothing the principles in the garb of poetry, and thus pre-
fers full-bodied gods to mere principles. A diet of straight
science, because science is power-knowledge, may contrib-
ute to *hubris;* whereas poetry (as an element of religion or
merely as poetry), because it forces on the attention ele-
ments which cannot be absorbed in a practical program,

constantly reminds man that the thing described lies outside man's control, and thus rebukes *hubris*.

To revert to terms already developed, poetic description involves a technique of inclusion rather than of exclusion. A civilization which has narrowed its sensibility with a regimen of power-knowledge, like Ralph, wakes to find that the world has become in a special and serious sense, stale, flat, and unprofitable. Ransom's poetry resolutely sets about to include "the other side." But it represents this other side, not by preachments, but by attempting to restore the total view. And the index of that totality is the ironic tone of the poem.

In emphasizing the center to which Ransom's irony refers, we must not give the impression that the special difficulty of the modern poet is his only theme, or that the rueful grin is the only gesture allowed to him as ironist. Having defined the central impulse of his poetry and his basic method, we shall have no difficulty in finding examples of an abundant variety of themes and attitudes. But the variety is a variety of ironies.

It is this method of indirection which allows Ransom to treat, with absolute sureness, subjects which most modern poets tend to shrink from—a child's first acquaintance with death ("Janet Waking") or the homesickness of one lover for another ("Winter Remembered"). To illustrate from the former poem, the poet begins by giving the exposition perfectly casually. The setting is that of typical American domesticity—even suburban:

Beautifully Janet slept
Till it was deeply morning. She woke then
And thought about her dainty-feathered hen,
To see how it had kept.

One kiss she gave her mother,
Only a small one gave she to her daddy
Who would have kissed each curl of his shining baby;
No kiss at all for her brother.

But Chucky, the pet hen, is dead. The poet treats its death mock-heroically:

And purply did the knot
Swell with the venom and communicate
Its rigour! Now the poor comb stood up straight
But Chucky did not.

No special importance attaches to Janet or to Chucky. The whole incident is perfectly ordinary. The poet implies that we are free to be amused at it—he is not trying to surround it with any special sanctity. And it is for this reason, that the pathos of the last stanzas seems to emerge legitimately from the incident—is not forced into the incident by the poet.

So there was Janet
Kneeling on the wet grass, crying her brown hen
(Translated far beyond the daughters of men)
To rise and walk upon it.

And weeping fast as she had breath
Janet inplored us, "Wake her from her sleep!"
And would not be instructed in how deep
Was the forgetful kingdom of death.

The poet, in effect, retains his tone of objectivity: he is willing to deal with the whole episode as an incident in Janet's education. Janet has difficulty with her lesson. She "would not be instructed." That Janet's difficulty is a universally human one does not need to be underscored by the poet. The effect is made indirectly.

The method of indirection renders successful the poems on the Old South, poems which one might think would surely offer this poet his most severe tests in maintaining firmness of tone. "The Old Mansion," for instance, suggests to the poet that

Here age seemed newly imaged for the historian
After his monstrous châteaux on the Loire,
A beauty not for depicting by old vulgarian
Reiterations which gentle readers abhor.

Consequently, the poet goes on to describe the old house in terms which avoid the "old vulgarian/Reiterations" (though the hard-boiled modern reader is embraced by the irony too in being characterized as "gentle"). The poet proceeds to develop the pathos in terms of an ironical commentary which keeps steadily in mind the fact that his reader has his mouth set for a succession of clichés.

It is an extreme indirection which contributes the obscurity to one of the most difficult of Ransom's poems, "Painting: a Head." The theme of this poem is roughly the same as that of "Two Gentlemen in Bonds": the human predicament of being divided into head and body. But the poem actually begins as a whimsical meditation on the portrait head on the wall.

The poet plays with the accidental symbolism involved in the fact that the portrait shows the head and no body—the head removed from the body by "dark severance." It is characteristic of heads, the poet observes, to attempt to be "absolute and to try decapitation." The face revealed in the portrait in question, however, it "too happy" and beautiful to have belonged to that class of heads. It is the head of a man of thirty and

> Discovers maybe thirty unwidowed years
> Of not dishonoring the faithful stem.

It is, moreover, the head of a nameless man, and thus has not been taken as a trophy by the "historian headhunters." For the artist to have painted it as removed from the body was, therefore, a piece of "capital irony."

But the poet, in the very process of pointing out that the portrait on which he meditates is not that of a man who was guilty of forcing abstraction, has made his case against abstraction, and is allowed to shift his tone from teasing whimsy into what amounts to the serious fantasy of fable:

> Beauty is of body.
> The flesh contouring shallowly on a head
> Is a rock-garden needing body's love
> And best bodiness to colorify

The big blue birds sitting and sea-shell flats
And caves and on the iron acropolis
To spread the hyacinthine hair and rear
The olive garden for the nightingales.

One may generalize by saying that Ransom's irony never becomes a stereotype. It is a function of the entire poem and consequently varies from poem to poem. At the one extreme, it does not flatten out into mere satire; at the other extreme, it does not fail to obtain altogether. It is always present, if only as a sense of aesthetic distance.

Indeed, Ransom's forte is the subtlety and firmness of tone which he achieves. His poems are as little amenable to paraphrase as are any poems that one can think of. It is probably because he is able to transmit so definitely shades of attitude which can be perceived and yet which defy exact description in prose commentary that critics are so often moved to metaphorical descriptions of his method —descriptions which sometimes convey little more than a recognition that something has been achieved in the poetry. Ransom's triumphs, like those of the poets of the early seventeenth century, are triumphs in the handling of tone. And his fundamental relation to those poets lies in the brilliance of his handling of tone—not in the use of a particular diction or "conceits" or in his taking a particular attitude toward certain themes. It is rather in the attention which he has given to the definition and communication of delicate shadings of attitude as a problem in itself. His poems bear their own self-criticism. And this is why they are unsentimental, tough-minded, and penetrating, and why the serious ones are powerful in the responses which they evoke.

Allen Tate's poetry, too, illustrates what we have called a structure of synthesis, and furnishes even more violent illustrations than does Ransom's. Tate constantly throws his words and images into active contrast. Almost every adjective in his poetry challenges the reader's imagination to follow it off at a tangent. For instance, in the "Ode to the Confederate Dead," November becomes not "drear" November, "sober" November, but

> *Ambitious* November with the humors of the year
>   [italics mine].

The "curiosity of an angel's stare" is not "idle" or "quiet" or "probing" or any other predictable adjective, but "brute" curiosity. This is the primary difficulty that Tate's poetry presents to the reader who is unacquainted with his dominant themes: the surface of the poem, in its apparently violent disorder, may carry him off at tangents.

There is some justification, therefore, for approaching Tate's poetry through an account of his basic themes—all the more since these themes are closely related to the poetic method itself. We may conveniently begin by examining a very important passage in his essay on "Humanism and Naturalism." In discussing attitudes toward history, he describes two ways of viewing the past. The first is that which gives what may be called the scientist's past, in which events form a logical series; the second is that which gives what Tate himself calls the "temporal past."

". . . the logical series is quantitative, the abstraction of space. The temporal series is, on the other hand, space concrete. Concrete, temporal experience implies the existence of a temporal past, and it is the foundation of the religious imagination; that is to say, the only way to think of the past independently of . . . naturalism is to think religiously; and conversely, the only way to think religiously is to think in time. Naturalistic science is timeless. A doctrine based upon it, whether explicitly or not, can have no past, no idea of tradition, no fixed center of life. The 'typically human' is a term that cannot exist apart from some other term; it is not an absolute; it is fluid and unfixed.

"To de-temporize the past is to reduce it to an abstract lump. To take from the present its concrete fullness is to refuse to let standards work from the inside. It follows

that 'decorum' must be 'imposed' from above. Thus there
are never specific moral problems (the subject matter of the
arts) but only fixed general doctrines without subject mat-
ter—that is to say, without 'nature.'"

In other words, the artist today finds that his specific
subject matter tends to be dissolved in abstractions of
various sorts. His proper subjects—specific moral problems
—are not to be found in an abstract, logical series, for in
such a series there are no standards of any sort—and noth-
ing specific, nothing concrete.

Tate's preoccupation with history and time in his poetry
is thus closely related to Ransom's characteristic problem:
that of man living under the dispensation of science—mod-
ern man suffering from a dissociation of sensibility.

Tate goes on to say in the same essay: "The 'historical
method' has always been the anti-historical method. Its
aim is to contemporize the past. Its real effect is to de-
temporize it. The past becomes a causal series, and time-
less . . ." Tate's concern here is with the neohumanists,
but the generalization may be applied to the arts without
distorting it too violently. Carl Sandburg, for example, will
supply an example pat to our purpose. Consider his "Four
Preludes on Playthings of the Wind."

After the first Prelude with its "What of it? Let the dead
be dead," and after the second Prelude which describes an
ancient city (Babylon?) with its cedar doors and golden
dancing girls and its ultimate destruction, Prelude Three
begins:

> It has happened before.
> Strong men put up a city and got
>   a nation together,
> And paid singers to sing and women
>   to warble: We are the greatest city,
>   the greatest nation,
>   nothing like us ever was.

But, as the poem goes on to point out, the ultimate dancers
are the rats, and the ultimate singers, the crows. The poet's

intention, presumably, is to contemporize the past. The real effect is to detemporize it. Babylon or Nineveh becomes interchangeable with Chicago. Chicago receives a certain access of dignity from the association; Babylon, a certain humanity and reality; and the poet is allowed to imply, with a plausible finality, that human nature fundamentally doesn't change.

Sandburg's primary impulse seems to be a revulsion from the "literary" past—the people of the past, too, hired singers, ran night-clubs, and joined booster societies. But Sandburg's contemporizing of the past springs also—probably unconsciously—from the fact that he is immersed in a scientific civilization.

Tate not only cannot accept Sandburg's detemporized past; he must strive actively to ascertain what meaning the past can have for modern man who has so many inducements to consider it merely as a logical series. This, I take it, is the primary theme of "The Mediterranean," "Aeneas at Washington," and even—in a varied form—of the "Ode to the Confederate Dead." Aeneas possessed a concrete past— moved from a particular Troy to found a particular Rome. We, on the other hand, who have "cracked the hemispheres with careless hand," in abolishing space have also abolished time. The poem is not a lament, nor is it a "sighing for vanished glories." It is a recognition and an exploration of our dilemma. Modern man, like the Aeneas of Tate's poem, is obsessed with the naturalistic view of history— history as an abstract series. He sees

> . . . all things apart, the towers that men
> Contrive I too contrived long, long ago.

But Aeneas has been acquainted with another conception of history.

> Now I demand little. The singular passion
> Abides its object and consumes desire
> In the circling shadow of its appetite.

(We may gloss the last quoted lines as follows: In his "Religion and the Old South," Tate argues that the naturalistic view of history is intent on utility; but in the case of concrete history, the "images are only to be contemplated, and perhaps the act of contemplation after long exercise initiates a habit of restraint, and the setting up of absolute standards which are less formulas for action than an interior discipline of the mind.")

Modern man with his tremendous historical consciousness is thus confronted with a dilemma when asked for the meaning of his actions:

> . . . Stuck in the wet mire
> Four thousand leagues from the ninth buried city
> I thought of Troy, what we had built her for.

The problem of history receives a somewhat similar treatment in the fine "Message from Abroad." The form into which the problem is cast is peculiarly that of the American confronted with the lack of "history" of his own land and thrown up against the immense "history" of Europe. Stated in somewhat altered form, it is the problem of man, who requires a history in which he can participate personally, lost in the vast museum galleries of western civilization.

>   Provençe,
> The Renascence, the age of Pericles, each
> A broad, rich-carpeted stair to pride
> . . . they're easy to follow
> For the ways taken are all notorious,
> Lettered, sculptured and rhymed. . . .

But "those others," the ways taken by his ancestors, are

>   . . . incuriously complete, lost,
> Not by poetry and statues timed,
> Shattered by sunlight and the impartial sleet.

He can find, to mark those ways,

> Now only
> The bent eaves and the windows cracked,
> The thin grass picked by the wind,
> Heaved by the mole. . . .

The tall "red-faced" man cannot survive the voyage back to Europe:

> With dawn came the gull to the crest,
> Stared at the spray, fell asleep
> Over the picked bones, the white face
> Of the leaning man drowned deep. . . .

And the poet is finally forced to admit that he cannot see the ancestors, and can merely conjecture

> What did you say mornings?
> Evenings, what?
> The bent eaves
> On the cracked house,
> That ghost of a hound . . .
> The man red-faced and tall
> Will cast no shadow
> From the province of the drowned.

Obviously Tate's poetry is not occupied exclusively with the meaning of history. But his criticism of merely statistical accounts of reality serves as an introduction to the special problems of his poetry in much the same way that Ransom's comments on the relation of science to the myth serve as an approach to his.

Attention to his criticism will illuminate, for example, the positive position from which he comments on our present disintegration:

> The essential wreckage of your age is different,
> The accident the same; the Annabella
> Of proper incest, no longer incestuous:
> In an age of abstract experience, fornication
> Is self-expression, adjunct to Christian euphoria. . . .
>   —"Causerie"

Or, to make the application to the subject of poetry itself, one may quote from the same poem:

> We have learned to require
> In the infirm concessions of memory
> The privilege never to hear too much.
> What is this conversation, now secular,
> A speech not mine yet speaking for me in
> The heaving jelly of my tribal air?
> It rises in the throat, it climbs the tongue,
> It perches there for secret tutelage
> And gets it, of inscrutable instruction. . . .

The situation described is peculiarly that of the modern poet. His speech is a mass of clichés—of terms which with their past associations seem too grandiloquent and gaudy, or, with their past content emptied, now seem meaningless. "Vocabulary/ Becomes confusion," and without vocabulary man is lost.

> Heredity
> Proposes love, love exacts language, and we lack
> Language. When shall we speak again? When shall
> The sparrow dusting the gutter sing? When shall
> This drift with silence meet the sun? When shall
>   I wake?

We may state the situation in still other terms: Man's religion, his myths, are now merely private fictions. And as Tate has remarked in one of his essays, ". . . a myth should be in conviction immediate, direct, overwhelming, and I take it that the appreciation of this kind of imagery is an art lost to the modern mind." The lover in Tate's "Retroduction to American History," has lost his appreciation of such imagery. He "cannot hear. . . . His very eyeballs fixed in disarticulation. . . . his metaphors are dead."

Tate's metaphors are very much alive; it is through the production of energetic metaphor, of live "myths" that the poet attempts to break through the pattern of "abstract

9480

experience" and give man a picture of himself as man. Hence his preoccupation with time and mortality and "specific moral problems." But as a matter of integrity, he cannot take the short cut which Tennyson tends to take to these subjects. One cannot find a living relation between the present and the past without being honest to the present —and that involves taking into account the anti-historical character of our present.

In his "Retroduction to American History," the poet asks why "in such serenity of equal fates"—that is, why, if life is merely a causal sequence, merely abstract experience— has Narcissus "urged the brook with questions?" In a naturalistic world, the brook, like Mr. Ransom's cataract, is only so much water; and we have the absurdity which the poet proceeds to point out:

> Merged with the element
> Speculation suffuses the meadow with drops to tickle
> The cow's gullet; grasshoppers drink the rain.

Self-scrutiny, introspection, in a purely mechanistic universe, is merely a romantic gesture—"Narcissism." In the "Ode to the Confederate Dead," Narcissism figures again, though without a specific symbol.

As Tate has said in a recent article: "The poem is 'about' solipsism or Narcissism, or any other *ism* that denotes the failure of the human personality to function properly in nature and society. Society (and 'nature' as modern society constructs it) appears to offer limited fields for the exercise of the whole man, who wastes his energy piecemeal over separate functions that ought to come under a unity of being. . . . Without unity we get *the remarkable self-consciousness* of our age [italics mine]."

In the "Ode," the Narcissism of the present forms one term of the contrast; the "total" world in which the dead soldiers fulfilled themselves, the other. But the poet refuses to take the easy romantic attitude toward the contrast. The world which the dead soldiers possessed is not available to the speaker of the poem, for that kind of world is the function of a society, not something which can be wrought out by the private will. Moreover, the poet is honest: the leaves, for him, *are* merely leaves.

The irony expressed in the poem, then, is not the romantic irony of the passage quoted from Tate's criticism in Chapter III. It is a more complex irony, and almost inevitably, a self-inclusive irony. Such an irony is found also in "Last Days of Alice," "The Sonnets at Christmas," "The Meaning of Life," and "The Meaning of Death."

Before considering these poems, however, it is well to note a further criticism of naturalism in Tate's prose. The naturalistic view of experience (history as an abstract series) suggests an "omnipotent human rationality." It can only predict success. The poet (who, by virtue of being a poet, is committed to the concrete and particular) is thus continually thrown into the role of Tiresias.

A number of Tate's poems are ironical treatments of rationality, "The Eagle," for example. It is not the heart which fears death, but the mind, "the white eagle." And in the "Epistle to Edmund Wilson,"

> The mind's a sick eagle taking flight. . . .

The theme is most powerfully stated in the last of the "Sonnets of the Blood." The brother is cautioned to

> Be zealous that your numbers are all prime,
> Lest false division with sly mathematic
> Plunder the inner mansion of the blood. . . .
> . . . the prime secret whose simplicity
> Your towering engine hammers to reduce,
> Though driven, holds that bulwark of the sea
> Which breached will turn unspeaking fury loose
> To drown out him who swears to rectify
> Infinity. . . .

If the blood is a symbol of the nonrational, concrete stuff of man which resists abstract classification, by the same token it symbolizes man's capacity to be more than an abstract integer, and therefore signifies man's capacity for sin. In an age of abstract experience sin is meaningless.

In "Last Days of Alice," the logical, self-consistent but inhuman world of *Through the Looking-Glass* becomes an ironical symbol of the modern world. The poet maintains most precisely the analogy between Alice gazing "learnedly down her airy nose" into the abstract world of the mirror, and modern man who has also turned his world into abstraction. The subsidiary metaphors—"Alice grown . . . mammoth but not fat," symbolizing the megalomania of the modern; Alice "turned absent-minded by infinity" who "cannot move unless her double move," symbolizing the hypostasis of the modern—grow naturally out of the major symbolism. The poem is witty in the seventeenth-century sense; the reference to the Cheshire cat with his abstract grin, a witty comparison. But the wit, the sense of precision and complexity, is functional. It contributes the special quality of irony necessary to allow the poet to end his poem with the positive outcry:

> O God of our flesh, return us to Your Wrath,
> Let us be evil could we enter in
> Your grace, and falter on the stony path!

Man's capacity for error, his essential unpredictability, is referred to in a number of Tate's poems. It is the basis of the beautiful "Ode to Fear."

> My eldest companion present in solitude,
> Watch-dog of Thebes when the blind hero strove:
> 'Twas your omniscience at the cross-road stood
> When Laius, the slain dotard, drenched the grove.
>
> Now to the fading, harried eyes immune
> Of prophecy, you stalk us in the street
> From the recesses of the August noon,
> Alert world over, crouched on the air's feet.

> You are the surety to immortal life,
> God's hatred of the universal stain. . . .

There is an especially rich development of this theme in the twin poems, "The Meaning of Life," and "The Meaning of Death." The first opens with a dry statement of the point as if in a sort of apologetic monotone:

> Think about it at will; there is that
> Which is the commentary; there's that other,
> Which may be called the immaculate
> Conception of its essence in itself.

But the essence must not be turned into mere abstraction by the commentary, even though the commentary is so necessary that the essence is speechless without it. The poet goes on to apologize for the tone of tedious explication:

> I was saying this more briefly the other day
> But one must be explicit as well as brief.
> When I was a small boy I lived at home
> For nine years in that part of old Kentucky
> Where the mountains fringe the Blue Grass,
> The old men shot at one another for luck;
> It made me think I was like none of them.
> At twelve I was determined to shoot only
> For honor; at twenty not to shoot at all;
> I know at thirty-three that one must shoot
> As often as one gets the rare chance—*
> In killing there is more than commentary.

Our predicament is that the opportunity for any meaningful action rarely offers itself at all.

With the last lines the poet shifts the tone again, modulating from the half-whimsical, personal illustration into a brilliant summarizing figure:

* I shall expect some one to wrench this statement into a symptom of the poet's "Fascism." A prominent critic, in order to make such a point, has already twisted out of its context Tate's statement that the Southerner can only take hold of his tradition "by violence." In the context in which it occurs, it obviously means "by politics" as opposed to "by religion."

> But there's a kind of lust feeds on itself
> Unspoken to, unspeaking; subterranean
> As a black river full of eyeless fish
> Heavy with spawn; with a passion for time
> Longer than the arteries of a cave.

The symbol of the concrete, irrational essence of life, the blood, receives an amazing amplification by its association with the cave. The two symbols are united on the basis of their possession of "arteries." The blood is associated with "lust," is "subterranean" (buried within the body), is the source of "passion." But the added metaphor of the cave extends the associations from those appropriate to an individual body to something general and eternal. The reference to the fish may be also a fertility symbol. But the fish are "eyeless" though "heavy with spawn." The basic stuff of life lacks eyes—cannot see even itself; and filled with infinite potentialities, runs its dark, involved, subterranean course. The metaphor is powerful and rich, but it gives no sense of having been spatchcocked on to the poem. The blood symbol is worked out only in terms of the cave symbol; the two cannot be broken apart. Moreover, it has been prepared for in the casual personal allusion which precedes it. It too is a part of "old Kentucky/ Where the mountains fringe the Blue Grass."

"The Meaning of Death" also begins quietly, as "An After-Dinner Speech." The speech is addressed to us, the moderns, who have committed ourselves to commentary—complete, lucid, and full. We have no passion for time—have abolished time.

> Time, fall no more.
> Let that be life—time falls no more. The threat
> Of time we in our own courage have foresworn.
> Let light fall, there shall be eternal light
> And all the light shall on our heads be worn
>
> Although at evening clouds infest the sky
> Broken at base from which the lemon sun
> Pours acid of winter on a useful view. . . .

The concession announced by "although" is important in developing the tone. Incorrigible optimists that we are, we say hopefully that there shall be eternal light although one must admit that the evening light does not suggest the warmth of life but freezes the landscape with cold, pours acid upon it, turns it into something which is a vanity and meaningless. (The psychological basis for the symbolism here is interesting. The "lemon sun" indicates primarily the color of the evening sun, but "lemon" carries on over into a suggestion of something acid and astringent.)

But, the poet observes, our uneasiness is really groundless. Tomorrow surely will bring "jocund day" and the colors of spring. If one in boyhood connected fear with the coming on of the dark at evening, that was merely because one was a small boy. We, at least, have given up that past with its irrationalities and superstitions:

> Gentlemen! let's
> Forget the past, its related errors, coarseness
> Of parents, laxities, unrealities of principle.
>
> Think of tomorrow. Make a firm postulate
> Of simplicity in desire and act
> Founded on the best hypotheses;
> Desire to eat secretly, alone, lest
> Ritual corrupt our charity . . .

Ritual implies a respect for the thing as thing; it implies more than an abstract series—implies a breach in our strict naturalism. That naturalism must be maintained

> Lest darkness fall and time fall
> In a long night . . .

and thus spoil our plans for the conquest of time—spoil our plans for the reduction of everything to abstraction where, we hope,

> . . . learned arteries
> Mounting the ice and sum of barbarous time
> Shall yield, without essence, perfect accident.

The past phrase suggests the final metaphor of "The Meaning of Life," and with the final line of this poem, the speaker drops his ironical pretense of agreement with the "gentlemen" and shifts into another quality of irony, a deeper irony, returning to the cave metaphor:

> We are the eyelids of defeated caves.

We are the generation that has broken with history, the generation that has closed the mouth of the cave. The word "eyelids" indicates the manner of the closing: the suggestion is that the motion is one of languor and weariness as one might close his eyelids in sleep. The vitality is gone.

A similar theme is to be found in "The Oath" though the setting and the treatment of the theme in this poem are very different. The two friends are sitting by the fire in the gathering twilight.

> It was near evening, the room was cold,
> Half-dark; Uncle Ben's brass bullet-mould
> And powder-horn and Major Bogan's face
> Above the fire in the half-light plainly said:
> There's naught to kill but the animated dead.
> Horn nor mould nor major follows the chase.

Then one of the friends proposes the question, "Who are the dead?"

> And nothing more was said. . . .
> So I leaving Lytle to that dream
> Decided what it is in time that gnaws
> The aging fury of a mountain stream
> When suddenly, as an ignorant mind will do,
> I thought I heard the dark pounding its head
> On a rock, crying: *Who are the dead?*
> Then Lytle turned with an oath—By God it's true!

The thing that is true is obvious that *we* are the dead. The dead are those who have given in to abstraction, even though they may move about and carry on their business and be—to use the earlier phrase in the poem—the "animated dead." A mountain stream ceases to be a mountain stream when its bed has become worn level. It might even be termed a "defeated" mountain stream when it has lost the activity which gave its career meaning.

6

FROST, MACLEISH,

AND AUDEN

ROBERT FROST is a regionalist and a traditionalist. Yet his poetry differs sharply from that of the poets discussed in the previous chapters. And in the popular mind it differs more sharply still. He is popularly supposed to be homely, salty, direct, whereas poets like Ransom and Tate are reputed to be tortured intellectual obscurantists. The presumption is that the structure of his poetry differs radically from the structure of theirs.

A thoughtful reading will show that Frost's poetry, however salty and homely, is scarcely direct. The casual reader may receive an impression of directness because Frost works so constantly in terms of anecdote, incident, and character sketch—elements which have no special associations with the pure technique of poetry. But the *poetry* of Frost does not inhere in these elements; on the contrary, he employs these elements as means to the end of poetry. The reader, then, should ask himself how they are related to the central method, and should not consider them as ends in themselves. (In fairness to the reader, it ought to be said that Frost has encouraged this misapprehension by his frequent laxity in building his elements into a form.)

Frost's anecdotes, incidents, character sketches do have a surface directness; but, as poet, he employs them for purposes of indirection. What sets him off from the poets already discussed is not, for example, a lack of irony, but, first, the context in which the irony appears, and second, the level at which it operates. Characteristically, it appears at the level of licensed whimsy, or of dry understatement.

The whimsy is licensed by being made a mannerism of the New England character. That character (it does not concern the present issue whether it is Frost's own character or merely a mask which he adopts as poet) may be described as follows: the sensitive New Englander, possessed of a natural wisdom; dry and laconic when serious; genial and whimsical when not; a character who is uneasy with hyperbole and prefers to use understatement to risking possible overstatement.

The range of Frost's poetry is pretty thoroughly delimited by the potentialities for experience possessed by such a character. The poetry will rarely lapse into sentimentality. It will not allow itself to become grandiose. But on the other hand, because of its fear of overreaching itself, it will rarely aspire to any great intensity. The virtues of Frost's poetry, in short, are solid ones—virtues produced by a strong sense of dramatic decorum.

Much of Frost's poetry hardly rises above the level of the vignette of rural New England. Consider the genre piece, "The Code." The incident related occurs in the New England haying season. The theme is that the New England yeoman has his code of honor too: he will not be "told" to hurry or take pains. But the ironic tension is pretty well limited to the title itself. Except for the idiomatic and flexible blank verse, Frost makes use of no resources in the poem not available to the accomplished short story writer. The poetry is diluted and diffuse. A significant symptom of the diffuseness is the absence of metaphor. The very minimum of imagery is used.

In general, Frost's metaphors are few and tame; and the occasional bold metaphor is confined to his very lightest poems: for example, to such a sally of self-ironic whimsy as "Canis Major." Frost does not think through his images; he requires statements. The audacity of his metaphor is thus in inverse proportion to the seriousness of the experience.

This same basic timidity often prevents the anecdotes from developing into fables or symbols. Frost's themes are frequently stated overtly, outside the symbolical method; the poet comes downstage to philosophize explicitly.

Thus, in "Two Tramps in Mud-Time," the point of the poem is explicitly stated in the last stanza:

> My object in life is to unite
> My avocation and my vocation. . . .
> Only where love and need are one,
> And the work is play for mortal stakes,
> Is the deed ever really done. . . .

The statement, of course, is given a *raison d'être* in terms of an incident. The speaker is chopping wood and having a great deal of pleasure in his activity when two tramps from the lumber-camps come by and pause to ask for the job. He enjoys the work, but he realizes that he has no moral right to deprive the men of a job which they need.

The first stanza sketches in the situation. The poet does not hurry on to moralize on it. He toys with what is to be his decision while he goes on to chatter about the changeableness of the northern spring, the satisfaction of making the beech blocks fall

> . . . splinterless as a cloven rock

and the pleasure of the physical exercise. There is the mildly ironic self-deprecation of

> The blows that a life of self-control
> Spares to strike for the common good
> That day, giving a loose to my soul,
> I spent on the unimportant wood.

The poet even risks a little conceit in describing the season:

> Be glad of water, but don't forget
> The lurking frost in the earth beneath
> That will steal forth after the sun is set
> And show on the water its crystal teeth.

These stanzas establish the character of the speaker so that the generalization which he utters in the end is dramatically justified—it is in character and in tone.

The generalization states a doctrine which I admire, and I have suggested the devices used by the poet to provide a dramatic frame for it. It may not be invidious therefore to point out that it is made finally in the mode of prose rather than in terms of symbol. The same censure applies to "Birches," and more severely still, to "Mending Wall." Frost prefers to dilute his poetry in contrast to the poets treated earlier in this study; and if dilution will account for his greater popularity, it will also indicate why he fails to realize full dramatic intensity. Compare with the conclusion to "Two Tramps in Mud-Time" the "generalization" with which Yeats concludes "Among School Children":

> Labor is blossoming or dancing where
> The body is not bruised to pleasure soul,
> Nor beauty born out of its own despair,
> Nor blear-eyed wisdom out of midnight oil.
> O chestnut tree, great rooted blossomer,
> Are you the leaf, the blossom or the bole?
> O body swayed to music, O brightening glance,
> How can we know the dancer from the dance?

At his best, of course, Frost does not philosophize. The anecdote is absorbed into symbol. The method of indirection operates fully: the sense of realistic detail, the air of casual comment, are employed to build up and intensify a serious effect.

Consider "The Woodpile," for example. The poem is ostensibly the account of a winter walk, and, on the surface, the poem is as rambling and directionless as the walk. On the walk the poet scares up a bird, which is afraid of him and keeps flying on ahead:

> He thought that I was after him for a feather—
> The white one in his tail; like one who takes
> Everything said as personal to himself.

(The bird becomes a New England character just as the colt in "The Runaway" becomes a New England urchin.) Finally, the walker comes upon the abandoned woodpile itself:

> Clematis
> Had wound strings round and round it like a bundle.
> What held it though on one side was a tree
> Still growing, and on one a stake and prop,
> These latter about to fall.

But the woodpile is burning and therefore warming the frozen swamp (rotting is oxidation, a kind of burning). Nature has picked up the abandoned task and is completing it. Nothing is lost. This is the point of the poem, but it is suggested merely. The poet does not even make it the central aspect of the thought with which he concludes the poem: What sort of person would go to the trouble of cutting and cording wood, only to leave it to warm the frozen swamp?

In the more ambitious poems Frost's central problem is to develop depth of feeling without seeming to violate the realistic and matter-of-fact elements of the situation with which the poem deals.

His successful poems are thus successes in the handling of tone. Some of Frost's admirers, in insisting on the poet as a sort of kindly homespun philosopher, neglect the far more important matter: that popular poetry of this sort usually becomes pretentious or sentimental, and have thus failed to see that Frost's really remarkable achievement has been to maintain integrity of tone as he has. The pitch is considerably lower, the problem simpler, but the method is essentially that of the poets earlier discussed.

One of his best examples of management of tone occurs in "After Apple-Picking," a poem in which he extends his symbolism further, and achieves more intensity, than is usual for him. But to demonstrate this is to indicate that the poem is in reality a symbolist poem.

The concrete experience of apple-picking is communicated firmly and realistically; but the poem invites a metaphorical extension. The task of apple-picking, it is suggested, is any task; it is life.

The drowsiness which the speaker feels after the completion of the task is associated with the cycle of the seasons. Its special character is emphasized by a bit of magic, even though the magic is whimsical:

> Essence of winter sleep is on the night,
> The scent of apples: I am drowsing off.
> I cannot rub the strangeness from my sight
> I got from looking through a pane of glass
> I skimmed this morning from the drinking trough
> And held against the world of hoary grass.
> It melted, and I let it fall and break.

The speaker goes on to speculate playfully on the form that his dreaming will take. It will surely be about apples, for his instep arch still feels the pressure of the ladder rung, and his ears are still full of the rumble of apples rolling into the cellar bin. But he returns to the subject of his drowsiness, and the phrase, "whatever sleep it is," renews the suggestion that his sleepiness may not be merely ordinary human sleepiness:

> Were he not gone,
> The woodchuck could say whether it's like his
> Long sleep, as I describe its coming on,
> Or just some human sleep.

The end of the labor leaves the speaker with a sense of completion and fulfillment—in short, with a sense of ripeness which savors of the fruit with which he has been working and of the season in which the work has been done. The ice sheet through which he has looked signals the termination of the harvest and the summons to the winter sleep of nature. The woodchuck has already begun his hibernation. The speaker does not overemphasize his own connection with nature—the reference to the woodchuck is merely one more piece of whimsy—but the connection is felt.

The poem even suggests that the sleep is like the sleep of death. We are not to feel that the speaker is necessarily conscious of this. But perhaps we are to feel that, were the analogy to present itself to him, he would accept it. In the context defined in the poem, death might be considered as something eminently natural, as a sense of fulfillment mixed with a great deal of honest weariness and a sense of something well done—though with too much drowsiness for one to bother that every one of the apples had not been picked. The theme thus turns out to be a sort of rustic New England version of "Ripeness is all," though the theme is arrived at casually—stumbled over, almost—and with no effect of literary pretentiousness.

Frost's best poetry thus exhibits the structure of symbolist-metaphysical poetry—much more clearly, indeed, than does that of a poet like Archibald MacLeish, who on casual inspection would appear to be far more modern.

The basic method and impulse of MacLeish's poetry, in fact, resembles that of Carl Sandburg. There are great differences to be sure. Certainly MacLeish's verse reveals a competence which makes any comparison of the two seem at first glance absurd. Yet there is a basic resemblance. And an examination of this common element may provide us with the most fruitful approach to MacLeish's poetry.

MacLeish, like Sandburg, deals in a detemporized past. His longer poems are rather consistently "histories" and the world which they reveal is timeless—with the emphasis, not like Sandburg's on a timeless present, but on a timeless past. Sandburg tends to be brash and topical, and he is obsessed with the immediacy of his point, namely, that the real past was the world of ourselves—the trivial, tawdry, and yet somehow glorious world that we know in common experience. MacLeish has more delicacy and restraint. His

imagery is richer, his canvas broader, his control of rhythms
far more profound. Compare with "Four Preludes on Play-
things of the Wind" MacLeish's "Men":

> Our history is grave noble and tragic
> We trusted the look of the sun on the green leaves
> We built our towns of stone with enduring ornaments
> We worked the hard flint for basins of water. . . .

The poem continues with a recitation of a miscellany of
items typical of the life of men:

> We planted corn grapes apple-trees rhubarb . . .
> We believed in the promises made by the brows of
>   women . . .
> We fought at the dikes in the bright sun for the pride
>   of it . . .

to conclude with the lines,

> Many cities are gone and their channels broken
> We have lived a long time in this land and with honor.

The poem is typical of all men everywhere. It might be
spoken by Assyrians or Greeks or modern Americans. It
is a tribute to MacLeish's skill in the use of imagery that
the items, though sharp and distinct, give no clue—do not
date or locate (and therefore, in this case, limit) the poem.

The images, of course, do a great deal more than this.
They establish and sustain a certain tone. The history has
its dignity and its simple seriousness. Man's foolishness
and knavery are an integral part of that history—

> We were drunk and lay with our fine dreams in the
>   straw . . .

They need not be, and are not, glossed over. In turn, the
frank and even casual mention of such items removes any
tinge of vaingloriousness from the recital. The poem is
thoroughly successful; but the technique of the poem (and
it is typical of MacLeish) is stringently limited.

Consider the way in which the poem is built. The poem is made up of a series of parallel statements, apparently stacked together with no effort at subordination or order of any sort. The naïve parallelism is, of course, part of the artistic method: it sorts with the character of the men who speak, men who see no pattern in their history and who have no point to make but merely set forward, simply and seriously, the memorable items of that history.

Thoroughly parallel to this method of organization is the piling up of nouns and noun phrases in *Conquistador:*

Palms ragged with sea-gust . . .
                              all careened with the
Weed in the rusty chains and the keelsons splin-
    tered . . .
Bleaching with sun and the . . .
                              nights in . . .
                                        elegant knees
        like the
Girls in Spain and the sand still hot from the sun and
    the
Surf slow . . .
            wind over . . .
                        palm-trees sweeping the . . .

Or consider the imagery in "The Epistle to be Left in the Earth":

The earth is round
                    there are springs under the orchards
The loam cuts with a blunt knife
                              beware of
Elms in thunder . . .

It is the kind of imagery that dominates long sections of the "Hamlet" and "The Pot of Earth," and is the staple of the "Land's End" poems.

This piling up of separate items of detail is often, on the level of direct evocation, extremely successful, and in many of the poems it is dramatically justified. An index of its potentialities is one means of arriving at the scope and limitations of the poet himself. For MacLeish is in one sense an Imagist—though he surpasses the poets conventionally known as Imagists at every point.

For example, the passage quoted above from *Conquistador*—and many other passages from that poem—makes the Imagists seem very thin indeed. Moreover, in *Conquistador* the structure of detail set upon detail, loosely held together with and's and then's, admirably suits the conditions of narration. The succession of images, each momentarily held and illuminated for an instant by the mind, represents very well the process of memory as the old soldier lives back over his campaign.

But the poem is essentially reverie, not drama; the final effect pathos, not tragedy.

The point of this observation is not to censure *Conquistador* for failing to be something which the poet did not attempt. The poem is what it is, and surely must be judged one of the finer accomplishments of modern American poetry. The point of the remark is to define more narrowly the terms in which the poem achieves its success.

MacLeish's poetry, in this poem and elsewhere, is essentially a poetry of the noun, not of the verb. His images, far more than those of the Imagists, do tend to become symbols; but the symbols are relatively static, lack dynamic quality. MacLeish's sensibility is rich but lacks principles. His poetry does not have the intricacy of idea necessary to the poetry of a poet like Yeats. One may sum up by saying that his poetry lacks dramatic tension.

This fact may explain why his successful poems so often deal with a primitive people going about the essential concerns of human life, and why the imagery stresses only those things which are the common denominator of all peoples. In such "histories," there are no meanings, no interpretations, apart from the fact that the histories are "grave noble and tragic." Or to make the application to *Conquistador*, there can be no meaning to the history of the conquest of

Mexico apart from the meaning of the campaign to Bernal
Diaz as a man.

The poet asks in the prologue to this poem:

What are the dead to us in the world's wonder?
Why (and again now) on their shadowy beaches
Pouring before them the slow painful blood

Do we return to force the truthful speech of them
Shrieking like snipe along their gusty sand . . .

The lines are noble, but no truth is forced from the dead.
The parallel to Odysseus is superficial: what Bernal brings
back from Hades is a personal possession—not wisdom but
memory. The poem in essence is lyric, and a very fine one
it is, but it is not an epic of the conquest of Mexico.

If we are to raise the question of MacLeish's lack of
dramatic quality, it may be well to test the statement against
an explicit attempt at drama, MacLeish's play, *Panic*. Here,
as in nearly all his work, there is much to admire. The
external items are handled well. The poet is successful in
evoking the sense of the modern scene: the frenzy, the half-
crazed crowds, the atmosphere of panic. But there is no
dramatic relation between the civilization which is going to
pieces and the central character of the play, the banker
McGafferty. McGafferty is merely a special instance of the
panic. He does not supply a focus for the forces which are
supposed to dominate the play.

In the first place, McGafferty is too passive. We are con-
stantly told by his employees and colleagues and the crowds
on the street that he is an all-powerful financial force; and
the poet does try to give us a sense of his fighting against
the panic. But the picture does not carry conviction.
McGafferty's gestures seem essentially empty, and, as he
admits later, are bewildered. Most of all, he makes no
decision which commits him definitely to an issue involved
in the tragic effect. He is rather the man who falls prey
to a disease, an epidemic infection.

A consideration of the dramatic situation is revealing. McGafferty's position is almost precisely that of a man whose expensive car breaks down. He raises the hood and does some tinkering with the carburetor. But he does not really understand the engine and he cannot repair it. There is first mere annoyance, then a dawning knowledge of the true state of affairs, then a sort of despair. The situation is basically comic, and merely to make the issues more serious is not enough to turn it into tragedy.

McGafferty is after all another one of the characters from "Men." Everything he has done "has been faithful and dangerous." The dikes in the bright sun have given place to skyscrapers but nothing is changed. Consequently MacLeish can summon up for his protagonist a kind of pathos; but any further attempt to secure more intensity would merely have resulted in sentimentality. This is why the reproval of McGafferty's *hubris* is not sufficient to make the play a tragedy and why McGafferty's death (because he does not wish to be forced to admit his ignorance of the financial machine) is finally the effect of a private and irrelevant pride, and therefore meaningless in the tragic sense.

Most revealing of all is an examination of the kind of irony accorded to McGafferty in the last scenes of the play. It is romantic irony—the irony of the disillusioned strong man—not tragic irony. Romantic irony and a fairly obvious external and satiric irony—see "Memorial Rain" and the *Frescoes*—these are the kinds of irony which MacLeish is capable of. Irony of the sort described in the earlier chapters of this study, irony which maintains an equilibrium between opposed attitudes, irony which acts as a stabilizing force, is hardly to be found in MacLeish's poetry at all. His best poetry is of a kind to which such irony is irrelevant.

Examination of MacLeish's most successful poems will bear out this generalization. His best poems are "palpable and mute . . . motionless in time." They are remarkably solid, but they are as static as statuary. They do not involve shifts in tone; there is little or no development in the poet's attitude. This static quality holds true, even when, as in the celebrated "You, Andrew Marvell," the specific theme is the poet's sense of the passage of time.

The poem is a brilliant example of the philosophy of "Ars Poetica." The images are more than instances of the fall of the night; they suggest the tempo of the movement of the creeping shadow—

> . . . the always coming on
> The always rising of the night.

Moreover, through their organic relationship they bring together all sorts of enriching suggestions. The undertone of suggestion that the "rising of the night" is a flood is a simile which, though never explicitly declared, is sustained throughout the poem:

> And strange at Ecbatan the trees
> . . . .
> The flooding dark about their knees
>
> . . . and the bridge
> Across the silent river gone . . .
>
> And Spain go under and the shore
> Of Africa. . . .

But rich and full-bodied as the poem is, the suggestions are overtones, brilliantly controlled, of one rather simple theme. And it is significant that the poem uses MacLeish's typical structure: detail piled on detail.

Or consider the fine "Memorial Rain." Fragments of the fatuous and pompous speech of the ambassador at the memorial service are played off against the stream of thought of the dead soldier's brother, thus:

> —Reflects that these enjoy
> Their country's gratitude, that deep repose,
> That peace no pain can break, no hurt destroy,
> That rest, that sleep—

> At Ghent the wind rose.
> There was a smell of rain and a heavy drag
> Of wind in the hedges but not as the wind blows
> Over fresh water when the waves lag
> Foaming and the willows huddle and it will rain:
> I felt him waiting.

The tension is built up, to be suddenly released when the rain descends and breaks up the memorial service:

> Seeping in the sand under the grass roots, seeping
> Between cracked boards to the boːs of a clenched
>   hand:
> The earth relaxes, loosens; he is sleeping,
> He rests, he is quiet, he sleeps in a strange land.

One of the most subtle devices used here may be analyzed as follows: The poet builds up the tension in the living brother (and in us as audience, since we see the poem from the living brother's standpoint)—builds it up to the point of irritation, and then suddenly breaks it with the gust of rain. The sense of relaxation—as secured by the control of imagery and rhythms—for the reader (and the living brother) is very real; and it is this sense of relief and relaxation which, by a deft psychological transfer, is attributed to the dead man. The bold predication with which the poem ends and which gives it its power is thus made to work.

But the resolution of the poem is typical of MacLeish. The strength of the poem lies in its applicability to all wars —there is no special relation to the Great War or to our own civilization. The Memorial rain is like Sandburg's grass:

> Pile the bodies high at Austerlitz and Waterloo.
> Shovel them under and let me work—
> I am the grass; I cover all.

Both perform the same service: Nature does what man cannot do. That is not to say that the poems have the same theme or that Sandburg's is comparable to MacLeish's in excellence. "Memorial Rain" is not only richer and more powerful: the theme is given a personal reference around which it is organized as an experience. But they both possess about the same intellectual content.

Outside of the lyrics of the sort just discussed, probably the most successful of MacLeish's poems is the *Frescoes for Mr. Rockefeller's City*. It will not be difficult to show why. Whether or not MacLeish's sense of history is defective, there can be no censure of his sense of the individuality of place. America has its own quality—

> She's a tough land under the corn mister:
> She has changed the bone in the cheeks of many races—

and the realization of the incommensurable character of the country, in the light of which all mere abstractions break down, is powerful enough to generate a theme which holds together the various parts of the poem. It is powerful enough to furnish MacLeish with an interpretation of history.

It is this theme which gives direction to the masses of rich detail which he is always able to assemble. For example, the legend of Crazy Horse is given in the sort of detail used in *Conquistador;* but there is an added meaning. Crazy Horse was fighting for something—

> My God should he not fight? It was his.

In the same way the journey of exploration carried out by Meriwether Lewis meant something to him over and above recovered memories of the "winter rattling in the brittle haws," and "the buffalo numberless," and "the quail calling."

In one sense, the poem is a pastiche of the various effects MacLeish deals in. But here, because the various sections bear an organic relation to a larger theme, the poem is literally greater than the sum of its parts. The satirical sections, for instance, because of their relation to the positive core of the poem, go deeper than merely cheap jesting, and take on, in the light of the earlier passages of the poem, the effect of bitter taunting. For the types satirized are defined, even as Crazy Horse and Lewis are defined, by their relation to the land—the empire builders to whom the land was merely an abstraction. It was all prices to them: they never looked at it—it was also merely an abstraction to the expatriate artist and the abstract revolutionaries * who have never looked at it either.

There are doubtless finer passages in some of MacLeish's other poems, but the *Frescoes* probably remains the most ambitious successful poem which MacLeish has written. And it represents a direction which one could wish he might follow up if his remarkable technical talents and his rich sensibility are to yield their best poetry.

The point is worth raising in view of the fact that Mac-Leish seems to have sensed a defect in his poetry, and seems to be searching for a theme, a controlling principle. The fruitful direction for him, in view of what has been said above, does not seem to lie in the direction of Sandburg; and his recent flourishing of the phrase, "— the people, yes," makes one apprehensive for his future career. For "the people" is too vague.

If MacLeish represents the unprincipled sensibility, Auden represents, possibly, the sensibility fortified with principles, or perhaps, changing the viewpoint, the sensibility at the mercy of a set of principles—the artist working in the service of a cause. Suffice it to say here, by anticipation, that Auden, for all of his reputation as a left-wing poet, seems to me to call for no modification of what has already been said in an earlier chapter on this subject. At his best his poetry reveals what we have called the structure of inclusion, with a maximum density and firmness and with no glib oversimplifications.

* Some of the left-wing critics have pretty well disgraced themselves as critics by failing to see this point. Or is their objection that abstract revolutionaries are better than concrete ones and that MacLeish should know this; or, is their objection that no revolutionary who quotes Marx could possibly be abstract?

But there may be questions as to what is his best. The central impulse of Auden's poetry may be defined by quoting the last stanzas from Poem XX:

> And all emotions to expression came,
> Recovering the archaic imagery:
> The longing for assurance takes the form
>
> Of a hawk's vertical stooping from the sky;
> These tears, salt for a disobedient dream,
> The lunatic agitation of the sea;
>
> While this despair with hardened eyeballs cries
> "A Golden Age, a Silver . . . rather this,
> Massive and taciturn years, the Age of Ice."

Auden's surest triumphs represent a recovery of the archaic imagery—fells, scarps overhung by kestrels, the becks with their pot-holes left by the receding glaciers of the age of ice. His dominant contrast is the contrast between this scene and the modern age of ice: foundries with their fires cold, flooded coal-mines, silted harbors—the débris of the new ice age. The advent of the new age of ice, a "polar peril," supplies the background for his finest poetry. In this poetry the archaic imagery is recovered—not as items of the picturesque but in the service of a fine irony. It is an irony which comprehends the poet himself and the class to which he belongs.

The poetry is thin in proportion as the irony tends to dissolve into external topical satire—e.g., "The Dance of Death" —not because it is topical, since his best poetry is often topical, but because the center is external to the poetry. In general, Auden's poetry weakens as he tries to rely upon an external framework—a doctrine or ideology.

The following passage, for instance, is an example of Auden's dominant theme and his most successful method: the satire is directed at an essential frivolousness of mind —a stodgy, comfortable, unconscious complacency which

makes men disguise losses and injuries, or even accept them
as a part of the natural order of things.

> It is later than you think; nearer that day
> Far other than that distant afternoon
> Amid rustle of frocks and stamping feet
> They gave the prizes to the ruined boys.
> You cannot be away, then, no
> Not though you pack to leave within an hour,
> Escaping humming down arterial roads. . . .

The sense of grim understatement native to the tradition of
Old English poetry is used to point up mercilessly the
desiccation of College Quad and Cathedral Close. "It is
later than you think. . . ." (An English gentleman is
never late to appointments—even the ruling classes will
listen to an indictment couched in these terms, the poet
implies.) "Nearer that day. . . ." (The description is
ominously vague. Suffice it to say that it is not at all like that
"distant afternoon" with its rustling of frocks and stamping
of feet and the prize-giving. But the mention of the after-
noon suggests what has brought to pass the day so different
from it, and perhaps suggests also why the financier and
his friends have lost their sense of time and do not realize
the lateness of the hour.)

The phrase, "the ruined boys," is also menacingly vague.
It means primarily boys ruined for living, boys moulded for
other distant afternoons, not for that day, etc. But it sug-
gests "sexually perverted," too, literally perhaps and cer-
tainly symbolically. They have been emasculated, made
infertile and incapable of producing any healthy growth.

Perhaps the neatest effect of the grim humor is achieved
in the last three lines where it is suggested that the descent
of the whirlwind will find the gentlemen incapable of re-
acting even to catastrophe except in terms of their class and
code. "Not though you pack . . ." (as for a week-end in
the country. The gentlemen have had at least in their ex-
perience sudden invitations.)

But the final sardonic picture of the financier and his friends escaping in their saloon cars down arterial roads does not become flat and heavy-handed, for it is intimately related to the whole texture of the experience. The relationship between the elements in this passage is as intricate as in any other kind of poetry. The satire rises into a more serious mode.

This picture of spiritual decay finds its complement in the glimpses of the decayed industries of the North Country:

> Below him sees dismantled washing-floors,
> Snatches of tramline running to the wood,
> An industry already comatose,
> Yet sparsely living. A ramshackle engine
> At Cashwell raises water; for ten years
> It lay in flooded workings until this. . . .

This is the new ice age realized in terms of the land itself. The two pictures are constantly juxtaposed: on occasion, in a passage so brilliant as the following:

> Pass on, admire the view of the massif
> Through plate-glass windows of the Sport Hotel;
> Join there the insufficient units
> Dangerous, easy, in furs, in uniform
> And constellated at reserved tables
> Supplied with feelings by an efficient band
> Relayed elsewhere to farmers and their dogs
> Sitting in kitchens in the stormy fens.

The passage takes on, in view of the larger context of Auden's work, a symbolical character. The Alpine scene represents the remnants of Europe's last glacial period. The ruling classes use it as their playground; it is beautiful and safe, seen through the plate-glass windows of the luxury hotel. As representatives of the new ice age it is ironically appropriate that they should choose such a playground. They are part of the age: they are frozen—they have to be

"supplied with feelings. . . ." But on another level of
irony it is appropriate too: the new glaciers, not tame ones
now, are to crush them.

The visitors at St. Moritz are contrasted with the farmers
in their kitchens. The nexus is superficial; the farmers in
the stormy fens have in common with the visitors merely
the fact that they are listening to the same music, via radio.
But the suggested connection is deeper. We are really
dealing with understatement. That which the radios im-
ply—the whole technical-industrial age—binds the two
groups very tightly together indeed. The ruling classes are
really being very foolish in ignoring the other classes. The
term "stormy" is applied to the fens, but the suggestion
carries over to the farmers too: they represent the storm
which will overwhelm the top-heavy civilization. And the
term "fens" itself takes place in the irony. The visitors at
St. Moritz would do well to look for the new glaciers, not
in the Alpine mountains—these do not matter—but in the
last place one would think to look—the stormy fens.

If the account just given seems overingenious, one need
not insist on it. Least of all do I intend to imply that the
sets of contrasts were *consciously* contrived by the poet, or
that the reader, in order to understand the poem, must
work out such an analysis. But if one attempts to explain
the added fullness and solidity of much of Auden's best
work, he is driven back on such accounts as this: the con-
nections which lace together the various parts of the poem,
on inspection become more and more complex; the symbol-
ism, more and more rich; the analogies and contrasts, more
and more detailed.

Certainly, it is the use of sharp contrasts which gives
vitality to Auden's verse. It is by way of becoming a hall-
mark of his poetry. Obviously, it is a device which can be
overworked, and in the verse of many of Auden's followers
and in some of the weaker verse of Auden himself, it has
become a stereotype.

The temptation to use shocking contrasts is particularly

strong when satire is directed at smugness and compla-
cency. The real criticism is, however, to be directed not
at the degree of shock but at the fact that often in such
verse the shocking and discordant is used merely for its
own sake. In the passages dealt with earlier, as we have
seen, the contrasts are involved in the central pattern: they
are not aimless or irresponsible but are legitimate exten-
sions from a center which they illuminate. Auden is not
always so careful: the center to which the satire refers is
sometimes negligible or confused. Take the following
passage, for example (which, by the way, seems to owe
something to Lindsay's "Bryan, Bryan, Bryan, Bryan"):

> Hearing the arrival of his special train,
> Hearing the fireworks, the saluting and the guns,
> Bob and Miss Belmairs spooning in Spain,
> Where is the trained eye? Under the sofa.
> Where is Moxon? Dreaming of nuns.
> Their day is over, they shall decorate the Zoo
> With Professor Jeans and Bishop Barnes at 2d a view,
> Or be ducked in a gletcher, as they ought to be,
> With the Simonites, the Mosleyites and the I.L.P.

In fairness to the poem, Auden is consciously using a
method of broad satire with its complement, obviously ex-
aggerated praise, in order to set up the positive matter
which he means to convey, and which comes, with a change
of tone, in a short passage at the end of the poem. Even so,
the method is coarser, easier, than that used in the earlier
passages commented upon.

The satire is broader still in sections of "The Dance of
Death," where the poet relies more heavily on the external
framework—and the external doctrine—to pull the poem
together. The gain in clarity is immense, but the gain is
at the expense of the poetry, as a comparison with some
of the poetry in the more obscure "Paid on Both Sides" and
"The Orators" will demonstrate.

It is some of Auden's disciples, however, whose work

represents a real abuse of the use of contrasts. Mere contrast, obviously, becomes monotonous, and a continual dealing in heterogeneity soon becomes as flat as the collecting of resemblances. To fall into mere heterogeneity is the temptation of the poet who wishes to portray disintegration.

Oddly enough, it may be used with the same vagueness to portray the antithesis of disintegration, lusty growth. Whitman, for example, often uses heterogeneity for this purpose. In the catalogue passages we are given hunks of American variety:

> The mate stands braced in the whale-boat, lance and
>   harpoon are ready,
> The duck-shooter walks by silent and cautious stretches,
> The deacons are ordain'd with cross'd hands at the
>   altar,
> The spinning-girl retreats and advances to the hum of
>   the big wheel,
> The farmer stops by the bars as he walks on a First-day
>   loaf and looks at the oats and rye,
> The lunatic is carried at last to the asylum a confirm'd
>   case. . . .

The heterogeneity is used by Whitman to celebrate formlessness. The tone asks us to note how tremendous, how various the continent is, and the discords are ironical at the expense of categories of any kind. The implication is that any classifications which one possesses are made to seem shabby and inadequate when called in to take account of the enormous teeming variety of the new country.

But the game is too easy for Whitman as the proponent of nebulous bonhommie and fraternity. The poetry is thin and diluted. The game is too easy also for the celebrants of a rather vague communism—or in their negative and satiric mode, the mockers at vague confusion and disintegration.

Auden shows his superiority by his ability to assimilate the discords into a meaningful pattern. In this connection

it may be well to comment on the extent to which Auden
has relied constantly on a method of assimilation and syn-
thesis.   The method has resulted in charges of obscurity—
some of them quite justified, many of them unjustified; but
it is this method which essentially makes him a far better
poet than poets often linked with him, Day Lewis and
Stephen Spender.   Indeed, the faults of these two poets
are the result of oversimplification.   Lewis, in his weaker
moments, furnishes obvious cases of a flat didacticism;
Spender, of sentimentality.   Auden, on the contrary, even
in his less tightly knit verse, works continually in a pattern
of synthesis, and the ambiguity as to his attitude is a func-
tion of this pattern.

For example, note the ambivalence of his attitude toward
the English public school.   In some of the poems, it is the
nursery of English complacency; in others, the system—the
schoolmaster's advice, the Rugby team—is accepted to be
made the vehicle of the poet's statement.   There is, of
course, no real contradiction, but the attitude in which the
apparent contradictions are resolved is far more complex
than blanket acceptance or rejection.   To give some in-
stances, the poet is allowed to parody the schoolmasterish
style, and to develop a tone of ragging, scolding, cheering
up, coaxing, which fits his purpose admirably.   The real
seriousness of his advice is protected from oversolemnity by
the fact that its expression is an obvious parody of boy-
scoutism.   This is to put it crudely, but consider:

Do you think that because you have heard that on
    Christmas Eve
In a quiet sector they walked about on the skyline,
Exchanged cigarettes, both learning the words for "I
    love you"
    In either language:
You can stroll across for a smoke and a chat any eve-
    ning?
    Try it and see.

On one level, the passage represents a debunking of the heroism and chivalry of war; but on another, it is a statement of the seriousness of taking sides in a conflict which is much too grim for such fraternizing. On one level, it stands as an ironical parody of the tone of the schoolmaster to the pupil or the veteran to the recruit; but in addition, it has its measure of seriousness (and is the more serious because the poet has shown himself conscious of the ludicrous aspects of such advice).

The many passages in Auden which deal with the devoted band of conspirators function in much the same way. Some seem to be parodies, ironical and sometimes pitying, of fascism; and others seem to be fantasies which contain hints of what the proper sort of fascism (revolutionary communism?) ought to be. The constantly suggested connection between the school gang and the fascist conspirators is really intricate and important. The poet is allowed to imply: fascism is juvenile—ought to appeal really to school boys. And yet he also is allowed to imply: these appeals have their validity—there is sloth and complacency which are to be combatted. I am far from suggesting that Auden wavers in his political views or that he is indifferent to political views. I am concerned to show that his attitude is one which accommodates in a dramatic unity the various elements which in our practical oversimplification are divided and at war with one another.

This quality is Auden's best certification as a first-rate poet though it will hardly recommend him to propagandists of one sort or another, or to proponents of an immediate cause. (It is interesting that he has already been called a fascist by at least one of the sterner American left-wing magazines.) The proponent of the cause will prefer to the complexity of drama with its real conflicts the knocking over of a straw man—will prefer to Poem XVI, "The Dance of Death" with its literal straw-man, the dancer, who can be ticketed and labeled.

But Poem XVI is fine enough to warrant a little further

attention, and sections of it will furnish some of the best illustrations of Auden's positive virtues. The kind of unity which he achieves at his best is well illustrated by such a passage as the following:

> It is time for the destruction of error.
> The chairs are being brought in from the garden,
> The summer talk stopped on that savage coast
> Before the storms, after the guests and birds:
> In sanatoriums they laugh less and less,
> Less certain of cure; and the loud madman
> Sinks now into a more terrible calm.
>
> The falling leaves know it, the children,
> At play on the fuming alkali-tip
> Or by the flooded football ground, know it—
> This is the dragon's day, the devourer's. . . .

The poetry recommends itself at once by a certain fullness and richness of tone and by the organic quality of the rhythm. But if we are to be more precise we shall have little difficulty in showing how the contrasts among the various items serve to build up the quiet but powerful irony which is achieved. The chairs are brought in because it is the season of storms, but, as stated in the poem, it is suggested that this simple act is a reaction to the threat of destruction. The classes who can afford the gardens can make only trivial responses. They can view the "destruction of error" as only a storm to be avoided by seasonal migration. There is another irony in the fact that the "savage coast" has attracted the gentle folk because it *is* savage —with the conventional associations of the romantic and the picturesque.

Further lines of resemblance emerge on inspection: The summer hotel is a sort of sanatorium, at least in the lightest sense of the word "recreation." The summer talk of the hotel is thus allied with the laughter of the patients in the sanatorium; and to the madman's ravings, for the asylum is still another kind of sanatorium.

The summer talk, the patients' laughter, and the cries of the madman are ironically linked together in an insight which involves the nature of the whole civilization, an insight which sets up a new relation among aspects of civilization which are usually regarded as discordant and antithetical.

In the same way consider the relationship of the images in the section which follows. The children are like the falling leaves, natural—in a sense in which the fuming alkali-tip is not "natural," and yet it is natural that the children should play upon it. They have no place but the industrial rubbish heaps on which to play. The children pull it into the relevant world of the poem. The fuming alkali is a significant part of the world upon which the storm is to descend, and for which the visitors at the summer hotel are responsible, whether or not they care to acknowledge it. The children with their innocent play do acknowledge it, and in a sense know what is to occur as the adults of the ruling classes do not.

Moreover, the reference to the children prepares for and acclimatizes the dragon reference. Children believe in dragons as adults do not, and ironically, therefore—as well as literally—it is appropriate that it should be they who know that the dragon's day is at hand. As these ironies develop, further relationships emerge: the children, the madman, the sick, the leaves become related in their sharing of a knowledge which, ironically, is withheld from the mature, the sane, the healthy, and the human.

It is quite idle at this time to try to predict Auden's future career. His best work revolves around one rather narrow theme. Other themes will undoubtedly bring their special problems. What it does seem relevant to insist on here, and especially relevant in connection with the principles argued in this book, is that Auden's best poetry represents the structure which we discussed in the first chapters of this study.

7

THE WASTE LAND:

CRITIQUE OF THE MYTH

THOUGH MUCH has been written on *The Waste Land,* it will not be difficult to show that most of its critics misconceive entirely the theme and the structure of the poem. There has been little or no attempt to deal with it as a unified whole. F. R. Leavis and F. O. Matthiessen have treated large sections of the poem in detail, and I am obviously indebted to both of them. I believe, however, that Leavis makes some positive errors of interpretation. I find myself in almost complete agreement with Matthiessen in his commentary on the sections which he deals with in his *Achievement of T. S. Eliot,* but the plan of his book does not allow for a complete consecutive examination of the poem.

In view of the state of criticism with regard to the poem, it is best for us to approach it frankly on the basis of its theme. I prefer, however, not to raise just here the question of how important it is for the reader to have an explicit intellectual account of the various symbols and a logical account of their relationships. It may well be that such rationalization is no more than a scaffolding to be got out of the way before we contemplate the poem itself as poem. But many readers (including myself) find the erection of such a scaffolding valuable—if not absolutely necessary—and if some readers will be tempted to lay more stress upon the scaffolding than they should, there are perhaps still more readers who, without the help of such a scaffolding, will be prevented from getting at the poem at all.

The basic symbol used, that of the waste land, is taken of course, from Miss Jessie Weston's *From Ritual to Romance*. In the legends which she treats there, the land has been blighted by a curse. The crops do not grow and the animals cannot reproduce. The plight of the land is summed up by, and connected with, the plight of the lord of the land, the Fisher King, who has been rendered impotent by maiming or sickness. The curse can be removed only by the appearance of a knight who will ask the meanings of the various symbols which are displayed to him in the castle. The shift in meaning from physical to spiritual sterility is easily made, and was, as a matter of fact, made in certain of the legends. As Eliot has pointed out, a knowledge of this symbolism is essential for an understanding of the poem.

Of hardly less importance to the reader, however, is a knowledge of Eliot's basic method. *The Waste Land* is built on a major contrast—a device which is a favorite of Eliot's and is to be found in many of his poems, particularly his later poems. The contrast is between two kinds of life and two kinds of death. Life devoid of meaning is death; sacrifice, even the sacrificial death, may be life-giving, an awakening to life. The poem occupies itself to a great extent with this paradox, and with a number of variations upon it.

Eliot has stated the matter quite explicitly himself in one of his essays. In his "Baudelaire" he says: "One aphorism which has been especially noticed is the following: *la volupté unique et suprême de l'amour gît dans la certitude de faire le mal*. This means, I think, that Baudelaire has perceived that what distinguishes the relations of man and woman from the copulation of beasts is the knowledge of Good and Evil (of *moral* Good and Evil which are not natural Good and Bad or puritan Right and Wrong). Having an imperfect, vague romantic conception of Good, he was at least able to understand that the sexual act as evil is more dignified, less boring, than as the natural, 'life-giving,' cheery automatism of the modern world. . . . So far as we are human, what we do must be either evil or good; so far as we do evil or good, we are human; and it is better, in a paradoxical way, to do evil than to do nothing: at least, *we exist* [italics mine]." The last statement is highly important for an understanding of *The Waste Land.* The fact that men have lost the knowledge of good and evil, keeps them from being alive, and is the justification for viewing the modern waste land as a realm in which the inhabitants do not even exist.

This theme is stated in the quotation which prefaces the poem. The Sybil says: "I wish to die." Her statement has several possible interpretations. For one thing, she is saying what the people who inhabit the waste land are saying. But she may also be saying what the speaker of "The Journey of the Magi" says: ". . . this Birth was/Hard and bitter agony for us, like Death, our death/. . . I should be glad of another death."

I

The first section of "The Burial of the Dead" develops the theme of the attractiveness of death, or of the difficulty in rousing oneself from the death in life in which the people of the waste land live. Men are afraid to live in reality. April, the month of rebirth, is not the most joyful season but the cruelest. Winter at least kept us warm in forgetful snow. The idea is one which Eliot has stressed elsewhere. Earlier in "Gerontion" he had written

> In the juvescence of the year
> Came Christ the tiger
> . . . .
> The tiger springs in the new year. Us he devours.

More lately, in *Murder in the Cathedral,* he has the chorus say

> We do not wish anything to happen.
> Seven years we have lived quietly,
> Succeeded in avoiding notice,
> Living and partly living.

And in another passage: "Now I fear disturbance of the quiet seasons." Men dislike to be roused from their death-in-life.

The first part of "The Burial of the Dead" introduces this theme through a sort of reverie on the part of the protagonist—a reverie in which speculation on life glides off into memory of an actual conversation in the Hofgarten and back into speculation again. The function of the conversation is to establish the class and character of the protagonist. The reverie is resumed with line 19.

> What are the roots that clutch, what branches grow
> Out of this stony rubbish?

The protagonist answers for himself:

> Son of man,
> You cannot say, or guess, for you know only
> A heap of broken images, where the sun beats,
> And the dead tree gives no shelter, the cricket
>   no relief,
> And the dry stone no sound of water.

In this passage there are references to Ezekiel and to Ecclesiastes, and these references indicate what it is that men no longer know: The passage referred to in Ezekiel 2, pictures a world thoroughly secularized:

1. And he said unto me, Son of man, stand upon thy feet, and I will speak unto thee.

2. And the spirit entered into me when he spake unto me, and set me upon my feet, that I heard him that spake unto me.

3. And he said unto me, Son of man, I send thee to the children of Israel, to a rebellious nation that hath rebelled

against me: they and their fathers have transgressed against me, even unto this very day.

Other passages from Ezekiel are relevant to the poem, Chapter 37 in particular, which describes Ezekiel's waste land, where the prophet, in his vision of the valley of dry bones, contemplates the "burial of the dead" and is asked: "Son of man, can these bones live? And I answered, O Lord God, thou knowest. 4. Again he said unto me, Prophesy over these bones, and say unto them, O ye dry bones, hear the word of the Lord."

One of Ezekiel's prophecies was that Jerusalem would be conquered and the people led away into the Babylonian captivity. That captivity is alluded to in Section III of *The Waste Land,* line 182, where the Thames becomes the "waters of Leman."

The passage from Ecclesiastes 12, alluded to in Eliot's notes, describes the same sort of waste land:

1. Remember now thy Creator in the days of thy youth, while the evil days come not, nor the years draw nigh, when thou shalt say, I have no pleasure in them;

2. While the sun, or the light, or the moon, or the stars, be not darkened, nor the clouds return after the rain;

3. In the day when the keepers of the house shall tremble, and the strong men shall bow themselves, and the grinders cease because they are few, and those that look out of the windows be darkened,

4. And the doors shall be shut in the streets, when the sound of the grinding is low, and he shall rise up at the voice of the bird, and all the daughters of musick shall be brought low;

5. Also when they shall be afraid of that which is high, and fears shall be in the way, and the almond tree shall flourish, and the grasshopper shall be a burden, *and desire shall fail* [italics mine]: because man goeth to his long home, and the mourners go about the streets;

6. Or ever the silver cord be loosed, or the golden bowl be broken, or the pitcher be broken at the fountain, or the wheel broken at the cistern.

7. Then shall the dust return to the earth as it was: and the spirit shall return unto God who gave it.

8. Vanity of vanities, saith the preacher; all is vanity.

A reference to this passage is also evidently made in the nightmare vision of Section V of the poem.

The next section of "The Burial of the Dead" which begins with the scrap of song quoted from Wagner (perhaps another item in the reverie of the protagonist), states the opposite half of the paradox which underlies the poem: namely, that life at its highest moments of meaning and intensity resembles death. The song from Act I of Wagner's *Tristan und Isolde*, "*Frisch weht der Wind*," is sung in the opera by a young sailor aboard the ship which is bringing Isolde to Cornwall. The "*Irisch kind*" of the song does not properly apply to Isolde at all. The song is merely one of happy and naïve love. It brings to the mind of the protagonist an experience of love—the vision of the hyacinth girl as she came back from the hyacinth garden. The poet says

> . . . my eyes failed, I was neither
> Living nor dead, and I knew nothing,
> Looking into the heart of light, the silence.

The line which immediately follows this passage, "*Oed' und leer das Meer*," seems at first to be simply an extension of the last figure: that is, "Empty and wide the sea [of silence]." But the line, as a matter of fact, makes an ironic contrast; for the line, as it occurs in Act III of the opera, is the reply of the watcher who reports to the wounded Tristan that Isolde's ship is nowhere in sight; the sea is empty. And, though the "*Irisch kind*" of the first quotation is not Isolde, the reader familiar with the opera will apply it to Isolde when he comes to the line "*Oed' und leer das Meer*." For the question in the song is in essence Tristan's question in Act III: "My Irish child, where dwellest thou?" The two quotations from the opera which frame the ecstasy-of-love passage thus take on a new meaning in the altered con-

text. In the first, love is happy; the boat rushes on with a
fair wind behind it. In the second, love is absent; the sea
is wide and empty. And the last quotation reminds us that
even love cannot exist in the waste land.

The next passage, that in which Madame Sosostris figures,
calls for further reference to Miss Weston's book. As Miss
Weston has shown, the Tarot cards were originally used to
determine the event of highest importance to the people,
the rising of the waters. Madame Sosostris has fallen a long
way from the high function of her predecessors. She is
engaged merely in vulgar fortune-telling—is merely one
item in a generally vulgar civilization. But the symbols of
the Tarot pack are still unchanged. The various characters
are still inscribed on the cards, and she is reading in reality
(though she does not know it) the fortune of the protagon-
ist. She finds that his card is that of the drowned Phoeni-
cian Sailor, and so she warns him against death by water,
not realizing any more than do the other inhabitants of the
modern waste land that the way into life may be by death
itself. The drowned Phoenician Sailor is a type of the
fertility god whose image was thrown into the sea annually
as a symbol of the death of summer. As for the other
figures in the pack: Belladonna, the Lady of the Rocks, is
woman in the waste land. The man with three staves,
Eliot says he associates rather arbitrarily with the Fisher
King. The term "arbitrarily" indicates that we are not to
attempt to find a logical connection here. (It may be in-
teresting to point out, however, that Eliot seems to have
given, in a later poem, his reason for making the associa-
tion. In "The Hollow Men" he writes, speaking as one of
the Hollow Men:

> Let me also wear
> Such deliberate disguises
> Rat's coat, crowskin, crossed staves
> In a field
> Behaving as the wind behaves.

The figure is that of a scarecrow, fit symbol of the man who possesses no reality, and fit type of the Fisher King, the maimed, impotent king who ruled over the waste land of the legend. The man with three staves in the deck of cards may thus have appealed to the poet as an appropriate figure to which to assign the function of the Fisher King, although the process of identification was too difficult to expect the reader to follow and although knowledge of the process was not necessary to an understanding of the poem.)

The Hanged Man, who represents the hanged god of Frazer (including the Christ), Eliot states in a note, is associated with the hooded figure who appears in "What the Thunder Said." That he is hooded accounts for Madame Sosostris' inability to see him; or rather, here again the palaver of the modern fortune-teller is turned to new and important account by the poet's shifting the reference into a new and serious context. The Wheel and the one-eyed merchant will be discussed later.

After the Madame Sosostris passage, Eliot proceeds to complicate his symbols for the sterility and unreality of the modern waste land by associating it with Baudelaire's "*fourmillante cité*" and with Dante's Limbo. The passages already quoted from Eliot's essay on Baudelaire will indicate one of the reasons why Baudelaire's lines are evoked here. In Baudelaire's city, dream and reality seem to mix, and it is interesting that Eliot in "The Hollow Men" refers to this same realm of death-in-life as "death's dream kingdom" in contradistinction to "death's other kingdom."

The references to Dante are most important. The line, "I had not thought death had undone so many," is taken from the Third Canto of the *Inferno;* the line, "Sighs, short and infrequent, were exhaled," from the Fourth Canto. Mr. Matthiessen has already pointed out that the Third Canto deals with Dante's Limbo which is occupied by those who on earth had "lived without praise or blame." They share this abode with the angels "who were not rebels, nor were faithful to God, but were for themselves." They ex-

emplify almost perfectly the secular attitude which domi-
nates the modern world. Their grief, according to Dante,
arises from the fact that they "have no hope of death; and
their blind life is so debased, that they are envious of every
other lot." But though they may not hope for death, Dante
calls them "these wretches who never were alive." The
people described in the Fourth Canto are those who lived
virtuously but who died before the proclamation of the
Gospel—they are the unbaptized. They form the second of
the two classes of people who inhabit the modern waste
land: those who are secularized and those who have no
knowledge of the faith. Without a faith their life is in
reality a death. To repeat the sentence from Eliot pre-
viously quoted: "So far as we do evil or good, we are
human; and it is better, in a paradoxical way, to do evil than
to do nothing: at least, we exist."

The Dante and Baudelaire references, then, come to the
same thing as the allusion to the waste land of the medi-
eval legends; and these various allusions, drawn from
widely differing sources, enrich the comment on the modern
city so that it becomes "unreal" on a number of levels: as
seen through "the brown fog of a winter dawn"; as the
medieval waste land and Dante's Limbo and Baudelaire's
Paris are unreal.

The reference to Stetson stresses again the connection
between the modern London of the poem and Dante's hell.
After the statement, "I could never have believed death
had undone so many," follow the words, "After I had dis-
tinguished some among them, I saw and knew the shade of
him who made, through cowardice, the great refusal."
The protagonist, like Dante, sees among the inhabitants of
the contemporary waste land one whom he recognizes.
(The name "Stetson" I take to have no ulterior significance.
It is merely an ordinary name such as might be borne by
the friend one might see in a crowd in a great city.) Mylae,
as Mr. Matthiessen has pointed out, is the name of a battle
between the Romans and the Carthaginians in the Punic

War. [The Punic War was a trade war—might be considered a rather close parallel to our late war. At any rate, it is plain that Eliot in having the protagonist address the friend in a London street as one who was with him in the Punic War rather than as one who was with him in the World War is making the point that all the wars are one war; all experience, one experience.] As Eliot put the idea in *Murder in the Cathedral*:

> We do not know very much of the future
> Except that from generation to generation
> The same things happen again and again

I am not sure that Leavis and Matthiessen are correct in inferring that the line, "That corpse you planted last year in your garden," refers to the attempt to bury a memory. But whether or not this is true, the line certainly refers also to the buried god of the old fertility rites. It also is to be linked with the earlier passage—"What are the roots that clutch, what branches grow," etc. This allusion to the buried god will account for the ironical, almost taunting tone of the passage. [The burial of the dead is now a sterile planting—without hope. But the advice to "keep the Dog far hence," in spite of the tone, is, I believe, well taken and serious. The passage in Webster goes as follows

> But keep the wolf far thence, that's foe to men,
> For with his nails he'll dig them up again.

Why does Eliot turn the wolf into a dog? And why does he reverse the point of importance from the animal's normal hostility to men to its friendliness? If, as some critics have suggested, he is merely interested in making a reference to Webster's darkest play, why alter the line? I am inclined to take the Dog (the capital letter is Eliot's) as Humanitarianism * and the related philosophies which, in their

* The reference is perhaps more general still: it may include Naturalism, and Science in the popular conception as the new magic which will enable man to conquer his environment completely.

concern for man, extirpate the supernatural—dig up the corpse of the buried god and thus prevent the rebirth of life. For the general idea, see Eliot's essay, "The Humanism of Irving Babbitt."

The last line of "The Burial of the Dead"—"You! hypocrite lecteur!—mon semblable,—mon frère!" the quotation from Baudelaire, completes the universalization of Stetson begun by the reference to Mylae. Stetson is every man including the reader and Mr. Eliot himself..

II

If "The Burial of the Dead" gives the general abstract statement of the situation, the second part of *The Waste Land,* "A Game of Chess," gives a more concrete illustration. The easiest contrast in this section—and one which may easily blind the casual reader to a continued emphasis on the contrast between the two kinds of life, or the two kinds of death, already commented on—is the contrast between life in a rich and magnificent setting, and life in the low and vulgar setting of a London pub. But both scenes, however antithetical they may appear superficially, are scenes taken from the contemporary waste land. In both of them life has lost its meaning.

I am particularly indebted to Mr. Allen Tate's comment on the first part of this section. To quote from him, "The woman . . . is, I believe, the symbol of man at the present time. He is surrounded by the grandeurs of the past, but he does not participate in them; they don't sustain him." And to quote from another section of his commentary: "The rich experience of the great tradition depicted in the room receives a violent shock in contrast with a game that symbolizes the inhuman abstraction of the modern mind." Life has no meaning; history has no meaning; there is no answer to the question: "What shall we ever do?" The only thing that has meaning is the abstract game which they are to play, a game in which the meaning is assigned

and arbitrary, meaning by convention only—in short, a game
of chess.

This interpretation will account in part for the pointed
reference to Cleopatra in the first lines of the section. But
there is, I believe, a further reason for the poet's having
compared the lady to Cleopatra. The queen in Shake-
speare's drama—"Age cannot wither her, nor custom stale/
Her infinite variety"—is perhaps the extreme exponent of
love for love's sake, the feminine member of the pair of
lovers who threw away an empire for love. But the in-
finite variety of the life of the woman in "A Game of Chess"
has been staled. There is indeed no variety at all, and love
simply does not exist. The function of the sudden change
in the description of the carvings and paintings in the room
from the heroic and magnificent to "and other withered
stumps of time" is obvious. But the reference to Philomela
is particularly important, for Philomela, it seems to me, is
one of the major symbols of the poem.

Miss Weston points out (in *The Quest of the Holy Grail*)
that a section of one of the Grail manuscripts, which is
apparently intended to be a gloss on the Grail story, tells
how the court of the rich Fisher King was withdrawn from
the knowledge of men when certain of the maidens who
frequented the shrine were raped and had their golden cups
taken from them. The curse on the land follows from this
act. Miss Weston conjectures that this may be a statement,
in the form of a parable, of the violation of the older mys-
teries which were probably once celebrated openly, but
were later forced underground. Whether or not Mr. Eliot
noticed this passage or intends a reference, the violation of
a woman makes a very good symbol of the process of
secularization. John Crowe Ransom makes the point very
neatly for us in *God Without Thunder*. Love is the aes-
thetic of sex; lust is the science. Love implies a deferring
of the satisfaction of the desire; it implies a certain asceti-
cism and a ritual. Lust drives forward urgently and sci-

entifically to the immediate extirpation of the desire. Our contemporary waste land is in large part the result of our scientific attitude—of our complete secularization. Needless to say, lust defeats its own ends. The portrayal of "the change of Philomel, by the barbarous king" is a fitting commentary on the scene which it ornaments. The waste land of the legend came in this way; the modern waste land has come in this way.

This view is corroborated by the change of tense to which Edmund Wilson has called attention: "And still she *cried*, and still the world *pursues* [italics mine]." Apparently the "world" partakes in the barbarous king's action, and still partakes in that action.

To "dirty ears" the nightingale's song is not that which filled all the desert with inviolable voice—it is "jug, jug." Edmund Wilson has pointed out that the rendition of the bird's song here represents not merely the Elizabethans' neutral notation of the bird's song, but carries associations of the ugly and coarse. The passage is one, therefore, of many instances of Eliot's device of using something which in one context is innocent but in another context becomes loaded with a special meaning.

The Philomela passage has another importance, however. If it is a commentary on how the waste land became waste, it also repeats the theme of the death which is the door to life, the theme of the dying god. The raped woman becomes transformed through suffering into the nightingale; through the violation comes the "inviolable voice." The thesis that suffering is action, and that out of suffering comes poetry is a favorite one of Eliot's. For example, "Shakespeare, too, was occupied with the struggle—which alone constitutes life for a poet—to transmute his personal and private agonies into something rich and strange, something universal and impersonal." Consider also his statement with reference to Baudelaire: "Indeed, in his way of suffering is already a kind of presence of the supernatural and of the superhuman. He rejects always the purely nat-

ural and the purely human; in other words, he is neither
'naturalist' nor 'humanist.'" [The theme of the life which is
death is stated specifically in the conversation between the
man and the woman. She asks the question, "Are you alive,
or not?" Compare the Dante references in "The Burial of
the Dead." (She also asks, "Is there nothing in your head?"
He is one of the Hollow Men—"Headpiece filled with
straw.") These people, as people living in the waste land,
know nothing, see nothing, do not even live.

But the protagonist, after this reflection that in the waste
land of modern life even death is sterile—"I think we are in
rats' alley/Where the dead men lost their bones"—remem-
bers a death that was transformed into something rich and
strange, the death described in the song from *The Tempest*
—"Those are pearls that were his eyes."

The reference to this section of *The Tempest* is, like the
Philomela reference, one of Eliot's major symbols. A gen-
eral comment on it is therefore appropriate here, for we are
to meet with it twice more in later sections of the poem.
The song, one remembers, was sung by Ariel in luring
Ferdinand, Prince of Naples, on to meet Miranda, and thus
to find love, and through this love, to effect the regeneration
and deliverance of all the people on the island. Ferdinand,
hearing the song, says:

> The ditty does remember my drowned father.
> This is no mortal business, nor no sound
> That the earth owes . . .

The allusion is an extremely interesting example of the de-
vice of Eliot's already commented upon, that of taking an
item from one context and shifting it into another in which
it assumes a new and powerful meaning. The description
of a death which is a portal into a realm of the rich and
strange—a death which becomes a sort of birth—assumes in
the mind of the protagonist an association with that of the
drowned god whose effigy was thrown into the water as a
symbol of the death of the fruitful powers of nature but

which was taken out of the water as a symbol of the revivi-
fied god. (See *From Ritual to Romance.*)   The passage
therefore represents the perfect antithesis to the passage in
"The Burial of the Dead": "That corpse you planted last
year in your garden," etc.   It also, as we have already
pointed out, finds its antithesis in the sterile and unfruitful
death "in rats' alley" just commented upon.   (We shall find
that this contrast between the death in rats' alley and the
death in *The Tempest* is made again in "The Fire Sermon.")

We have yet to treat the relation of the title of the second
section, "A Game of Chess," to Middleton's play, *Women
Beware Women,* from which the game of chess is taken.
In the play, the game is used as a device to keep the widow
occupied while her daughter-in-law is being seduced.   The
seduction amounts almost to a rape, and in a *double en-
tendre,* the rape is actually described in terms of the game.
We have one more connection with the Philomela symbol,
therefore.   The abstract game is being used in the con-
temporary waste land, as in the play, to cover up a rape and
is a description of the rape itself.

In the latter part of "A Game of Chess" we are given a
picture of spiritual emptiness, but this time, at the other
end of the social scale, as reflected in the talk between two
cockney women in a London pub.   (It is perhaps unneces-
sary to comment on the relation of their talk about abortion
to the theme of sterility and the waste land.)

The account here is straightforward enough, and the only
matter which calls for comment is the line spoken by
Ophelia in *Hamlet,* which ends the passage.   Ophelia, too,
was very much concerned about love, the theme of conver-
sation between the women in the pub.   As a matter of fact,
she was in very much the same position as that of the
woman who has been the topic of conversation between the
two ladies whom we have just heard.   And her poetry, like
Philomela's, had come out of suffering.   We are probably
to look for the relevance of the allusion to her here rather
than in an easy satiric contrast between Elizabethan glories

and modern sordidness. After all, Eliot's criticism of the present world is not merely the sentimental one that this happens to be the twentieth century after Christ and not the seventeenth.

III

["The Fire Sermon" makes much use of several of the symbols already developed. The fire is the sterile burning of lust, and the section is a sermon, although a sermon by example only.] This section of the poem also contains some of the most easily apprehended uses of literary allusion. The poem opens on a vision of the modern river. In Spenser's "Prothalamion" the scene described is also a river scene at London, and it is dominated by nymphs and their paramours, and the nymphs are preparing for a wedding. The contrast between Spenser's scene and its twentieth century equivalent is jarring. The paramours are now "the loitering heirs of city directors," and, as for the nuptials of Spenser's Elizabethan maidens, in the stanzas which follow we learn a great deal about those. At the end of the section the speech of the third of the Thames-nymphs summarizes the whole matter for us.

The waters of the Thames are also associated with those of Leman—the poet in the contemporary waste land is in a sort of Babylonian Captivity.

The castle of the Fisher King was always located on the banks of a river or on the sea shore. The title "Fisher King," Miss Weston shows, originates from the use of the fish as a fertility or life symbol. This meaning, however, was often forgotten, and so his title in many of the later Grail romances is accounted for by describing the king as fishing. Eliot uses the reference to fishing for reverse effect. The reference to fishing is part of the realistic detail of the scene—"While I was fishing in the dull canal." [But to the reader who knows the Weston references, the reference is to that of the Fisher King of the Grail legends. The protagonist is the maimed and impotent king of the legends.]

Eliot proceeds now to tie the waste-land symbol to that of *The Tempest*, by quoting one of the lines spoken by Ferdinand, Prince of Naples, which occurs just before Ariel's song, "Full Fathom Five," is heard. But he alters *The Tempest* passage somewhat, writing not, "Weeping again the king my father's wreck," but

> Musing upon the king my brother's wreck
> And on the king my father's death before him.

It is possible that the alteration has been made to bring the account taken from *The Tempest* into accord with the situation in the Percival stories. In Wolfram von Eschenbach's *Parzival*, for instance, Trevrezent, the hermit, is the brother of the Fisher King, Anfortas. He tells Parzival, "His name all men know as Anfortas, and I weep for him evermore." Their father, Frimutel, is dead.

The protagonist in the poem, then, imagines himself not only in the situation of Ferdinand in *The Tempest* but also in that of one of the characters in the Grail legend; and the wreck, to be applied literally in the first instance, applies metaphorically in the second.

After the lines from *The Tempest*, appears again the image of a sterile death from which no life comes, the bones, "rattled by the rat's foot only, year to year." (The collocation of this figure with the vision of the death by water in Ariel's song has already been commented on. The lines quoted from *The Tempest* come just before the song.)

The allusion to Marvell's "To His Coy Mistress" is of course one of the easiest allusions in the poem. Instead of "Time's winged chariot" the poet hears "the sound of horns and motors" of contemporary London. But the passage has been further complicated. The reference has been combined with an allusion to Day's "Parliament of Bees." "Time's winged chariot" of Marvell has not only been changed to the modern automobile; Day's "sound of horns and hunting" has changed to the horns of the motors. And Actaeon will not be brought face to face with Diana, goddess of chastity; Sweeny, type of the vulgar bourgeois, is to be brought to Mrs. Porter, hardly a type of chastity. The reference in the ballad to the feet "washed in soda water" reminds the poet ironically of another sort of foot-washing, the sound of the children singing in the dome heard at the ceremony of the foot-washing which precedes the restoration of the wounded Anfortas (the Fisher King) by Parzival and the taking away of the curse from the waste land. The quotation thus completes the allusion to the Fisher King commenced in line 189—"While I was fishing in the dull canal."

The pure song of the children also reminds the poet of the song of the nightingale which we have heard in "The Game of Chess." The recapitulation of symbols is continued with a repetition of "Unreal city" and with the reference to the one-eyed merchant.

Mr. Eugenides, the Smyrna merchant, is the one-eyed merchant mentioned by Madame Sosostris. The fact that the merchant is one-eyed apparently means, in Madame Sosostris' speech, no more than that the merchant's face on the card is shown in profile. But Eliot applies the term to Mr. Eugenides for a totally different effect. The defect corresponds somewhat to Madame Sosostris' bad cold. He is a rather battered representative of the fertility cults: the prophet, the *seer*, with only one eye.

The Syrian merchants, we learn from Miss Weston's book, were, along with slaves and soldiers, the principal carriers of the mysteries which lie at the core of the Grail legends. But in the modern world we find both the representatives of the Tarot divining and the mystery cults in decay. What he carries on his back and what the fortune-teller is forbidden to see is evidently the knowledge of the mysteries (although Mr. Eugenides himself is hardly likely to be more aware of it than Madame Sosostris is aware of the importance of her function). Mr. Eugenides, in terms of his former function, ought to be inviting the protagonist into the esoteric cult which holds the secret of life, but on the realistic surface of the poem, in his invitation to "a weekend at the Metropole" he is really inviting him to a homosexual debauch. The homesexuality is "secret" and now a "cult" but a very different cult from that which Mr. Eugenides ought to represent. The end of the new cult is not life but, ironically, sterility.

In the modern waste land, however, even the relation between man and woman is also sterile. The incident between the typist and the carbuncular young man is a picture of "love" so exclusively and practically pursued that it is not love at all. The tragic chorus to the scene is Tiresias, into whom perhaps Mr. Eugenides may be said to modulate, Tiresias, the historical "expert" on the relation between the sexes.

The fact that Tiresias is made the commentator serves a further irony. In *Oedipus Rex*, it is Tiresias who recognizes that the curse which has come upon the Theban land has been caused by the sinful sexual relationship of Oedipus and Jocasta. But Oedipus' sin has been committed in ignorance, and knowledge of it brings horror and remorse. The essential horror of the act which Tiresias witnesses in the poem is that it is not regarded as a sin at all—is perfectly casual, is merely the copulation of beasts.

The reminiscence of the lines from Goldsmith's song in the description of the young woman's actions after the departure of her lover, gives concretely and ironically the utter break-down of traditional standards.

It is the music of her gramophone which the protagonist hears "creep by" him "on the waters." Far from the music which Ferdinand heard bringing him to Miranda and love, it is, one is tempted to think, the music of "O O O O that Shakespeherian Rag."

But the protagonist says that he can *sometimes* hear "the pleasant whining of a mandoline." Significantly enough, it is the music of the fishmen (the fish again as a life symbol) and it comes from beside a church (though—if this is not to rely too much on Eliot's note—the church has been marked for destruction). Life on Lower Thames Street, if not on the Strand, still has meaning as it cannot have meaning for either the typist or the rich woman of "A Game of Chess."

The song of the Thames-daughters brings us back to the opening section of "The Fire Sermon" again, and once more we have to do with the river and the river-nymphs. Indeed, the typist incident is framed by the two river-nymph scenes.

The connection of the river-nymphs with the Rhine-daughters of Wagner's *Götterdämerung* is easily made. In the passage in Wagner's opera (to which Eliot refers in his note), the opening of Act III, the Rhine-daughters bewail the loss of the beauty of the Rhine occasioned by the theft of the gold, and then beg Siegfried to give them back the Ring made from this gold, finally threatening him with death if he does not give it up. Like the Thames-daughters they too have been violated; and like the maidens mentioned in the Grail legend, the violation has brought a curse on gods and men. The first of the songs depicts the modern river, soiled with oil and tar. (Compare also with the description of the river in the first part of "The Fire Sermon.") The second song depicts the Elizabethan river, also evoked in the first part of "The Fire Sermon." (Leicester and Elizabeth ride upon it in a barge of state. Incidentally, Spenser's "Prothalamion" from which quotation is made in the first part of "The Fire Sermon" mentions Leicester as having formerly lived in the house which forms the setting of the poem.)

In this second song there is also a definite allusion to the passage in *Antony and Cleopatra* already referred to in the opening line of "A Game of Chess."

> Beating oars
> The stern was formed
> A gilded shell

And if we still have any doubt of the allusion, Eliot's note on the passage with its reference to the "barge" and "poop"

should settle the matter. We have already commented on
the earlier allusion to Cleopatra as the prime example of
love for love's sake. The symbol bears something of the
same meaning here, and the note which Eliot supplies does
something to reinforce the "Cleopatra" aspect of Elizabeth.
Elizabeth in the presence of the Spaniard De Quadra,
though negotiations were going on for a Spanish marriage,
"went so far that Lord Robert at last said, as I [De Quadra
was a bishop] was on the spot there was no reason why they
should not be married if the queen pleased." The passage
has a sort of double function. It reinforces the general con-
trast between Elizabethan magnificence and modern sordid-
ness: in the Elizabethan age love for love's sake has some
meaning and therefore some magnificence. But the passage
gives something of an opposed effect too: the same sterile
love, emptiness of love, obtained in this period too: Eliza-
beth and the typist are alike as well as different. (One of
the reasons for the frequent allusion to Elizabethan poetry
in this and the preceding section of the poem may be the
fact that with the English Renaissance the old set of super-
natural sanctions had begun to break up. See Eliot's various
essays on Shakespeare and the Elizabethan dramatists.)

The third Thames-daughter's song depicts another sordid
"love" affair, and unites the themes of the first two songs.
It begins "Trams and *dusty* trees." With it we are definitely
in the waste land again. Pia, whose words she echoes in
saying "Highbury bore me. Richmond and Kew/Undid
me" was in Purgatory and had hope. The woman speaking
here has no hope—she too is in the Inferno: "I can con-
nect/Nothing with nothing." She has just completed, float-
ing down the river in the canoe, what Eliot has described
in *Murder in the Cathedral* as

. . . the effortless journey, to the empty land

. . . .

Where those who were men can no longer turn the
    mind

Where the soul is no longer deceived, for there are no
    objects, no tones,
To distraction, delusion, escape into dream, pretence,
No colours, no forms to distract, to divert the soul
From seeing itself, foully united forever, nothing with
    nothing,
Not what we call death, but what beyond death is not
    death . . .

Now, "on Margate Sands," like the Hollow Men, she stands
"on this beach of the tumid river."

The songs of the three Thames-daughters, as a matter of
fact, epitomize this whole section of the poem.   With ref-
erence to the quotations from St. Augustine and Buddha
at the end of "The Fire Sermon" Eliot states that "the col-
location of these two representatives of eastern and western
asceticism, as the culmination of this part of the poem, is
not an accident."

It is certainly not an accident.   The moral of all the inci-
dents which we have been witnessing is that there must be
an asceticism—something to check the drive of desire.   The
wisdom of the East and the West comes to the same thing
on this point.   Moreover, the imagery which both St. Augus-
tine and Buddha use for lust is fire.   What we have wit-
nessed in the various scenes of "The Fire Sermon" is the
sterile burning of lust.   Modern man, freed from all re-
straints, in his cultivation of experience for experience's
sake burns, but not with a "hard and gemlike flame."   One
ought not to pound the point home in this fashion, but to
see that the imagery of this section of the poem furnishes
illustrations leading up to the Fire Sermon is the necessary
requirement for feeling the force of the brief allusions here
at the end to Buddha and St. Augustine.

IV

Whatever the specific meaning of the symbols, the general
function of the section, "Death by Water," is readily ap-
parent.   The section forms a contrast with "The Fire Ser-

mon" which precedes it—a contrast between the symbolism of fire and that of water. Also readily apparent is its force as a symbol of surrender and relief through surrender.

Some specific connections can be made, however. The drowned Phoenician Sailor recalls the drowned god of the fertility cults. Miss Weston tells that each year at Alexandria an effigy of the head of the god was thrown into the water as a symbol of the death of the powers of nature, and that this head was carried by the current to Byblos where it was taken out of the water and exhibited as a symbol of the reborn god.

Moreover, the Phoenician Sailor is a merchant—"Forgot . . . the profit and loss." The vision of the drowned sailor gives a statement of the message which the Syrian merchants originally brought to Britain and which the Smyrna merchant, unconsciously and by ironical negatives, has brought. One of Eliot's notes states that the "merchant . . . melts into the Phoenician Sailor, and the latter is not wholly distinct from Ferdinand Prince of Naples." The death by water would seem to be equated with the death described in Ariel's song in *The Tempest*. There is a definite difference in the tone of the description of this death—"A current under sea/Picked his bones in whispers," as compared with the "other" death—"bones cast in a little low dry garret,/Rattled by the rat's foot only, year to year."

Further than this it would not be safe to go, but one may point out that whirling (the whirlpool here, the Wheel of Madame Sosostris' palaver) is one of Eliot's symbols frequently used in other poems (*Ash Wednesday*, "Gerontion," *Murder in the Cathedral*, and "Burnt Norton") to denote the temporal world. And I may point out, supplying the italics myself, the following passage from *Ash Wednesday*:

Although I do not hope to *turn* again

.   .   .   .

Wavering between the *profit and the loss*
In this brief transit where the dreams cross
The dreamcrossed twilight *between birth and dying.*

At least, with a kind of hindsight, one may suggest that "Death by Water" gives an instance of the conquest of death and time, the "perpetual recurrence of determined seasons," the "world of spring and autumn, birth and dying" through death itself.

V

The reference to the "torchlight red on sweaty faces" and to the "frosty silence in the gardens" obviously associates Christ in Gethsemane with the other hanged gods. The god has now died, and in referring to this, the basic theme finds another strong restatement:

> He who was living is now dead
> We who were living are now dying
> With a little patience

The poet does not say "We who *are* living." It is "We who *were* living." It is the death-in-life of Dante's Limbo. Life in the full sense has been lost.

The passage on the sterility of the waste land and the lack of water provides for the introduction later of two highly important passages:

> There is not even silence in the mountains
> But dry sterile thunder without rain—

lines which look forward to the introduction later of "what the thunder said" when the thunder, no longer sterile, but bringing rain, speaks.

The second of these passages is, "There is not even solitude in the mountains," which looks forward to the reference to the Journey to Emmaus theme a few lines later: "Who is the third who walks always beside you?" The god has returned, has risen, but the travelers cannot tell whether it is really he, or mere illusion induced by their delirium.

The parallelism between the "hooded figure" who "walks always beside you," and the "hooded hordes" is another instance of the sort of parallelism that is really a contrast.

In the first case, the figure is indistinct because spiritual; in the second, the hooded hordes are indistinct because completely *unspiritual*—they are the people of the waste land—

> Shape without form, shade without colour,
> Paralysed force, gesture without motion—

to take two lines from "The Hollow Men," where the people of the waste land once more appear. Or to take another line from the same poem, perhaps their hoods are the "deliberate disguises" which the Hollow Men, the people of the waste land, wear.

Eliot, as his notes tell us, has particularly connected the description here with the "decay of eastern Europe." The hordes represent, then, the general waste land of the modern world with a special application to the breakup of Eastern Europe, the region with which the fertility cults were especially connected and in which today the traditional values are thoroughly discredited. The cities, Jerusalem, Athens, Alexandria, Vienna, like the London of the first section of the poem are "unreal," and for the same reason.

The passage which immediately follows develops the unreality into nightmare, but it is a nightmare vision which is something more than an extension of the passage beginning, "What is the city over the mountains"—in it appear other figures from earlier in the poem: the lady of "A Game of Chess," who, surrounded by the glory of history and art, sees no meaning in either and threatens to rush out into the street "With my hair down, so," has here let down her hair and fiddles "whisper music on those strings." One remembers in "A Game of Chess" that it was the woman's hair that spoke:

> . . . her hair
> Spread out in fiery points
> Glowed into words, then would be savagely still.

The hair has been immemorially a symbol of fertility, and Miss Weston and Frazer mention sacrifices of hair in order to aid the fertility god.

As we have pointed out earlier, this passage is also to be connected with the twelfth chapter of Ecclesiastes. The doors "of mudcracked houses," and the cisterns in this passage are to be found in Ecclesiastes, and the woman fiddling music from her hair is one of "the daughters of musick" brought low. The towers and bells from the Elizabeth and Leicester passage of "The Fire Sermon" also appear here, but the towers are upside down, and the bells, far from pealing for an actual occasion or ringing the hours, are "reminiscent." The civilization is breaking up.

The "violet light" also deserves comment. In "The Fire Sermon" it is twice mentioned as the "violet hour," and there it has little more than a physical meaning. It is a description of the hour of twilight. Here it indicates the twilight of the civilization, but it is perhaps something more. Violet is one of the liturgical colors of the Church. It symbolizes repentance and it is the color of baptism. The visit to the Perilous Chapel, according to Miss Weston, was an initiation—that is, a baptism. In the nightmare vision, the bats wear baby faces.

The horror built up in this passage is a proper preparation for the passage on the Perilous Chapel which follows it. The journey has not been merely an agonized walk in the desert, though it is that; nor is it merely the journey after the god has died and hope has been lost; it is also the journey to the Perilous Chapel of the Grail story. In Miss Weston's account, the Chapel was part of the ritual, and was filled with horrors to test the candidate's courage. In some stories the perilous cemetery is also mentioned. Eliot has used both: "Over the tumbled graves, about the chapel." In many of the Grail stories the Chapel was haunted by demons.

The cock in the folk-lore of many people is regarded as the bird whose voice chases away the powers of evil. It is significant that it is after his crow that the flash of lightning comes and the "damp gust/Bringing rain." It is just possible that the cock has a connection also with *The Tempest* symbols. The first song which Ariel sings to Ferdinand as he sits "Weeping again the king my father's wreck" ends

> The strain of strutting chanticleer,
> Cry, cock-a-doodle-doo.

The next stanza is the "Full Fathom Five" song which Eliot has used as a vision of life gained through death. If this relation holds, here we have an extreme instance of an allusion, in itself innocent, forced into serious meaning through transference to a new context.

As Miss Weston has shown, the fertility cults go back to a very early period and are recorded in Sanscrit legends. Eliot has been continually, in the poem, linking up the Christian doctrine with the beliefs of as many peoples as he can. Here he goes back to the very beginnings of Aryan culture, and tells the rest of the story of the rain's coming, not in terms of the setting already developed but in its earliest form. The passage is thus a perfect parallel in method to the passage in "The Burial of the Dead":

> You who were with me in the ships *at Mylae!*
> That corpse you planted *last year* in your garden . . .

The use of Sanscrit in what the thunder says is thus accounted for. In addition, there is of course a more obvious reason for casting what the thunder said into Sanscrit here: onomatopoeia.

The comments on the three statements of the thunder imply an acceptance of them. The protagonist answers the first question, "What have we given?" with the statement:

> The awful daring of a moment's surrender
> Which an age of prudence can never retract
> By this, and this only, we have existed.

Here the larger meaning is stated in terms which imply the sexual meaning. Man cannot be absolutely self-regarding. Even the propagation of the race—even mere "existence"— calls for such a surrender. Living calls for—see the passage already quoted from Eliot's essay on Baudelaire—belief in something more than "life."

The comment on *dayadhvam* (sympathize) is obviously connected with the foregoing passage. The surrender to something outside the self is an attempt (whether on the sexual level or some other) to transcend one's essential isolation. The passage gathers up the symbols previously developed in the poem just as the foregoing passage reflects, though with a different implication, the numerous references to sex made earlier in the poem. For example, the woman in the first part of "A Game of Chess" has also heard the key turn in the door, and confirms her prison by thinking of the key:

> Speak to me. Why do you never speak. Speak.
> What are you thinking of? What thinking? What?
> I never know what you are thinking. Think.

The third statement made by the thunder, *damyata* (control), follows the condition necessary for control, sympathy. The figure of the boat catches up the figure of control already given in "Death by Water"—"O you who turn the wheel and look to windward"—and from "The Burial of the Dead" the figure of happy love in which the ship rushes on with a fair wind behind it: *"Frisch weht der Wind . . ."*

I cannot accept Mr. Leavis' interpretation of the passage, "I sat upon the shore/Fishing, with the arid plain behind me," as meaning that the poem "exhibits no progression." The comment upon what the thunder says would indicate, if other passages did not, that the poem does "not end where it began." It is true that the protagonist does not witness a revival of the waste land; but there are two important relationships involved in his case: a personal one as well as a general one. If secularization has destroyed, or is likely to destroy, modern civilization, the protagonist still has a private obligation to fulfill. Even if the civilization is breaking up—"London Bridge is falling down falling down falling down"— there remains the personal obligation: "Shall I at least set my lands in order?" Consider in this connection the last sentences of Eliot's "Thoughts After Lambeth": "The World is trying the experiment of attempting to form a civilized but non-Christian mentality. The experiment will fail; but we must be very patient in awaiting its collapse; meanwhile redeeming the time: so that the Faith may be preserved alive through the dark ages before us; to renew and rebuild civilization, and save the World from suicide."

The bundle of quotations with which the poem ends has a very definite relation to the general theme of the poem and to several of the major symbols used in the poem. Before Arnaut leaps back into the refining fire of Purgatory with joy he says: "I am Arnaut who weep and go singing; contrite I see my past folly, and joyful I see before me the day I hope for. Now I pray you by that virtue which guides you to the summit of the stair, at times be mindful of my pain." This theme is carried forward by the quotation from *Pervigilium Veneris*: "When shall I be like the swallow." The allusion is also connected with the Philomela symbol. (Eliot's note on the passage indicates this clearly.) The sister of Philomela was changed into a swallow as Philomela was changed into a nightingale. The protagonist is asking therefore when shall the spring, the time of love, return, but also when will he be reborn out of his sufferings, and—with the special meaning which the symbol takes on from the preceding Dante quotation and from the earlier contexts already discussed—he is asking what is asked at the end of one of the minor poems: "When will Time flow away."

The quotation from "El Desdichado," as Edmund Wilson has pointed out, indicates that the protagonist of the poem has been disinherited, robbed of his tradition. The ruined tower is perhaps also the Perilous Chapel, "only the wind's home," and it is also the whole tradition in decay.   The protagonist resolves to claim his tradition and rehabilitate it.

The quotation from *The Spanish Tragedy*—"Why then Ile fit you. Hieronymo's mad againe"—is perhaps the most puzzling of all these quotations. It means, I believe, this: The protagonist's acceptance of what is in reality the deepest truth will seem to the present world mere madness. ("And still she cried . . . 'Jug Jug' to dirty ears.") Hieronymo in the play, like Hamlet, was "mad" for a purpose. The protagonist is conscious of the interpretation which will be placed on the words which follow—words which will seem to many apparently meaningless babble, but which contain the oldest and most permanent truth of the race:

> Datta. Dayadhvam. Damyata.

Quotation of the whole context from which the line is taken confirms this interpretation.   Hieronymo, asked to write a play for the court's entertainment, replies:

> Why then, I'll fit you; say no more.
> When I was young, I gave my mind
> And plied myself to fruitless poetry;
> Which though it profit the professor naught,
> Yet it is passing pleasing to the world.

He sees that the play will give him the opportunity he has been seeking to avenge his son's murder.   Like Hieronymo, the protagonist in the poem has found his theme; what he is about to perform is not "fruitless."

After this repetition of what the thunder said comes the benediction:

> Shantih   Shantih   Shantih

The foregoing account of *The Waste Land* is, of course, not to be substituted for the poem itself.   Moreover, it certainly . is not to be considered as representing *the method by which the poem was composed*.   Much which the prose expositor must represent as though it had been consciously contrived obviously was arrived at unconsciously and concretely.

The account given above is a statement merely of the "prose meaning," and bears the same relation to the poem as does the "prose meaning" of any other poem. But one need not perhaps apologize for setting forth such a statement explicitly, for *The Waste Land* has been almost consistently misinterpreted since its first publication. Even a critic so acute as Edmund Wilson has seen the poem as essentially a statement of despair and disillusionment, and his account sums up the stock interpretation of the poem. Indeed, the phrase, "the poetry of drouth," has become a cliché of left-wing criticism. It is such a misrepresentation of *The Waste Land* as this which allows Eda Lou Walton to entitle an essay on contemporary poetry, "Death in the Desert"; or which causes Waldo Frank to misconceive of Eliot's whole position and personality. But more than the meaning of one poem is at stake. If *The Waste Land* is not a world-weary cry of despair or a sighing after the vanished glories of the past, then not only the popular interpretation of the poem will have to be altered but also the general interpretations of post-War poetry which begin with such a misinterpretation as a premise.

Such misinterpretations involve also misconceptions of Eliot's technique. Eliot's basic method may be said to have passed relatively unnoticed. The popular view of the method used in *The Waste Land* may be described as follows: Eliot makes use of ironic contrasts between the glorious past and the sordid present—the crashing irony of

> But at my back from time to time I hear
> The sound of horns and motors, which shall bring
> Sweeney to Mrs. Porter in the spring.

But this is to take the irony of the poem at the most superficial level, and to neglect the other dimensions in which it operates. And it is to neglect what are essentially more

important aspects of his method. Moreover, it is to over-
emphasize the difference between the method employed by
Eliot in this poem and that employed by him in later poems.

The basic method used in *The Waste Land* may be
described as the application of the principle of complexity.
The poet works in terms of surface parallelisms which in
reality make ironical contrasts, and in terms of surface con-
trasts which in reality constitute parallelisms. (The second
group sets up effects which may be described as the obverse
of irony.) The two aspects taken together give the effect
of chaotic experience ordered into a new whole, though the
realistic surface of experience is faithfully retained. The
complexity of the experience is not violated by the apparent
forcing upon it of a predetermined scheme.

The fortune-telling of "The Burial of the Dead" will
illustrate the general method very satisfactorily. On the
surface of the poem the poet reproduces the patter of the
charlatan, Madame Sosostris, and there is the surface irony:
the contrast between the original use of the Tarot cards and
the use made by Madame Sosostris. But each of the details
(justified realistically in the palaver of the fortune-teller)
assumes a new meaning in the general context of the poem.
There is then, in addition to the surface irony, something of
a Sophoclean irony too, and the "fortune-telling," which is
taken ironically by a twentieth-century audience, becomes
true as the poem develops—true in a sense in which
Madame Sosostris herself does not think it true. The surface
irony is thus reversed and becomes an irony on a deeper
level. The items of her speech have only one reference in
terms of the context of her speech: the "man with three
staves," the "one-eyed merchant," the "crowds of people,
walking round in a ring," etc. But transferred to other
contexts they become loaded with special meanings. To
sum up, all the central symbols of the poem head up here;
but here, in the only section in which they are explicitly
bound together, the binding is slight and accidental. The
deeper lines of association only emerge in terms of the

total context as the poem develops—and this is, of course, exactly the effect which the poet intends.

This transference of items from an "innocent" context into a context in which they become charged and transformed in meaning will account for many of the literary allusions in the poem. For example, the "change of Philomel" is merely one of the items in the decorative detail in the room in the opening of "A Game of Chess." But the violent change of tense—"And still she cried, and still the world pursues"—makes it a comment upon, and a symbol of, the modern world. And further allusions to it through the course of the poem gradually equate it with the general theme of the poem. The allusions to *The Tempest* display the same method. The parallelism between Dante's Hell and the waste land of the Grail legends is fairly close; even the equation of Baudelaire's Paris to the waste land is fairly obvious. But the parallelism between the death by drowning in *The Tempest* and the death of the fertility god is, on the surface, merely accidental, and the first allusion to Ariel's song is merely an irrelevant and random association of the stream-of-consciousness:

> Is your card, the drowned Phoenician Sailor,
> (Those are pearls that were his eyes. Look!)

And on its second appearance in "A Game of Chess" it is still only an item in the protagonist's abstracted reverie. Even the association of *The Tempest* symbol with the Grail legends in the lines

> While I was fishing in the dull canal
>
> .   .   .   .
> Musing upon the king my brother's wreck

and in the passage which follows, is ironical merely. But the associations have been established, even though they may seem to be made in ironic mockery, and when we come to the passage, "Death by Water," with its change of tone, they assert themselves positively. We have a sense of revelation out of material apparently accidentally thrown together. I have called the effect the obverse of irony, for the method, like that of irony, is indirect, though the effect is positive rather than negative.

The melting of the characters into each other is, of course, an aspect of this general process. Elizabeth and the girl born at Highbury both ride on the Thames, one in the barge of state, the other supine in a narrow canoe, and they are both Thames-nymphs, who are violated and thus are like the Rhine-nymphs who have also been violated, etc. With the characters as with the other symbols, the surface relationships may be accidental and apparently trivial and they may be made either ironically or through random association or in hallucination, but in the total context of the poem the deeper relationships are revealed. The effect is a sense of the oneness of experience, and of the unity of all periods, and with this, a sense that the general theme of the poem is true. But the theme has not been imposed—it has been revealed.

This complication of parallelisms and contrasts makes, of course, for ambiguity, but the ambiguity, in part, resides in the poet's fidelity to the complexity of experience. The symbols resist complete equation with a simple meaning. To take an example, "rock" throughout the poem seems to be one of the "desert" symbols. For example, the "dry stone" gives "no sound of water"; woman in the waste land is "the Lady of the Rocks," and most pointed of all, there is the long delirium passage in "What the Thunder Said": "Here is no water but only rock," etc. So much for its general meaning, but in "The Burial of the Dead" occur the lines

> Only
> There is shadow under this red rock,
> (Come in under the shadow of this red rock).

Rock here is a place of refuge. (Moreover, there may also be a reference to the Grail symbolism. In *Parzival*, the

Grail is a stone: "And this stone all men call the grail . . .
As children the Grail doth call them, 'neath its shadow they
wax and grow.") The paradox, life through death, pene-
trates the symbol itself.

To take an even clearer case of this paradoxical use of
symbols, consider the lines which occur in the hyacinth girl
passage. The vision gives obviously a sense of the richness
and beauty of life. It is a moment of ecstasy (the basic
imagery is obviously sexual); but the moment in its in-
tensity is like death. The protagonist looks in that moment
into the "heart of light, the silence," and so looks into—not
richness—but blankness: he is neither "living nor dead."
The symbol of life stands also for a kind of death. This
duality of function may, of course, extend to a whole pas-
sage. For example, consider:

> Where fishmen lounge at noon: where the walls
> Of Magnus Martyr hold
> Inexplicable splendour of Ionian white and gold.

The function of the passage is to indicate the poverty into
which religion has fallen: the splendid church now sur-
rounded by the poorer districts. But the passage has an
opposed effect also: the fishmen in the "public bar in Lower
Thames Street" next to the church have a meaningful life
which has been largely lost to the secularized upper and
middle classes.

The poem would undoubtedly be "clearer" if every sym-
bol had a single, unequivocal meaning; but the poem would
be thinner, and less honest. For the poet has not been con-
tent to develop a didactic allegory in which the symbols are
two-dimensional items adding up directly to the sum of the
general scheme. They represent dramatized instances of
the theme, embodying in their own nature the fundamental
paradox of the theme.

We shall better understand why the form of the poem
is right and inevitable if we compare Eliot's theme to
Dante's and to Spenser's. Eliot's theme is not the state-

ment of a faith held and agreed upon (Dante's *Divine Comedy*) nor is it the projection of a "new" system of beliefs (Spenser's *Faerie Queene*). Eliot's theme is the rehabilitation of a system of beliefs, known but now discredited. Dante did not have to "prove" his statement; he could assume it and move within it about a poet's business. Eliot does not care, like Spenser, to force the didacticism. He prefers to stick to the poet's business. But, unlike Dante, he cannot assume acceptance of the statement. A direct approach is calculated to elicit powerful "stock responses" which will prevent the poem's being *read* at all. Consequently, the only method is to work by indirection. The Christian material is at the center, but the poet never deals with it directly. The theme of resurrection is made on the surface in terms of the fertility rites; the words which the thunder speaks are Sanscrit words.

We have been speaking as if the poet were a strategist trying to win acceptance from a hostile audience. But of course this is true only in a sense. The poet himself is audience as well as speaker; we state the problem more exactly if we state it in terms of the poet's integrity rather than in terms of his strategy. He is so much a man of his own age that he can indicate his attitude toward the Christian tradition without falsity only in terms of the difficulties of a rehabilitation; and he is so much a poet and so little a propagandist that he can be sincere only as he presents his theme concretely and dramatically.

To put the matter in still other terms: the Christian terminology is for the poet a mass of clichés. However "true" he may feel the terms to be, he is still sensitive to the fact that they operate superficially as clichés, and his method of necessity must be a process of bringing them to life again. The method adopted in *The Waste Land* is thus violent and radical, but thoroughly necessary. For the renewing and vitalizing of symbols which have been crusted over with a distorting familiarity demands the type of organization which we have already commented on in dis-

cussing particular passages: the statement of surface simi-
larities which are ironically revealed to be dissimilarities,
and the association of apparently obvious dissimilarities
which culminates in a later realization that the dissimilari-
ties are only superficial—that the chains of likeness are in
reality fundamental. In this way the statement of beliefs
emerges *through* confusion and cynicism—not in spite of
them.

8

YEATS: THE POET AS

MYTH-MAKER

WILLIAM BUTLER YEATS has produced in his *Vision* one of the most remarkable books of the last hundred years. It is the most ambitious attempt made by any poet of our time to set up a "myth." The framework is elaborate and complex; the concrete detail constitutes some of the finest prose and poetry of our time. But the very act of boldly setting up a myth will be regarded by most critics as an impertinence, or, at the least, as a fantastic vagary. And the latter view will be reinforced by Yeats's account of how he received the system from the spirits through the mediumship of his wife.

The privately printed edition of *A Vision* appeared so long ago as 1925, but it has been almost completely ignored by the critics even though there has been, since the publication of *The Tower* in 1928, a remarkable resurgence of interest in Yeats's poetry. Indeed, Edmund Wilson has been the only critic thus far to deal with *A Vision* in any detail. His treating it in any detail is all the more admirable in view of his general interpretation of the significance of Yeats's system. For Wilson, as we have already seen, considers the symbolist movement as a retreat from science and reality; and Yeats's system, with its unscientific paraphernalia, its gyres and cones, its strange psychology described in terms of Masks and Bodies of Fate, and most of all its frank acceptance of the supernatural, is enough to try the patience of any scientific modernist.

A very real regard for the fineness of Yeats's later poetry has kept him from carrying too far the view of Yeats as an escapist. But to regard the magical system as merely a piece of romantic furniture is to miss completely the function which it has performed for Yeats.

The central matter is science, truly enough, and Edmund Wilson is right in interpreting the symbolist movement as an antiscientific tendency. But the really important matter to determine is the grounds for Yeats's hostility to science. The refusal to accept the scientific account in matters where the scientific method is valid and relevant is unrealistic, but there is nothing "escapist" about a hostility to science which orders science off the premises as a trespasser when science has taken up a position where it has no business to be. For example, Victorian poetry will illustrate the illegitimate intrusion of science, and Yeats in his frequent reprehension of the "impurities" in such poetry —far from being a romantic escapist—is taking a thoroughly realistic position. The formulas which Edmund Wilson tends to take up—scientific, hard-headed, realistic; antiscientific-romantic, escapist—are far too simple.

We have argued in earlier chapters that all poetry since the middle of the seventeenth century has been characterized by the impingement of science upon the poet's world. Yeats, after a brief enthusiasm for natural science as a boy, came, he tells us, to hate science "with a monkish hate." "I am," Yeats tells us, "very religious, and deprived by Huxley and Tindall . . . of the simple-minded religion of my childhood, I had made a new religion, almost an infallible church of poetic tradition, of a fardel of stories, and of personages, and of emotions, inseparable from their first expression, passed on from generation to generation by poets and painters with some help from philosophers and theologians." Here is the beginning of Yeats's system.

It is easy, when one considers the system as expressed in A Vision to argue that Yeats's quarrel with science was largely that the system of science allowed no place for the

supernatural—visions, trances, and incredible happenings
—which began to manifest itself to Yeats at a very early
period in his life. Undoubtedly Yeats wished for an ac-
count of experience which would make room for such hap-
penings. But if we insist on this aspect of the matter, as
most critics have done, we neglect elements which are far
more important. Granting that Yeats had never had a
single supernatural manifestation, many of his objections
to science would have remained. The account given by
science is still abstract, unconcerned with values, and af-
fording no interpretations. Yeats wished for an account
of experience which would surmount such defects: as he
once put it, a philosophy which was at once "logical and
boundless." The phrase is an important one. Had Yeats
merely been content to indulge himself in fairy tales and
random superstitions, he would never, presumably, have
bothered with a system of beliefs at all. A philosophy
which was merely "boundless" would allow a person to live
in a pleasant enough anarchy. The "logical" quality de-
mands a systematization, though in Yeats's case one which
would not violate and oversimplify experience.

The whole point is highly important. If Yeats had
merely been anxious to indulge his fancy, not caring
whether the superstition accepted for the moment had any
relation to the world about him—had he been merely an
escapist, no system would have been required at all. For
the system is an attempt to make a coherent formulation of
the natural and the supernatural. The very existence of
the system set forth in *A Vision* therefore indicates that
Yeats refused to run away from life.

But if he refused to run away from life he also refused
to play the game with the counters of science. For the
abstract, meaningless, valueless system of science, he pro-
posed to substitute a concrete, meaningful system, substi-
tuting symbol for concept. As he states in the introduction
to *A Vision*, "I wished for a system of thought that would
leave my imagination free to create as it chose and yet

make all it created, or could create, part of the one history, and that the soul's." *   Or if we prefer Mr. Eliot's terms, Yeats set out to build a system of references which would allow for a unification of sensibility. Yeats wanted to give the authority of the intellect to attitudes and the intensity of emotion to judgments. The counsel of I. A. Richards is to break science and the emotions cleanly apart—to recognize the separate validity and relevance of "statements" (scientific propositions) on the one hand and of "pseudo-statements" (unscientific but emotionally valid statements) on the other.

Yeats, on the contrary, instead of breaking science and poetry completely apart, has preferred to reunite these elements in something of the manner in which they are fused in a religion. His system has for him, consequently, the authority and meaning of a religion, combining intellect and emotion as they were combined before the great analytic and abstracting process of modern science broke them apart. In short, Yeats has created for himself a myth. He says so frankly in the closing paragraphs of *A Vision* (1925 edition): "A book of modern philosophy may prove to our logical capacity that there is a transcendental portion of our being that is timeless and spaceless . . . and yet our imagination remain subjected to nature as before. . . . It was not so with ancient philosophy because the ancient philosopher had something to reinforce his thought,—the Gods, the Sacred Dead, Egyptian Theurgy, the Priestess Diotime. . . . I would restore to the philosopher his mythology."

It is because most of us misunderstand and distrust the myth and because we too often trust science even when it has been extended into contexts where it is no longer science that most of us misunderstand the function of Yeats's

* This statement occurs in the privately printed edition of *A Vision* which appeared in 1925. The new edition does not differ from the earlier fundamentally in the system that it sets forth, though it has many omissions and revisions of statement, and some extensions.

mythology. A further caution is in order. Yeats has called his system "magical," and the term may mislead us. Yeats even claims for the system a capacity for prediction. In 1917, in his "Anima Hominis," he wrote: "I do not doubt those heaving circles, those winding arcs, whether in one man's life or in that of an age, are mathematical, and that some in the world, or beyond the world, have foreknown the event and pricked upon the calendar the life-span of a Christ, a Buddha, a Napoleon"; and in the earlier edition of *A Vision*, there actually occurs a prophecy of the next two hundred years. But the system does not serve the ends of "vulgar magic." Yeats obviously does not propose to use his system to forecast the movements of the stock market, or to pick the winner of the Grand National. The relation of the system to science and the precise nature of Yeats's belief in it will be discussed later. For the present, the positive qualities of the myth may be best discussed by pointing out its relation to Yeats's poetry.

The system may be conveniently broken up into three parts: a picture of history, an account of human psychology, and an account of the life of the soul after death. The theory of history is the easiest aspect of the system. It bears a close resemblance to Spengler's cyclic theory. (Yeats takes notice of this, but he points out that his system was complete before he had read Spengler.) Civilizations run through cycles of two thousand-odd years, periods of growth, of maturity, and lastly, of decline; but instead of Spengler's metaphor of the seasons, spring-summer-autumn-winter, Yeats uses a symbolism drawn from the twenty-eight phases of the moon. For example, whereas Spengler speaks of the springtime of a culture, Yeats speaks of phases 1 to 8 (the first quarter of the moon). A civilization reaches its zenith at the full moon (phase 15) and then gradually declines, passing through phases 16 to 28 (the dark of the moon) again. Yeats further complicates his scheme by dividing his cycle into two subcycles of twenty-eight phases and of one thousand-odd years each.

The phases 15 of these two subcycles which make up the two thousand years of Christian civilization are, for example, Byzantine civilization under Justinian and the Renaissance. Our own period is at phase 23 of the second subcycle; the moon is rapidly rounding toward the dark when the new civilization to dominate the next two thousand years will announce itself—"the Second Coming."

The full moon (phase 15) symbolizes pure subjectivity, the height of what Yeats calls the "antithetical" which predominates from phase 8 (the half moon of the first quarter) to the full moon and on to phase 22 (the half moon of the last quarter). The dark of the moon ("full sun") symbolizes pure objectivity, the height of what Yeats calls the "primary," which dominates from phase 22 to phase 8. The critical phases themselves, 8 and 22, since they represent equal mixtures of primary and antithetical, are periods of great stress and change. So much for the four cardinal phases. Each of the various twenty-eight phases, indeed, is assigned a special character in like manner.

An account of phase 23 will be sufficient illustration—all the more since this phase is the subject of several of Yeats's poems. Yeats regards phase 22 as always a period of abstraction. Synthesis is carried to its furthest lengths and there comes "synthesis for its own sake, organization where there is no masterful director, books where the author has disappeared, painting where some accomplished brush paints with an equal pleasure, or with a bored impartiality, the human form or an old bottle, dirty weather and clean sunshine" (*A Vision*). In the next phase, phase 23, which the present world has already entered upon (Yeats gives the year of transition as 1927) "in practical life one expects the same technical inspiration, the doing of this or that not because one would, or should, but because one can, consequent license, and with those 'out of phase' anarchic violence with no sanction in general principles." *

---

* From the earlier edition. The account of history in the 1938 edition breaks off after the discussion of phase 22.

It is a vision of this period which Yeats gives us in what is perhaps the best known of his historical poems, "The Second Coming":

> Turning and turning in the widening gyre
> The falcon cannot hear the falconer;
> Things fall apart; the center cannot hold;
> Mere anarchy is loosed upon the world . . .

In "Meditations in Time of Civil War" Yeats gives another vision of the same period, one which employs again the symbol of the hawk but this time joined with the symbol of the darkening moon itself. In Section VII of this poem the poet has a vision of abstract rage, "The rage-driven . . . troop" crying out for vengeance for Jacques Molay, followed by a vision of perfect loveliness—ladies riding magical unicorns. But both visions fade out and

> Give place to an indifferent multitude, give place
> To brazen hawks. Nor self-delighting reverie,
> Nor hate of what's to come, nor pity for what's gone,
> Nothing but grip of claw, and the eye's complacency,
> The innumerable clanging wings that have put out the
>   moon.

The moon is used as a symbol of the imagination in its purity, of the completely subjective intellect. It has this general meaning in many of Yeats's poems—for example, in the poem, "Blood and the Moon," where it is played off against blood (which is comparable to the sun, or the dark of the moon) as a symbol of active force—of the objective, or the primary.

An examination of the various meanings of blood in this poem will indicate how flexible and subtle the "meanings" attached to one of Yeats's concrete images can be. The symbol first occurs in the phrase, "A bloody, arrogant power." The tower on which the poet stands has been built by such a force and the symbolic meaning of the term is partially indicated by the characterization of the power as "bloody," shedding blood. But the meaning is extended and altered somewhat in the reference to Swift's heart: "in his blood-sodden breast" which "dragged him down into mankind." Blood here is associated with elemental sympathy, though the reference to Swift's particular quality of sympathy qualifies it properly—a sympathy grounded in one's elemental humanity which cannot be escaped and which—from the standpoint of the pure intellect—may be said to drag one down. The third reference to blood occurs in the phrase, "blood and state," and a third connection emerges—the connection of blood with nobility and tradition.

These references, it is important to notice, do not so much define the meaning of the symbol as indicate the limits within which the meaning(or manifold of meanings) is to be located. That meaning emerges fully only when we reach the last two sections of the poem where the symbols of blood and moon enter into active contrast: action contrasted with contemplation, power with wisdom, the youth of a civilization with its age.

> The purity of the unclouded moon
> Has flung its arrowy shaft upon the floor.
> Seven centuries have passed and it is pure,
> The blood of innocence has left no stain.
> There, on blood-saturated ground, have stood
> Soldier, assassin, executioner,
> Whether for daily pittance or in blind fear
> Or out of abstract hatred, and shed blood,
> But could not cast a single jet thereon.
> Odor of blood on the ancestral stair!
> And we that have shed none must gather there
> And clamour in drunken frenzy for the moon.
>
> Upon the dusty, glittering windows cling,
> And seem to cling upon the moonlit skies,
> Tortoiseshell butterflies, peacock butterflies,
> A couple of night-moths are on the wing.

Is every modern nation like the tower,
Half dead at the top? No matter what I said,
For wisdom is the property of the dead,
A something incompatible with life; and power,
Like everything that has the stain of blood,
A property of the living; but no stain
Can come upon the visage of the moon
When it has looked in glory from a cloud.

The development is very rich, and even though the poet
in the last stanza has apparently reduced his meaning to
abstract statement, the meaning is fuller than the statement
taken as mere statement. We must read the lines in their
full context to see how their meaning is made more com-
plex, and, if one likes, more "precise" by the development
of the symbols already made.

The tower itself, it is probably unnecessary to add, is
the symbol of the poet's own old age and the old age of
the civilization to which he belongs—

Is every modern nation like the tower,
Half dead at the top?

The poem itself is a very fine example of the unification of
sensibility. As we have said, the poem refuses to be re-
duced to allegory—allegory which is perhaps the first at-
tempt which man makes to unite the intellect and the emo-
tions when they begin to fall apart—Spenser's *Faerie
Queene*, for example. Moreover, the poet has repudiated
that other refuge of a divided sensibility, moralization fol-
lowing on a piece of description—Tennyson's *Princess*, for
instance. One can imagine how the poem would probably
have been written by a Victorian: The old man standing
upon the tower surveys from its vantage point the scene
about him; then the poet, having disposed of the concrete
detail, moralizes abstractly on the scene to the effect that
wisdom and power are incompatibles. Instead, Yeats has
confidence in his symbols; the concrete and the abstract,
thought and feeling, coincide. The poet refuses to define

the moralization except in terms of the specific symbols and the specific situation given.

A more special and concentrated example of Yeats's contemplation of the cyclic movement of history is revealed in his "Two Songs from a Play." These poems really represent his account of "the First Coming," the annunciation to Mary of the birth of Christ, the dynamic force which was to motivate the two thousand year cycle of Christian civilization. The first stanza of the second song will further illustrate the close dependence of Yeats's poetry on his system.

> In pity for man's darkening thought
> He walked that room and issued thence
> In Galilean turbulence;
> The Babylonian starlight brought
> A fabulous, formless darkness in;
> Odor of blood when Christ was slain
> Made all Platonic tolerance vain
> And vain all Doric discipline.

We have already commented on the fact that, according to Yeats's system, new civilizations are born at the dark of the moon—at the first phase. When the moon is dark, the stars alone are to be seen—hence the "Babylonian starlight" may be said to have brought the new force in. But the phrase is used not merely to indicate that the time is that of the first phase of a civilization. Babylon is associated by Yeats with the early study of the stars, and more than this, with a mathematical, history-less measurement of events. The Babylonian starlight, then, is not only eastern starlight, but the starlight as associated with the objective and the "primary." (In his system Yeats indicates that he considers the West as dominantly antithetical, the East as dominantly primary; moreover, the two thousand years of Graeco-Roman civilization is dominantly antithetical; the cycle of Christian civilization, dominantly primary.) The phrase, "fabulous, formless darkness," one finds (in *A Vision*) to come from a pagan philosopher of the fourth century who described Christianity as "a fabulous, formless, darkness" that blotted out "every beautiful thing." The conception of the advent of Christianity on the rational, ordered classic world as a black cloud boiling up out of the ancient East is further developed in the last three lines of the stanza. "Blood," we have already seen, is another one of the symbols for the primary, and it is the odor of this blood which breaks up the order of classic thought and the classic discipline of action. The implied image, very powerful in its effect, is that of men made frantic and irrational by the smell of blood.

Examination of *A Vision* will also throw light on the first lines of the stanza. Yeats is describing man just before the advent of Christianity: "Night will fall upon man's wisdom now that man has been taught that he is nothing. He had discovered, or half-discovered, that the world is round and one of many like it, but now he must believe that the sky is but a tent spread above a level floor, and . . . blot out the knowledge or half-knowledge that he has lived many times.

"The mind that brought the change [that of Christ], if considered as man only, is a climax of whatever Greek and Roman thought was most a contradiction to its age; but considered as more than man He controlled what Neo-Pythagorean and Stoic could not—irrational force. He could announce the new age, all that had not been thought of or touched or seen, because He could substitute for reason, miracle.

"We say of Him because His sacrifice was voluntary that He was love itself, and yet that part of Him which made Christendom was not love but pity, and not pity for intellectual despair, though the man in Him, being *antithetical* like His age, knew it in the Garden, but *primary* pity, that for the common lot, man's death, seeing that He raised Lazarus, sickness, seeing that He healed many, sin, seeing that He died."

The celebrated poem, "Leda and the Swan," is of course related to this same general theme, for the annunciation to

Leda is felt by the poet to have ushered in the cycle of classic civilization. Leda and her swan are thus parallel to Mary and her dove. The power with which Yeats handles the old myth resides in part in the fact that his own myth allows him to take the older one in terms of *myth*, reincorporating it into itself. "Leda and the Swan," far from being merely a pretty cameo, a stray *objet d'art* picked up from the ruins of the older civilization, has a vital relation to Yeats in his own civilization of the twentieth century. (One may observe in passing that the section on history in *A Vision* includes the finest rhythmic prose written in English since that of Sir Thomas Browne.)

Remembering Yeats's expressed desire for a system which would make all history an imaginative history, "and that the soul's," one is not surprised to find that Yeats employs the symbolism of the moon also to describe the various types of men. Men are classified on the basis of their mixtures of the subjective and objective. There are not twenty-eight possible types of men, however, but only twenty-six; for phase 1, complete objectivity, and phase 15, complete subjectivity are not mixtures. These phases are therefore supernatural or superhuman and may characterize an age though not an individual person. Several possible misapprehensions may be anticipated here: The phase of an age does not determine the phase of men living in that age. A man of phase 20, for example, like Shakespeare, may live in some other historical phase than 20— Yeats assigns him, as a matter of fact, to historical phase 16. Moreover, the determination of a man's personality by the nature of his phase is by no means absolute. He is also influenced by his environment. The historical phase thus qualifies the individual phase.

The faculties involved in Yeats's system of psychology are four rather than the Aristotelian three. In Yeats's system, Man possesses: Will; Mask (image of what he wishes to become or reverence); Creative Mind (all the mind which is consciously constructive); and Body of Fate (physical and mental environment). One need not enter here into the modes for determining the precise relations of the four faculties to each other in a given personality. One relationship among them, however, is of great importance. The four faculties are divided into two sets, and each member of the pair is opposite to the other. A man is classified under the phase to which his Will belongs. The Mask is always opposite to this phase. Thus, if we imagine the twenty-eight phases of the moon drawn in the form of a circle, a man whose Will is of phase 17, will have his Mask directly across the circle at phase 3; in the same way, a man with Will at phase 18, will have his Mask at phase 4. Creative Mind and Body of Fate are paired in opposition in like manner.

The interplay of tensions among the four faculties is very intricate, and this also cannot be treated here. The important thing to notice, one repeats, is this: that the psychology is founded on the conflict of opposites. The basic form of the whole system is the gyre, the one end of which widens concomitantly as the other narrows. Will and Mask are fixed in such a relation in one gyre; Creative Mind and Body of Fate, in another. "All things are from antithesis," Yeats observes, "all things dying each other's life, living each other's death." Will and Mask, desire and the thing desired, among the other elements of Yeats's system, bear such a relationship.

The relationship of Will and Mask especially illuminates Yeats's theory of the artist. Men of the antithetical or subjective phases (8 to 22) must strive in their work to realize the Mask which is the opposite of all that they are in actual life. The poem, "Ego Dominus Tuus," gives an exposition of this view. Keats, for example, a man of phase 14, is described as follows:

> His art is happy, but who knows his mind?
> I see a schoolboy when I think of him,
> With face and nose pressed to a sweet-shop window,
> For certainly he sank into his grave

His senses and his heart unsatisfied,
And made—being poor, ailing and ignorant,
Shut out from all the luxury of the world,
The coarse-bred son of a livery-stable keeper—
Luxuriant song.

The case of Yeats himself, who apparently considers himself a man of phase 17, will also illustrate. He says of himself in his *Autobiographies* that he is "a gregarious man, going hither and thither looking for conversation, and ready to deny from fear or favor [his] dearest conviction." Frequently he chides himself for his interest in politics. Yet the Mask, the antiself of man of phase 17, hates "parties, crowds, propaganda" and delights in "the solitary life of hunters and of fishers and 'the groves pale passion loves.'" In his own great later poetry it is the "proud and lonely things" which he celebrates, and typically the fisherman:

I choose upstanding men
That climb the streams until
The fountain leap, and at dawn
Drop their cast at the side
Of dripping stone. . . .

So much for antithetical men, men whose Will is at phases dominantly antithetical; but primary men, on the other hand, men of phases 22 to 8, "must cease to desire *Mask* and Image by ceasing from self-expression, and substitute a motive of service for that of self-expression. Instead of the created *Mask* [they have] an imitative *Mask*. . . ." This condition may be illustrated by Synge (whom Yeats assigns to phase 23), a man who needed to plunge into the objective world to find his true self; or, to take another illustration, and one more extremely "primary," there is the saint (phase 27) who must renounce all desire. "His joy is to be nothing, to do nothing, to think nothing; but to permit the total life, expressed in its humanity, to flow in upon him and to express itself through his acts and thoughts."

If Yeats may appear to the reader to have fallen into a mechanical determinism quite as rigid as the scientific determinism which he tried to escape, and one which is fantastic to boot, one should notice that Yeats allows a considerable amount of free will. For each man of every phase, there is a False Mask as well as a True Mask—a course of action which is fatal for him to pursue as well as a course which he should pursue. Shelley, for example, (like Yeats, a man of phase 17 and "partisan, propagandist, and gregarious") too often sought his False Mask and wrote "pamphlets, and [dreamed] of converting the world." More will be said later about the effect of this psychology on Yeats's own development as a poet. For the present purpose it is easiest to pass on at this point to the relation of conscious to subconscious in Yeats's system.

In the first place, one may observe that Yeats accounts for the subconscious in his myth of the Daimon. "The *Four Faculties* are not the abstract categories of philosophy, being the result of the four memories of the *Daimon* or ultimate self of that man. His *Body of Fate*, the series of events forced upon him from without, is shaped out of the *Daimon's* memory of the events of his past incarnations; his *Mask* or object of desire or idea of the good, out of its memory of the moments of exaltation in his past lives; his *Will* or normal ego out of its memory of all the events of his present life, whether consciously remembered or not; his *Creative Mind* from its memory of ideas—or universals— displayed by actual men in past lives, or their spirits between lives." The man's Will is the Daimon's Mask; his Mask, the Daimon's Will; and so likewise with Creative Mind and Body of Fate. The mind of the man and his Daimon are thus related as the narrow and wide ends of a gyre are related. And Yeats had already told us in "Anima Mundi," that the Daimon "suffers with man as some firm-souled man suffers with the woman he but loves the better because she is extravagant and fickle." Moreover, "the Daemon, by using his mediatorial shades, brings

man again and again to the place of choice, heightening
temptation that the choice may be as final as possible . . .
leading his victim to whatever among works not impossible
is the most difficult." Man must not refuse the struggle.
To do so is to fall under automatism and so be "out of
phase." But the most powerful natures may occasionally
need rest from the struggle and may fall into such an au-
tomatism temporarily without becoming out of phase.

Yeats has apparently described such a rest in his own
life in his fine but obscure poem, "Demon and Beast."

> For certain minutes at the least
> That crafty demon and that loud beast
> That plague me day and night
> Ran out of my sight;
> Though I had long perned in the gyre,
> Between my hatred and desire,
> I saw my freedom won
> And all laugh in the sun.

The sun symbolizes, here, the primary life of the men of
early phases, instinctive acceptance of, and delight in, ob-
jective nature, in which Yeats as an antithetical man cannot
normally participate. The portraits of the dead seem to
smile at him and accept him, for their struggle is over, and
now that he has ceased to struggle, he is of them. He feels
an "aimless joy" at seeing a gull and a "portly green-pated"
duck on the lake.

> Being no more demoniac
> A stupid happy creature
> Could rouse my whole nature.

But man not only is influenced by his Daimon; he may
also be influenced by the dead, and partake in the *Anima
Mundi*, the great collective memory of the world. Here
one comes upon the third division of Yeats's system, that
which deals with the life after death. To deal with Yeats's
highly complicated account very summarily, one may say
that Yeats holds that the soul after death goes through cer-

tain cycles in which it relives its earthly life, is freed from pleasure and pain, is freed from good and evil, and finally reaches a state of beatitude. Unless it has finished the cycle of its human rebirths, it then receives the Cup of Lethe, and, having forgotten all of its former life, is reborn in a human body.

The soul remains in existence, therefore, after the death of the body, and under various conditions disembodied souls may communicate with the living—for example, in dreams—though on waking, the dreamer has substituted for the dream, some other image. The reader will remember that in *A Packet for Ezra Pound* Yeats claims, like Kusta Ben Luka in the poem, "The Gift of Harun Al-Rashid," to have received this system of thought itself from the spirits through the mediumship of his wife.

The relation of the artist to the souls of the dead is apparently a highly important one for Yeats, and two of Yeats's finest poems, the "Byzantium" poems, depend heavily upon a knowledge of this relationship.

Byzantium, as Mr. R. P. Blackmur has pointed out, is the heaven of man's mind. But more especially it is a symbol of the heaven of man's imagination, and pre-eminently of a particular kind of imagination, the nature of which Yeats suggests for us in the following passage from *A Vision*. "I think if I could be given a month of Antiquity and leave to spend it where I chose, I would spend it in Byzantium a little before Justinian opened St. Sophia and closed the Academy of Plato. I think I could find in some little wine-shop some philosophical worker in mosaic who could answer all my questions, the supernatural descending nearer to him than to Plotinus even. . . .

"I think that in early Byzantium, maybe never before or since in recorded history, religious, aesthetic and practical life were one, that architect and artificers—though not, it may be, poets, for language had been the instrument of controversy and must have grown abstract—spoke to the multitude and the few alike. . . .

"[In Byzantium of this period] . . . all about . . . is an incredible splendor like that which we see pass under our closed eyelids as we lie between sleep and waking, no representation of a living world but the dream of a somnambulist. Even the drilled pupil of the eye, when the drill is in the hand of some Byzantine worker in ivory, undergoes a somnambulistic change, for its deep shadow among the faint lines of the tablet, its mechanical circle, where all else is rhythmical and flowing, give to Saint or Angel a look of some great bird staring at miracle."

So much for the symbol of Byzantium itself. The poem "Sailing to Byzantium," as the less difficult of the two, may properly be considered first.

> That is no country for old men. The young
> In one another's arms, birds in the trees,
> —Those dying generations—at their song,
> The salmon-falls, the mackerel-crowded seas,
> Fish, flesh, or fowl, commend all summer long
> Whatever is begotten, born, and dies.
> Caught in that sensual music all neglect
> Monuments of unageing intellect.
>
> An aged man is but a paltry thing,
> A tattered coat upon a stick, unless
> Soul clap its hands and sing, and louder sing
> For every tatter in its mortal dress,
> Nor is there singing school but studying
> Monuments of its own magnificence;
> And therefore I have sailed the seas and come
> To the holy city of Byzantium.

The poet appeals to the

> . . . sages standing in God's holy fire
> As in the gold mosaic of a wall,

asking them to

> Come from the holy fire, perne in a gyre,
> And be the singing-masters of my soul.

A quotation from "Anima Mundi" is illuminating at this point: "There are two realities, the terrestrial and the condition of fire. All power is from the terrestrial condition, for there all opposites meet and there only is the extreme of choice possible, full freedom. And there the heterogeneous is, and evil, for evil is the strain one upon another of opposites; but in the condition of fire is all music and all rest. . . ." The dead whose souls have gone through all the sequences, and whose sequences have come to an end are in the condition of fire: ". . . the soul puts on the rhythmic or spiritual body or luminous body and contemplates all the events of its memory and every possible impulse in an eternal possession of itself in one single moment."

There is a close connection between the dead living in their passionate memories, and Yeats's theory of *Anima Mundi* or the Great Memory. In the same essay he tells us: "Before the mind's eye, whether in sleep or waking, came images that one was to discover presently in some book one had never read, and after looking in vain for explanation to the current theory of forgotten personal memory, I came to believe in a great memory passing on from generation to generation." From this great memory come two influences: First, "that inflowing coming alike to men and to animals is called natural." It is this, for example, that teaches a bird to build her nest or which shapes the child in the womb. But the second inflowing "which is not natural but intellectual . . . is from the fire. . . ." It is this inflow which the poet wishes to come to him and to transform him, shaping him to a "bodily form" which is not taken

> from any natural thing,
> But such a form as Grecian goldsmiths make
> Of hammered gold and gold enamelling . . .

And if we inquire why the symbol of this "unnatural" form is denoted by that of a bird, though a bird of metal, we may find the reason in reading further in "Anima

Mundi": "From tradition and perception, one thought of one's own life as symbolized by earth, the place of heterogeneous things [compare "the terrestrial condition" *supra*], the images as mirrored in water and the images themselves one could divine but as air; and beyond it all there was, I felt confident, certain aims and governing loves, the fire that makes all simple. Yet the images themselves were fourfold, and one judged their meaning in part from the predominance of one out of the four elements, or that of the fifth element, the veil hiding another four, a bird born out of the fire."

The poem can be taken on a number of levels: as the transition from sensual art to intellectual art; as the poet's new and brilliant insight into the nature of the Byzantine imagination; as the poet's coming to terms with age and death. The foregoing account of the development of the symbols in the poet's personal experience will not in itself explain the fineness of the poem, or even indicate its aesthetic structure: it will not indicate, for example, the quality of self-irony in his characterization of himself as a "monument of unageing intellect" or as a "tattered coat upon a stick" or the play of wit achieved in such a phrase as "the artifice of eternity." The account given will, for that matter, do no more than indicate the series of contrasts and paradoxes on which the poem is founded—it will not assess their function in giving the poem its power. But it may indicate the source of the authority which dictates the tone of the poem. The real importance of the symbolic system is that it allows the poet a tremendous richness and coherency.

"Sailing to Byzantium," as we have seen, derives its direction from the poet's own sense of loss and decay. The focus of the poem rests in the reader's sense that the poet is in Ireland, *not* Byzantium. The appeal to the sages of Byzantium is made in terms of the man whose soul is "fastened to a dying animal." "Byzantium," on the other hand, a more difficult poem, concerns itself directly with the "condition of fire" and the relation of the living to the living dead. It will furnish therefore perhaps the best illustration of the extent to which Yeats can successfully rely upon his system, for the poem is an undoubted success and yet its relation to the system is detailed and intricate.

BYZANTIUM *

The unpurged images of day recede;
The Emperor's drunken soldiery are abed;
Night resonance recedes, night-walkers' song
After great cathedral gong;
A starlit or a moonlit dome disdains
All that man is,
All mere complexities,
The fury and the mire of human veins.

Before me floats an image, man or shade,
Shade more than man, more image than a shade;
For Hades' bobbin bound in mummy-cloth
May unwind the winding path;
A mouth that has no moisture and no breath
Breathless mouths may summon;
I hail the superhuman;
I call it death-in-life and life-in-death.

Miracle, bird or golden handiwork,
More miracle than bird or handiwork,
Planted on the star-lit golden bough,
Can like the cocks of Hades crow,
Or, by the moon embittered, scorn aloud
In glory of changeless metal
Common bird or petal
And all complexities of mire or blood.

At midnight on the Emperor's pavement flit
Flames that no faggot feeds, nor steel has lit,
Nor storm disturbs, flames begotten of flame,
Where blood-begotten spirits come

* From *Collected Poems*. By permission of The Macmillan Co., publishers.

And all complexities of fury leave,
Dying into a dance,
An agony of trance,
An agony of flame that cannot singe a sleeve.

Astraddle on the dolphin's mire and blood,
Spirit after spirit! The smithies break the flood,
The golden smithies of the Emperor!
Marbles of the dancing floor
Break bitter furies of complexity,
Those images that yet
Fresh images beget,
That dolphin-torn, that gong-tormented sea.

Consider the lines

A starlit or a moonlit dome disdains
All that man is,
All mere complexities,
The fury and the mire of human veins.

A starlit dome, in contradistinction to a moonlit dome, is one at the dark of the moon (phase 1), and the implication of "moonlit dome" is one lighted by the full moon (phase 15).

Now, as we have already seen, at phase 1, complete objectivity, and phase 15, complete subjectivity, human life cannot exist; for all human life represents a mixture of the subjective and the objective, "complexities," "mere complexities" as compared with the superhuman purity of phases 1 or 15. The dependence on the system may also seem excessive. And yet, even in this instance, one may show that the use is not merely arbitrary. The poem describes an appeal to the superhuman, to the deathless images of the imagination; and the starlit or moonlit dome, freed of the "unpurged images of day," and silent with the "Emperor's drunken soldiery" abed, may seem a place unhuman and supernatural, and a place in which one might fittingly invoke the superhuman. Yeats's symbols, though they are interwoven into complex organizations, never give way to a merely allegorical construct; the proof that they do not lies in the fact that on their literal level they tend to take the reader in the direction of the system, as in the present case.

The second stanza will be much clarified by a consideration of a number of passages in Yeats's prose. For example, consider with regard to the first lines of the stanza—

> Before me floats an image, man or shade,
> Shade more than man, more image than a shade;
> For Hades' bobbin bound in mummy-cloth
> May unwind the winding path . . .

—the following passage from "Hodos Chameliontos" (Yeats is pondering in this passage on the possibility of a great memory of the world): "Is there nation-wide multiform reverie, every mind passing through a stream of suggestion, and all streams acting and reacting upon one another no matter how distant the minds, how dumb the lips? A man walked, as it were, casting a shadow, and yet one could never say which was man and which was shadow, or how many the shadows that he cast." The general idea we have already quoted above: "Before the mind's eye whether in sleep or waking, came images that one was to discover presently in some book one had never read. . . ." The image here, "man or shade," is such an image, and a part of the great memory. "Hades' bobbin bound in mummy-cloth" occurs in the earlier poem, "All Souls' Night," where Yeats again summons the dead:

> I need some mind that, if the cannon sound
> From every quarter of the world, can stay
> Wound in mind's pondering,
> As mummies in the mummy-cloth are wound.

All activity for Yeats, as we have seen, partakes of the whirling motion of the gyre, and the thread wound about the spool is continually used by Yeats as a symbol for experience wound up. Each age unwinds what the previous age has wound, and the life after death unwinds the thread wound on the spool by life. The "winding path" which "Hades' bobbin" may unwind is mentioned in "Anima Mundi." It is the "path of the Serpent" or the "winding movement of nature" as contrasted with the straight path open to the saint or sage. Once more, then, the natural and the human are contrasted with the supernatural and the superhuman. "Death-in-life and life-in-death" are of course the dead themselves, who are for Yeats more alive than the living: "It is even possible that being is only possessed completely by the dead. . . ."

The symbol of the bird in the third stanza, we have already come upon in "Sailing to Byzantium," and also in two passages quoted in this chapter from Yeats's prose—that in which he describes Byzantine art and that in which he uses the bird "born out of the fire" to symbolize the fifth element —the supernatural—the veil hiding another four. The allusion to the "cocks of Hades" is to be compared with the reference to the cockerel in the earlier poem, "Solomon and the Witch":

> A cockerel
> Crew from a blossoming apple bough
> Three hundred years before the Fall,
> And never crew again till now,
> And would not now but that he thought,
> Chance being at one with Choice at last,
> All that the brigand apple brought
> And this foul world were dead at last.

Chance is that which is Fated; Choice, that which is destined or chosen; and they coincide at phases 1 and 15, for at these phases Mask and Body of Fate are superimposed upon each other. "At Phase 15 mind [is] completely absorbed by Being"—at phase 1 "body is completely absorbed in its supernatural environment." The cockerel in the earlier poem "crowed out eternity [and]/Thought to have crowed it in again." The "miracle, bird or golden handiwork" may thus fittingly crow in "the artifice of eternity."

But we shall not understand the third stanza nor the fourth fully unless we understand something of Yeats's theory of spirits. For example the phrase "blood-begotten spirits" is explicable if we consider the following passage from "Anima Mundi": "All souls have a vehicle or body. . . . The vehicle of the human soul is what used to be called the animal spirits," and Yeats quotes from Hippocrates, "The mind of man is . . . not nourished from meats and drinks from the belly, but by a clear luminous substance that redounds by separation from the blood." These vehicles can be molded to any shape by an act of the imagination. Moreover, "our animal spirits or vehicles are but as it were a condensation of the vehicle of *Anima Mundi,* and give substance to its images in the faint materialisation of our common thought, or more grossly when a ghost is our visitor."

The description of the spirits as flames accords with the fact that they are in the condition of fire, but the additional phrase, "flames begotten of flame," requires reference to Yeats's statement that "the spirits do not get from it [the vehicle] the material from which their forms are made, but their forms take light from it as one candle takes light from another." Indeed, Yeats tells us in the earlier version of *A Vision* that spirits can actually be born of spirits. Beings called "arcons" are born from spirits which are at phases 15 and 1. Those born from spirits at phase 15 are antithetical arcons. The spirit at phase 15, desiring to rid itself of all traces of the primary, accomplishes this by "imposing upon a man or woman's mind an *antithetical* image. . . ." This image may be expressed as an action or as a work of art. The expression of it "is a harmonization which frees the Spirit from terror and the man from desire. . . ." So much from *A Vision.* In an essay published still earlier, Yeats says that Shelley "must have expected to receive thoughts and images from beyond his own mind, just in so far as that mind transcended its preoccupation with particular time and place, for he believed *inspiration a kind of death* [italics mine]; and he could hardly have helped perceiving that an image that has transcended particular time and place becomes a symbol, passes beyond death, as it were, and becomes a living soul." The passage from *A Vision* quoted above gives merely a schematization of this earlier thought: an explanation of what the dead man gives and what the living man receives, and the reason for the giving. One notices, however, that whereas Yeats gives in the poem a most complex theory of the relation of the dead to the Great Memory and of their relation to the living, the symbols form more than an exposition of the esoteric: they dramatize the emotional relationships. The spirits must be originally blood-begotten but the blood gives place to flame; the mere complexities give way to purity; the fire "makes all simple." Yet power is of the blood and the flames which "no faggot feeds" are powerless and cannot "singe a sleeve." The balance is maintained.

As for the dance of the spirits, another passage from "Anima Mundi" is relevant: "Then gradually they [the dead] perceive, although they are still but living in their memories, harmonies, symbols, and patterns, as though all were being refashioned by an artist, and they are moved by emotions, sweet for no imagined good but in themselves, like those of children dancing in a ring. . . . Hitherto shade has communicated with shade in moments of common memory that recur like the figures of a dance in terror or in joy, but now they run together like to like, and their Covens and Fleets have rhythm and pattern."

The fifth stanza is a recapitulation, but a recapitulation with the addition of a new and important image for the Great Memory, an image which Yeats has earlier used for it in his prose: the image of the sea. In "Anima Mundi," after speaking of the Great Memory, Yeats has written: "The thought was again and again before me that this study has created a contact or mingling with minds who had followed a like study in some other age, and that these minds still saw and thought and chose. Our daily thought was certainly but the line of foam at the shallow edge of a vast luminous sea; Henry More's *Anima Mundi,* Wordsworth's 'immortal sea which brought us hither. . . .' "

Again, in an essay on "The Tragic Theatre," Yeats has used the figure: "Tragic art, passionate art, the drowner of dykes, the confounder of understanding, moves us by setting us to reverie, by alluring us almost to the intensity of trance. . . . We feel our minds expand convulsively or spread out slowly like some moon-brightened image-crowded sea." The phrase, "gong-tormented," emphasizes the connection of the images of *Anima Mundi* with drama:

> All men are dancers and their tread
> Goes to the barbarous clangor of a gong.
> ("Nineteen Hundred and Nineteen")

The image of the Great Memory as a sea is introduced by the reference to Arion and the dolphin. The poet can travel in that sea, but only supported on the dolphin's mire and blood. The "golden smithies of the Emperor" are of course those referred to in "Sailing to Byzantium":

> Once out of nature I shall never take
> My bodily form from any natural thing,
> But such a form as Grecian goldsmiths make
> Of hammered gold and gold enamelling . . .

These artists—the Byzantine "painter, the worker in mosaic, the worker in gold and silver"—are those to whom, because of their craftsmanship, the "supernatural descended nearer . . . than to Plotinus even."

One can allow that much of the poem would be intelligible to a person entirely unacquainted with Yeats's system. But this rather detailed comparison of the poem with the passages from Yeats's prose given above is perhaps justified in showing how rich and intricate the poem becomes when a knowledge of the system is brought to bear on the poem. "Byzantium" is admittedly a somewhat special case, but many of Yeats's other poems—especially those written around 1917—are hardly less dependent on the system.

Most important of all, however, is to notice that from the poet's standpoint the richness and *precision* of such a poem as "Byzantium" is only made possible by the poet's possession of such a system. The system, in these terms, is an instrument for, as well as a symbol of, the poet's reintegration of his personality. It is the instrument through which Yeats has accomplished the unification of his sensibility.

A brief summary of the general function of Yeats's system may be in order here. We have already spoken of the advantages which the poet gains by using concrete symbols rather than abstract ideas and of traditional symbols which make available to him the great symbolism out of the past. The system, to put it concisely, allows Yeats to see the world as a great drama, predictable in its larger aspects (so that the poet is not lost in a welter of confusion), but in a pattern which allows for the complexity of experience and the apparent contradictions of experience (so that the poet is not tempted to oversimplify). The last point is highly important and bears directly on the dramatic aspect of the system, for the system demands, as it were, a continually repeated victory over the contradictory whereby the contradictory is recognized, and through the recognition, resolved into agreement. Yeats's finest poems not only state this thesis but embody such a structure, and his increasing boldness in the use of the contradictory and the discordant in his own poetry springs directly from his preoccupation with antithesis.

It is easy to see, at least from our vantage point of the present, the effect of this emphasis in making possible Yeats's break with Victorianism. The prime defect of Victorian poetry was that it subordinated the imaginative act of assimilating the incongruous to the logical act of matching the congruent. Yeats, in trying to write from his antiself, in trying to be all that he naturally was not—whatever we may think of his Doctrine of the Mask—broke away from Victorian optimism, decorum, and sentimentality, and disciplined his dramatic powers.

One may cite text and verse in corroboration. For example, in a highly illuminating passage in "Anima Hominis," Yeats has written: "The other self, the anti-self or the antithetical self . . . comes but to those who are no longer deceived, whose passion is reality. The sentimentalists are practical men who believe in money, in position, in a marriage bell, and whose understanding of happiness is to be so busy whether at work or play, that all is forgotten but the momentary aim." The antiself, then, is incompatible with sentimentality. And in "Hodos Chameliontos" Yeats writes of two such men who sought reality, Dante and Villon, saying of them that "had they lacked their Vision of Evil, had they cherished any species of optimism, they could but have found a false beauty. . . . They and their sort alone earn contemplation, for it is only when the intellect has wrought the whole of life to drama, to crisis, that we may live for contemplation, and yet keep our intensity." "Their sort" of poets is that to which Yeats himself must be certainly assigned. And his insistence on the dramatic element is fundamental. In "Anima Hominis" he says: "If we cannot imagine ourselves as different from what we are, and try to assume that second self, we cannot impose a discipline upon ourselves though we may accept one from others. Active virtue, as distinguished from the passive acceptance of a code, is therefore theatrical, consciously dramatic, the wearing of a mask. . . . Wordsworth, great poet though he be, is so often flat and heavy partly because his moral sense, being a discipline he had not created, a mere obedience, has no theatrical element."

So much for the general nature of Yeats's myth and for its relation to his own great poetry; and now, one further reference to the vexing question of Yeats's belief in his system. "The saner and greater mythologies," as Richards says, "are not fancies; they are the utterance of the whole soul of man and, as such, inexhaustible to meditation." The statement can be claimed for Yeats's myth. We have already uttered a warning against the use of the misleading term "magic" for Yeats's system. Magical in the sense that it proposes to use unscientific means to accomplish ends better accomplished by scientific means the system is not. Properly speaking it is a world-view or a philosophy—an "utterance of the whole soul of man" having for its object imaginative contemplation.

Yeats, as we have seen, apparently has no objection himself to referring to his system as a myth, but we are to remember that in calling it this, he is not admitting that it is trivial, or merely fanciful, or "untrue." And this is doubtless why Yeats, in answering the question of whether or not he believes in his system, can only reply with a counterquestion as to whether the word "belief," as the questioner will use it, belongs to our age. For the myth is not scientifically true, and yet though a fiction, though a symbolical representation, intermeshes with reality. It is imaginatively true, and if most people will take this to mean that it is after all trivial, this merely shows in what respect our age holds the imagination.

9

A NOTE ON THE DEATH OF

ELIZABETHAN TRAGEDY

WE HAVE argued in earlier chapters that the critical revolution in the seventeenth century which brought metaphysical poetry to an end was intimately bound up with the beginnings of the new science. The proponents of the new poetry and the proponents of the new science tend to overlap, with Thomas Hobbes standing in a dominant position in both parties. Ideally, the rise of science need not have injured poetry. Theoretical necessity did not force the critic of the seventeenth century to choose science *or* poetry. Ideally, each might have developed in terms of its appropriate principles, side by side. But confusion was natural, and, in view of the way in which the problem presented itself at this time, probably inevitable. The tendency toward order and simplification, taken over into a sphere in which it was inappropriate, succeeded in destroying metaphysical poetry. One is tempted to go on to say that it was this same tendency which brought about the destruction of Elizabethan tragedy.

The current explanations of the decline of that tragedy are not so convincing nor so thoroughgoing as to discourage further speculation. Most of the explanations that have been proposed deal with external changes—in social manners, political conditions, theatrical conventions—true enough in so far as they go, but not in themselves the main matter; or, they merely point to deeper changes which they do not in themselves define.

The closing of the theaters will obviously not serve as an explanation. Comedy survived this interruption to rise to more brilliant heights in the Restoration; and even the continuity of the tradition was not wholly broken. There is Shirley's *Hyde Park* on one side of the rupture, Etherege's *Love in a Tub* on the other. If the destructive force had been merely external, there is no reason why tragedy should not have experienced the same kind of revival.

A satisfactory interpretation of the decline of Elizabethan tragedy will have to deal with something which happened to the conception of tragedy itself. It will need to be more circumstantial, however, than the popular theory of internal decay which describes a natural cycle of, first, the vigorous youth of the movement, then, a period of brilliant maturity, and, finally, the inevitable decadence. This explanation depends for its force on the concealed metaphor; but if we refuse to be seduced by the plausibility of the metaphor, and inquire more closely, even the metaphor breaks down. How decadent, after all, was the Jacobean drama? Critics are more and more coming to agree that the charge of decadence rests ultimately on a moral judgment on some of the situations used by the Jacobean dramatists—situations made use of by Shakespeare himself; e.g., if Ford deals with incest, so does the Shakespeare of *Hamlet*.

Even if one admits the charge of decadence, however, there is still a larger question to be answered: Why does tragedy itself disappear after the seventeenth century? Why, after a temporary falling off, did no new tragedy arise, basing itself on new conventions and altered stage conditions? Why are the eighteenth and nineteenth centuries so notoriously undramatic? Surely, the tragic ingredient was not bound up with a curtainless theater? Or, are some of the devices which appear to us merely accidental indicative, after all, of a tragic structure which Addison and Lillo and Home could not recapture, and which even Otway and Rowe retain in only weakened form?

When the theater reopened in the Restoration, there was

no lack of attention given to the problem of tragedy. Dryden overhauled the Elizabethan achievement and contemporary practice on the Continent. Writers like D'Avenant and Hobbes reconstructed dramatic theory from a priori principles. The new drama did not lack theory; and, in their theorizing on it, the critics of the Restoration were well aware of its divergence from the older English drama. The divergence was calculated. The new dramatists had set about to "refine" tragedy even as in the role of new poets they had refined poetry.

Before discussing the specific refinements, however, it may be in order to restate some elementary propositions about the nature of tragedy. (For the effect of some of those "refinements" persists down to our own day—witness Mr. Eugene O'Neill.)

Tragedy involves the incongruous. There can be no tragedy, not even drama, if the fate of the protagonist is expected and predictable, the most natural thing in the world. We must feel that it is inappropriate, upsetting, incongruous. The incongruous is not necessary for *pathos*, of course; it is always possible to pity a young ass tethered near its mother, or a field mouse turned out of its home. But tragedy requires a definite upset in our normal expectations, for tragedy, as some of our modern dramatists seem to have forgotten, is something quite other than *pathos*. Everyone agrees that drama is based on conflict, but the specific conflict which grows out of the incongruity of tragedy exists on a deeper level even than the struggle of the protagonist with the other characters and with fate. In tragedy a conflict is set up within the mind of the auditor himself—a conflict between the impulse to condemn the protagonist as he breaks the moral laws in which the audience believes, and the impulse to sympathize with him in his struggle. The tragic attitude is complex. The tragic dramatist must not allow his audience too easily to reduce its attitude to simple approval or disapproval.

To assimilate incongruities requires, of course, a rather

vigorous act of synthesis. Such an act finds no counterpart in science, and it is definitely distasteful to a mind impregnated with science. Science, on principle, cannot tolerate the incongruous. Its method is analysis by which it attempts to reduce its world to congruities by an *act of abstraction*. The point need not be labored here. If tragedy involves essentially a complex of attitudes, one need merely suggest what happens when the tragic writer begins to apply Ockham's Razor.

One may put the matter in a slightly different way: tragedy does not easily yield clear and positive answers. Science on the contrary seeks to give answers and exults in their clarity and positiveness. A period like the middle seventeenth century, brought up on a didactic justification of the arts and flown with the prestige of the new science, might obviously do a great deal of damage to tragedy. So much for a hypothetical statement of the situation. An examination of the heroic drama of the Restoration will show that something of this sort actually happened.

The heroic tragedy, no longer content to pose questions about life, set out to present answers. As Bonamy Dobrée puts it in his brilliant *Restoration Tragedy*, "Tragedy, for a variety of causes, attempted to cure humanity of itself by presenting the exalted picture." The "variety of causes" need not concern us here; our concern is with the effect of the didacticism. Much of the tragedy of the past has been explicitly didactic, of course, but that of the Restoration was didactic with a difference. Consider Greek tragedy for a moment. It had grown out of religious rites, and the author had his allegiance to the moral order: justice had to be maintained by the punishment of the protagonist. But the protagonist was still linked to the author by the closest ties of sympathy. The protagonist had therefore to be so developed as to appear to the audience as both hero *and* criminal. Even Greek tragedy, therefore, called for the dramatist to sympathize with, and yet concur in the destruction of, his hero—to sympathize and yet detach himself from his sympathies.

It is interesting to notice the particular twist which the Restoration gave to the didacticism which it had inherited ultimately from classic sources. Hobbes, with the prestige of the new science behind him, hardens it and schematizes it. With characteristic neatness, he equates epic and tragedy as twin modes of the heroic poem. ". . . the Heroique Poem narrative . . . is called an *Epique Poem*. The Heroique Poem Dramatique is Tragedy. . . . The Figure therefore of an Epique Poem and of a Tragedy ought to be the same, for they differ no more but in that they are pronounced by one or many Persons." And what is the heroic poem? It derives its name from the fact that it deals with "princes and men of conspicious power, anciently called *Heroes*," who exert "a lustre and influence upon the rest of men. . . ." The purpose of the heroic poem is "to exhibit a venerable & amiable Image of Heroick virtue"; or, as Hobbes puts it in a later passage, "the work of an Heroick Poem is to raise admiration, principally, for three Vertues, Valour, Beauty, and Love." The didactic critic takes his didacticism seriously here, and he has specific recommendations.

Since the tragic or epic poem is to provoke admiration for the heroic virtues, mirth has no place. Even realism here is an impropriety: "the names of Instruments and Tools of Artificers, and words of Art, though of use in the Schools, are far from being fit to be spoken by a Heroe. He may delight in the Arts themselves, and have skill in some of them; but his Glory lies not in that, but in Courage, Nobility, and other Vertues of Nature, or in the Command he has over other men."

In general, the tragic poet is to keep clearly in mind that his poem is an instrument of virtue and that he is a teacher of virtue. The poet is to be careful that his purpose is not obscured by difficult expressions. For example, "A Metaphor . . . is not unpleasant; but when they are *sharp and extraordinary* [italics mine] they are not fit for an Heroique Poet, nor for a publique consultation, but only for an Accusation or Defence at the Bar [!]."

This theory of tragedy is so mechanically neat that one may wonder whether it was actually taken seriously by practicing playwrights. There is no need, however, to entertain any doubt on this point. In his critical essays, Dryden, for example, is willing to follow Hobbes, even in detail. He writes that "an heroic play ought to be an imitation, in little, of an heroic poem; and consequently, . . . Love and Valour ought to be the subject of it." In another essay he says frankly: "I have modelled my heroic plays by the rules of an heroic poem. And if that be the most noble, the most pleasant, and the most instructive way of writing in verse, and withal the highest pattern of human life . . . I shall need no other argument to justify my choice in this imitation." Consideration of the plays themselves will indicate that Dryden has built them, in the main, to Hobbes's specifications.*

With the transformation of tragedy into the "heroic poem dramatic," the attitude toward the protagonist is simplified. There is external conflict, but it hardly carries over into the auditor's mind. The issues are clear-cut, the threads of good and evil are disentangled; and this means that the characters have lost some of their integrity—that they are closer to abstractions, two-dimensional and thin, and that their actions are predictable and contrived.

The incongruous has been toned down—the tragic tension relaxed. When the Restoration playwright, aware of the necessity for some sort of conflict in his drama, insists on the polarity of love and valor, we have the incredibly valorous Almanzor burning with love for, yet unable to

---

* Elizabethan critics gave lip service to the didactic theory too, of course. But the Elizabethan dramatist did not approach his work on that basis. Elizabethan drama had its roots too deep in a tradition of the folk to allow it to conform to an abstract theory.

obtain, the incredibly beautiful and virtuous Almahide. But, as Dobrée observes, who but the brave deserves the fair? The complication is essentially that of melodrama.

The simplification of tragedy parallels almost exactly the Restoration's insistence on congruity of associations and uniformity of tone in poetry. The fact that critics of the period describe both processes as "refinements" need not blind us to their real character. Dryden's reprehension of the mechanic, the pedestrian, and the vulgar in literature is of a piece with Hobbes's insistence on scientific clarification. For Dryden's objection to words of "low" association in serious poetry (he did not object to them in satire) is based on the fact that he could not conceive of a complex unity wrought out of a tension between "low" and dignified materials.

Dryden assumes that earlier poets mixed the kinds from ignorance or carelessness: "Let us therefore admire the beauties and the heights of Shakespeare without falling after him into carelessness. . . ." But some of the mixtures of the incongruous practiced by the earlier poets were obviously willful. Dryden, as we have noted in an earlier chapter, complained that Donne, in his love poems, "perplexes" the fair sex, his appropriate readers. By using the term "perplexes" he frankly accepts Hobbes's basic objection. There was in Donne's poetry an ambiguity which went far deeper than the mere use of obscure and difficult references. There was—as there is in the case of tragedy— an ambiguity as to the poet's ultimate attitude. For, in a love scene, to take an example, logical propositions are out of place; so also are references to the ugly or the prosaic. Sweets to the sweet. To praise one's mistress by pretending to depreciate her, or to qualify that praise by an open-eyed recognition of some traits not wholly praiseworthy, or to seem to waver between praise and blame—these attitudes may be bewildering, particularly if one regards the poem as a *practical* instrument, as Dryden seems to; and the Augustans did not wish to bewilder or to be bewildered.

Better to avoid subtlety which might prove difficult or be misunderstood.

The exclusive association of wit, ingenuity, the pun, etc., with levity, then, is an aspect of the same process which broke apart the serious and the comic elements in tragedy. The Elizabethans had not reserved such elements merely for light verse or for satire, but then, neither had they kept low or comic elements out of their tragedies.

Dryden, it is true, was not prepared to take an extreme view on this point; and he defended Shakespeare's inclusion of comic elements in his tragedies. But the line which he, and later, the critics of the nineteenth century, took to defend the inclusion is revealing. The comic contrast was justified as affording relief to the mind taxed to the limit with suffering. As Dryden puts it in one of his prefaces: "The truth is, the audience are grown weary of continued melancholy scenes; and I dare venture to prophesy, that few tragedies except those in verse shall succeed in this age, if they are not lightened with a course of mirth. For the feast is too dull and solemn without the fiddles."

Aesthetics was deserted for psychology, and a limited and superficial psychology at that. Obviously, the mind does not really require comic relief. Sophocles, for instance, does not need to employ comic relief, and even the proponents of the theory do not attempt to justify the Fool in *Lear* as affording "relief." The jesting of the Fool has an integral part in the total effect. But the comic elements in any Elizabethan tragedy must be accounted to be integral to the total effect in so far as the play in question has a unity—has a total effect. We have already seen that the unity of tragedy is one that is founded on the resolution of disparities. The development of the theory of unintegrated comic relief is an indication that the age was losing sight of this conception.

William Empson, in his brilliant *English Pastoral Poetry*, has indicated some of the functions of the Elizabethan subplot in gaining the complex effect of the total play. "It is

an easy-going device, often used simply to fill out a play,
and has an obvious effect in the Elizabethans of making you
feel the play deals with life as a whole. . . . this may be
why criticism has not taken it seriously when it deserved
to be. Just because of this carelessness much can be put
into it; to those who miss the connections the thing still
seems sensible, and queer connections can be insinuated
powerfully and unobtrusively; especially if they fit in with
ideas the audience already has at the back of its mind.
The old quarrel about tragi-comedy, which deals with part
of the question, shows that the drama in England has al-
ways at its best had a certain looseness of structure; one
might almost say that the English drama did not outlive
the double plot."

Empson illustrates from such plays as *The Changeling,
Troilus and Cressida, Henry IV, Part I*. He even under-
takes to show that plots so remote from each other as those
used in Greene's *Friar Bacon and Friar Bungay* really act
to support each other. The low or comic underplot allows
a statement of the other side, and consequently gives by
its irony a sense of stability to the main plot. Empson
summarizes this effect as follows: "The value of the state
of mind which finds double irony natural is that it combines
breadth of sympathy with energy of judgment; it can keep
its balance among all the materials for judging. . . . The
Elizabethan feeling can be seen most clearly in the popular
rogue pamphlets, which express warm sympathy for the
villains while holding in mind both horror for their crimes
as such and pity and terror for the consequences. Stories
of successful cheats are 'merry' because the reader imagines
himself as the robber, so as to enjoy his courage, dexterity,
etc., and as the robbed—he can stand up to this trick now
that he has been told; a secret freedom kept the two from
obstructing each other. This fulness in the audience clearly
allowed of complex character-building; one need not put
hero and villain in black and white; though not everybody
in the audience understood such a character they did not

object when they only understood partial conflicting interpretations of it. . . . What is so impressive about the Elizabethans is that complexity of sympathy was somehow obvious to them; this same power, I think, made them feel at home with dramatic ambiguity and with the vague suggestiveness of the double plot."

With the Restoration, sensitiveness to a complex unity of the sort described by Empson became coarsened, or overridden by the all too explicit theories of decorum and correctness.

To consider the problem of irony as it applies both to dramatic and nondramatic poetry: later critics demanded that irony be more obvious. They could accept the ironic function of the Fool in *Lear* or the irony in certain of Hamlet's speeches; but they could hardly accept irony of a more subtle kind or in a context not overtly dramatic. The basic principle of irony is the same, however, whether in tragedy or the lyric. Tragedy, as we have already seen, grows out of the incongruous and, in one sense at least, like all incongruous things, is potentially comic. Were the issues less weighty, were he treated less sympathetically, Lear himself might become a comic figure: an arrogant, silly old fool. And Othello actually appeared to Rymer (who did not sympathize with Shakespeare's treatment and who applied the neoclassic prescriptions rigorously) as a comic character, a great clumsy oaf, bellowing in childish rage when he had stupidly destroyed his plaything. To those who still agree with the eighteenth- and nineteenth-century view that there is something in the play of wit which is intrinsically and ineradicably light, one may point out that a latent tendency toward levity lies at the heart of tragedy itself.

We have thus far considered the drama of the Elizabethan period as displaying the same structure as is found in the poetry of wit: specifically, the unity of both is a complex unity, founded on the resolution of the incongruous and the discordant. But one may reverse the comparison:

consider the poetry of wit as a *dramatization of the lyric*.

Donne's poems are dramatic—not only fundamentally but on the most obvious level. There are the dialogues: between the poet and his mistress, or between the poet and his God, or between the various selves of the poet. There are the swift, abrupt openings; there are the sudden shifts of tone. There is the use of shock, and the sudden turn of thought which leads to an unexpected climax. To turn to deeper and more significant characteristics, the poet's approach to any given subject, however abstract or general it may be, is always made through some concrete situation. But this characteristic is not an idiosyncracy of Donne's. It is shared by Carew and Marvell. And even the meditations of George Herbert are not ruminations; they are attempts made by the poet to explore his own religious experience. Modern poets like Yeats, Ransom, Eliot, of course, readily yield instances—and obvious instances—of highly "dramatic" poetry; and our treatment of them in earlier pages has emphasized this dramatic aspect.

As for the relation of the seventeenth-century poetry of wit to the early seventeenth-century drama, little more needs to be said. In his famous essay on the metaphysical poets, Eliot called attention to the fact that the qualities of their poetry are shared by the dramatic poets of the period. But if the poetry of wit is in essence dramatic, then it becomes clear that the poetry of the plays is of a piece with the other elements of the plays. One need only call attention to the fact that the relationship is not an accidental or superficial one, in order to understand what happened in the Restoration. If we realize that Shakespeare's use of conceits, puns, low subject matter and the like springs from the dramatic impulse itself, the meaning of the Restoration refinement becomes clear.

Dryden, speaking with a genuine admiration of Shakespeare, writes of him typically as follows: "He is many times flat, insipid; his Comick wit degenerating into clenches [puns], his serious swelling into Bombast. But he is alwayes great.". Obviously, the thing to do was to remove the "clenches" and the "Bombast." But to remove the method was to remove the dramatic element itself. What occurred may well go down in history as the classic example of throwing out the baby with the bath.

We have been speaking primarily of Restoration tragedy. The comedy of the period may be regarded as the apparent exception which tests the rule. Does it actually contradict our theory? We have already indicated that tragedy is relatively more complex than comedy—that, indeed, it represents something of a tension between unsympathetic laughter and sympathetic pity—between the impulse to condemn the protagonist and the impulse to feel pity for him. If in comedy we laugh at others, in tragedy we do some sort of equivalent of laughing at ourselves. By a simplification of attitudes toward either direct approval (Hobbes's "admiration") or downright disapproval, the Restoration, though cutting the ground from under its tragedy, retained a basis for comedy. In this comedy, wit continues to flourish, but a wit closer to our modern conception—a wit used not to intensify seriousness so much as to contribute to levity—satirical rather than ironical wit. The greatest comedy, of course, always approaches tragedy in the sense that there also we laugh at ourselves; it has a complexity of attitude because of the universal quality of the experience presented. Is it a coincidence that the greatest of the Restoration comedies, Congreve's *Way of the World*, was a failure on the stage? And do we find in the growing inflexibility of the age a possible reason for Congreve's retirement from comedy at the height of his brilliant powers? At any rate, by the end of the century comedy itself had become too complex. Satirical wit was too sharp an instrument; teaching by negative examples, too indirect, too equivocal for a literal-minded age. And so the sentimental comedy was born. Later attempts to resurrect Restoration comedy constitute the most striking testimonies to this point. Goldsmith and Sheridan were to revive Res-

toration comedy, but only with some admixture of senti-
mentality, and Lamb later was to choose to defend Restora-
tion comedy on the grounds that it was a sort of fairy tale
divorced from reality. All serious literature including
tragedy, of course, may be regarded as a sort of make-
believe; but the furious, deadly serious make-believe that is
drama was dead.

The nineteenth century, which worshipped Shakespeare,
was content to acquiesce in the condemnation of his serious
puns, his wit play, and his low imagery. If one felt puzzled
that this sort of thing should occur in the divine Shake-
speare, the low matter was explained as the "excess of the
age." The poets of the nineteenth century, like those of
the neoclassic period, failed to see that Shakespeare's poetry
was internally dramatic and therefore the fitting garb for the
dramas, and they failed to connect his poetry with the other
contemporary poetry of wit. What did remain to elicit a
sort of genteel bewilderment (a bewilderment which could
be, and was, turned to compliment) was Shakespeare's
ambiguity of attitude. With Tennyson the reader is as-
sured. He knows what attitude he is to adopt. So also with
Wordsworth, or even with Browning (whose dramatic
poems, though they exhibit a healthy vitality, hardly carry us
into the realm of dramatic ambiguity). The attitudes em-
bodied in the poems may be regarded as extensions of the
poet's own personal attitude. The contrast between Shake-
speare and the poets of the nineteenth century begot the
conception of Shakespeare as the man behind the mask—the
poet who kept his personal life inviolate.

This ambiguity may be restated, however, as a richness
and integrity with which the poet is able to endow his
symbols. He is able to cut the apron strings (or better, the
navel strings) of his characters so that they live a life of
their own. To take another example, Milton still possessed
enough of this quality in the middle of the seventeenth
century to endow the character Satan with so much vitality
that puzzled critics since that time have attempted to read

into Satan some secret expression of Milton himself. Milton is unconsciously on Satan's side, etc. A more robust conception simply regards Milton as possessing the qualities of a dramatic poet: he has a proper recognition of the variety and complexity of the world and he respects that complexity. Perhaps it is not too whimsical to call Milton's Lucifer an example of metaphysical wit. For the wit of Donne's "Valediction: Of My Name in the Window" or Shakespeare's "The expense of spirit in a waste of shame" may be described as an acute perception of the many, and even apparently contradictory, aspects of a given experience. It is dramatic in that it strives to overcome oppositions through struggle, and it is dramatic in that it represents a union of the subjective and the objective: the poet explores experience by separating his symbols from a personal allegiance to his own ego, and while infusing them with an active vitality, allows them to work out in accordance with their own logic and to develop in a life of their own. Milton's Lucifer is such a symbol.

One remembers, furthermore, that the nineteenth century gave its critical study primarily to Shakespeare's characters and Shakespeare's psychology of character. The poetry won thoroughly sincere praise and the poets borrowed phrases and imitated lines, but they failed to pay the higher compliment of building poetry with a structure like that of Shakespeare's. To overstate the matter somewhat, the nineteenth century tended to regard Shakespeare as the great *biographer* rather than as the great dramatist. There comes with this tendency an increasing interest in the off-stage life of the characters, and indeed the dramatic context itself comes to be treated as if it were biography: critics begin to speculate on Cordelia's girlhood or on Hamlet's life at Wittenberg.

In our revised interpretation of the history of English literature, the Romantic movement obviously is to be classed as an antiscientific revulsion. It retreated, as we know, from the rationalistic, the ordered, and the classified.

But it did not have the capacity to undo the damage done by Hobbes. In a sense it understood that the issue was science, but its reaction was confused. Hence we have on one hand Wordsworth's drivel about the botanist who would peek and botanize on his mother's grave, and on the other, Shelley's attempt to found a poetry of wonder and of humanitarianism on the latest findings of science. Moreover, as a reaction to neoclassicism, the movement was too much centered in the personal and the lyrical, and it had a cult of simplicity of its own. It substituted romantic subjectivism for neoclassic objectivism instead of fusing the two as they were fused in a great dramatic period such as the Elizabethan. Wordsworth has as little of the dramatic as does Shelley, and where we find an overt attempt at the dramatic, it is the personal self-dramatization of Byron—the self-conscious actor, not the objectifying dramatist. Keats, oddly enough, comes closest to giving us dramatic poems—in the great odes; and Keats himself had recognized before his death the need for a stiffening and toughening of his poetry. If, as Eliot has pointed out, wit is a quality that is lacking in the Romantic poets, one can point out a concomitant lack of the dramatic. And, as we have seen, the second statement is but a restatement of the first.

But, one may inquire, how does the re-emergence of a metaphysical poetry in our time fit into the scheme? I cannot but feel that it is more than mere coincidence that it should occur today when the course of science has come full circle from the age of Hobbes to the age of Einstein, and when the scientists themselves have come to point out that their science is, in one sense at least, a fiction—a construct. This perception, by removing the curse of *fiction* from poetry, allows the poet to develop *his* kind of *fiction* in accord with its own principles, unconfused by those of another.

To put the matter in slightly different terms: The concept of progress developed concomitantly with the advance of science and dominated men's imaginations in proportion as the scientific method won its successes. Thus, the doctrine of progress dominated the nineteenth century. It has not been until the twentieth century that the concept of progress has been seriously challenged. With the weakening of that concept, men are becoming ready once more to accept a poetry which will give a view of the human situation as total as that given by tragedy. To admit the advance of science (as all must) and yet to deny that the results of scientific advancement are automatically beneficial, is to take a more critical view of the nature of scientific description, and therefore, perhaps, open the way to a clearer, more just view of the nature of poetic description.

The principles of poetic organization, developed to their logical conclusion, we have argued, carry the poem over into drama, with the characteristics of tragedy—concreteness, dramatic ambiguity, irony, resolution through struggle —as perhaps their highest expression. Probably our best proof that the principles *are* essentially dramatic is the fact that one finds that the easiest introduction of a modern reader to the metaphysical poets today is made on the analogy of drama, and specifically, on the analogy of Shakespeare's drama. To conceive of the poem as a little drama may be the only way in which the overliteral-minded reader can proceed at all. Our sense of a poem as a dramatic context, in general, is slight; it has hardly been nourished by the poetry of the last two hundred years.

IO

NOTES FOR A REVISED

HISTORY OF ENGLISH

POETRY

I HAVE ASSERTED that the work of the modern poets already discussed implies a critical revolution in the light of which the current conception of the history of English poetry must be revised. The following sketch is merely suggestive, and it is possibly open to question on many points; still, to submit such a sketch may be the most vivid way of enforcing the point.

Logically, of course, such a sketch should begin with the beginnings of metaphysical poetry early in the sixteenth century. To begin here would make the sketch interesting but more ambitious than I propose to attempt. Allen Tate, in his "Note on Elizabethan Satire," has already made some brilliant suggestions, and has indicated the importance of Wyatt in a line of development which runs through the early Elizabethan poets to the work of Donne and Shakespeare. He is unquestionably right in seeing this line of development as affiliated with the development of the dramatic poetry of the period and as opposed to the allegorical poetry, like that of Spenser. It might be possible to trace the development back to Skelton himself.

Perhaps we shall do best to begin with the seventeenth century, and to begin by emphasizing the strength of the tradition of wit throughout the first third of that century.

The essential continuity of this tradition is a matter which the histories with their schools of Donne and schools of Jonson have tended to minimize.

The so-called schools of Donne and Jonson, on inspection, tend to coalesce. And the Cavalier poets are again witty poets, writing a poetry which has the same basic structure as that of Jonson and Donne, from whom they derive. The Spenserians do stand apart from the other groups; for these poets tended to approach the poem as an allegorical construct, that is, as an abstract framework of statement which was to be illustrated and ornamented by overlaying the framework with concrete detail. Their use of archaic diction indicates that they had a poetic diction (as opposed to a prose diction) rather fully developed; and their characteristic use of wit—as the ornamental elaboration of detail rather than as a structural device—indicates their separation from the other poets of the period.

But their misuse of wit in itself testifies to the strength of the tradition of wit which even they could not escape; and if they frequently misused wit, they sometimes employed it successfully. The "Epitaph on the Countess of Pembroke" by the Spenserian William Browne might well have been written by Jonson or Carew.

The poets differ in politics and in religion, but the poetry of the period, whether dramatic or nondramatic, secular or religious, light or serious, successful or unsuccessful, is basically and generally a poetry of wit.

The case of Herrick will serve as illustration. The literary historians usually set Herrick apart from the metaphysicals as the most devoted son of Ben Jonson. But the structure of Herrick's poetry is of a piece with theirs, as his use of conceits, his epigrams, his mixtures of the bawdy and the reverent, and of the fantastic and the decorous, will show. Anthologists are in the habit of representing him by his least "conceited" pieces. A glance at a complete text of the poems will reveal instances as striking as,

> Julia was carelesse, and withall,
> She rather took, than got a fall:
> The Wanton Ambler chanc'd to see
> Part of her legges sinceritie:

The use of the abstract word for the concrete is bold enough, but a moment's reflection will show that Herrick is also using "sincerity" as a pun. He must certainly have been familiar with the old fanciful etymology of "sincere": viz., *sine* plus *cerus*, without wax, applied to perfect marble which had not been chipped and patched with wax, and consequently applied to anything which was genuine. The exposure of the girl's legs in her fall from her horse is a revelation of perfect marble-white thighs as well as a frank exposure.

Or to take another example from Herrick, this time from a more serious poem, consider,

> 'Twill not be long (*Perilla*) after this,
> That I must give thee the *supremest* kisse.

"Supremest" represents the sort of verbal wit to be found in Donne or Shakespeare; for it means the "last" as well as the "most ecstatic," and the two meanings corroborate and support each other.

The contemporary prose is thoroughly in the tradition of wit. One may name such diverse writers as Bishop Lancelot Andrews, Thomas Fuller, Sir Thomas Browne, Bishop Earle, and Sir Thomas Overbury. Many of the "characters" by the last two writers are little more than extended conceits.

The prose of Sir Thomas Browne will furnish perhaps the most striking illustrations. His "quaintness" is anything but a naïve pedantry. Saintsbury was quite right in pointing out that there is in Browne's prose a quiet, but thoroughly conscious humor: a necessary revision of the views of critics like Hazlitt and Gosse. But we shall best dispose of the problem of his attitude toward his subject if we take his work as a prose of wit displaying the various levels of seriousness and the complexity of attitude which are to be found in the witty poets of the time. Browne is not trying to "bewilder his understanding," as Hazlitt thought; nor do we need to suppose, with Gosse, that "there was something abnormal in Browne's intellect . . . shown in the mad way in which he tossed words about." Browne is not more abnormal than are Shakespeare and Donne. If his genial, whimsical passages show the lighter uses of wit, his most magnificent passages will illustrate the complexity and intensity of serious wit. Browne's typical rhetoric may be illustrated by his phrase, "to lie immortal in the arms of fire." In addition to the main paradox involved, other contrasts and tensions are at work in the phrase. "To lie in the arms" suggests bliss or comfort—to lie in a lover's arms, or, like a child, to lie in a mother's arms. And these associations are played off against the associations of torment and suffering implied by the other half of the phrase: to lie in fire. The whole passage receives much of its resonance from this clash of opposed associations.

Or, to take another case, consider the famous "Time, which antiquates antiquities, and hath an art to make dust of all things, hath yet spared these minor monuments." The paraphrase, "These lowly urns have endured although greater monuments have perished" preserves the basic ironic fact. But the paraphrase leaves out of account that which gives the sentence its richness and vitality. The word "antiquates" is really used in a double sense. (1) Time is that which *makes* antiquities. But Browne suggests further, (2) Time is that which *unmakes* antiquities, i.e., even those things which have long withstood the force of Time. In addition, Time's ability to destroy is treated as if it were an art, a craft; and the destruction is thus described, ironically, as if it were really an act of construction.

There is no wonder that Dr. Johnson should have described Browne's characteristic method in almost precisely the same terms that he applied to the metaphysical poets: His style is *"a mixture of heterogeneous words,* brought together from distant regions, with terms appropriated to one art, and *drawn by violence* into the service of another [italics mine]."

A realization of the thorough-going influence of wit in the literature of the first third of the seventeenth century would throw into its proper importance the critical revolution which broke the tradition of wit. The nature of that revolution has been already discussed. Obviously, it did not do its work at once. The latter half of the century exhibits survivors from the earlier tradition like Vaughan and mixed cases like Dryden.

For convenience we may well go on to Pope and the eighteenth century, leaving further comment on poets like Dryden and Milton to later pages where we shall have occasion to mention them in connection with some of their imitators.

Pope, at the beginning of the eighteenth century, is usually taken to be the typical poet of the "Age of Reason." The critical revolution by this time had been thoroughly victorious and Pope's poetry indicates emphatically what had happened. He is not lacking in wit, but the wit has been relegated to satire and *vers de société.* (The delightful *Rape of the Lock* is monumental *vers de société.*) Where his wit is lacking—the "Elegy on an Unfortunate Lady"—he is a sentimentalist. And perhaps this was his essential character. One feels that he is often afraid to try to raise the emotional intensity of his poetry, for fear of becoming the sentimentalist—or, as he would have put it, "the enthusiast." Such qualities are concealed by the textbook phrase, the Age of Reason.

But though the scope has been narrowed, Pope's best poetry is that in which the wit can still be used to set up a tension between the various elements. The wit is being used in this fashion in the "Portrait of Atticus."

Willing to wound, and yet afraid to strike,
Just hint a fault, and hesitate dislike;
Alike reserv'd to blame, or to commend,
A tim'rous foe, and a suspicious friend.

The wit consists in the elaborately careful qualifications
which convey the sense of Pope's own cautiousness in giv-
ing judgment, and yet at the same time parody ironically
the hypocritical reserve of the man whom he is censuring!
We may consider the "Portrait" as an elementary instance
of the union of opposed impulses, and this may in part
account for our feeling that Pope here is more of the poet
than it is his usual habit to be.

The Rape of the Lock makes use of the same structure.
Pope is able to indulge in social satire and at the same time
do justice to the charm of the society which he censures.
The two judgments are not to be separated from each other.
The beauty of Belinda's dressing table—and it has a sort of
beauty—is pointed out in the very process of indicating its
artificial and even absurd luxury. In exposing the foibles
and pretenses of the conventions which govern the party
at Hampton Court, Pope manages to convey a sense of the
very real charm which these conventions, within certain
contexts, may possess. The poem achieves a genuine unity
of sensibility—far more than Pope can achieve with a con-
ventionally "big" subject such as he undertakes in *The Essay
on Man.*

James Thomson, though we are accustomed to think of
him as representing a totally different impulse in poetry,
will, no less than Pope, illustrate the effects of the critical
revolution which produced the Age of Reason. The ortho-
dox historians are, of course, quite right in emphasizing his
turning away from pictures of the drawing room and the
club, to pictures of the countryside; and they are right in
interpreting his poetry as a shift from the abstract to the
concrete, from ideas to objects. Indeed, one is tempted to
see the contemporary enthusiasm for *The Seasons* as analo-

gous to the twentieth century's liking for imagist poetry.
As examples of Thomson's imagist quality, consider:

> . . . the downy peach, the shining plum,
> With a fine blueish mist of animals
> Clouded . . .

> Anemones; auriculas, enriched
> With shining meal o'er all their velvet leaves;
> And full ranunculus, of glowing red.

Later critics are agreed that the return to the concrete
was in itself a relief; they came, of course, to feel that
Thomson's rural objects were somehow in themselves more
poetic than Pope's city objects. The really important
quality is the dichotomy between thought and feeling that
emerges in Thomson's poetry even more emphatically than
in Pope's. The vignettes of country life are sharply sepa-
rated from the passages of speculation; for example, Thom-
son's one-hundred-and-ninety-line dissertation on the origin
of springs in which he attempts dutifully to follow John
Woodward's *Natural History of the World*. The thought is
as scientific as Thomson could make it, but the poetry is
not "intellectual" as Donne's poetry is intellectual, nor is it
intellectual in the sense in which some of our moderns are
reproached with being intellectual.

When we examine Thomson's attitudes as reflected in
his thoughtful generalizations, we shall find that they tend
to be sentimental attitudes. This comes out clearly when
Thomson commits himself to statements of explicit ideas.
He can condemn hare-hunting as cruel, or grieve over
worms writhing on the hook (and thus recommend fishing
with artificial flies if one is to fish at all). Indeed, he would
turn out to be the "enthusiast" except for a certain tepidity
and gentlemanly reserve. It is these qualities which rescue
him from sentimentality rather than those qualifications of
attitude which define, and refine, metaphysical poetry.

In the eighteenth century these qualifying factors are

better represented in prose than in poetry. Swift's prose contains more of this quality of tension than does his poetry —and more than the poetry of any other writer of his time. The *Modest Proposal* will illustrate. The system of contrasts and tensions reveals itself almost violently.

The dry, precise observation and comment Swift did not use merely because he wished to write "correct" prose; he uses it functionally to intensify the horror of his indictment. It has a larger and more poetic function still: the prose style concentrates in itself the very structure of the politico-economic system which was grinding the Irish people to pieces.

The basic irony of the *Proposal* is, of course, relatively simple, and the general purpose of the *Proposal* may even be said to be didactic. But it is eighteenth century didacticism with a difference. It is not that of Darwin's *Botanical Garden*, say, or of the *Essay on Man*.

For Swift himself believes in the social classes, hates "enthusiasm," sees the necessity for a matter-of-fact, realistic attack on the various problems which beset a civilization. In a sense, then, the honest Dublin citizen, whom Swift creates to make the *Proposal*, represents Swift himself, at least an aspect of Swift, while at the same time serving as the ironic foil for Swift's basic attitude. We can reconcile these conflicting functions, as they are reconciled in the *Proposal* itself, by saying that Swift gives us the impression of a violent attack on the treatment of the Irish, but an attack in which the violence does not nullify his recognition that the problem is a complex one. We feel that the attack is realistic and level-headed, not hysterical and quixotic, and our very sense of this poise makes the indictment the more damning.

Not all Swift's readers, however, have been able to feel that a convincing reconciliation of attitudes has been achieved. Swift, after all, *must* have been a rather callous man for so horrifying a conception ever to have occurred to him at all, or for him to have been able to treat it so coolly, even as fantasy. The same objection has been raised even more pointedly in connection with his *Tale of a Tub*. Many readers of later centuries have joined Queen Anne in feeling that a sincerely religious man could not have referred to a religion in which he really believed with metaphors so coarse and irreverent as those used in this satire. Swift was, therefore, something of a cynic. It was by precisely the same reasoning that Donne came to be regarded as a cynical love poet.

The *Modest Proposal* succeeds in being more passionate than any poem of the period, and its passion, in large part, is due to the method it employs, which is as indirect as Donne's. One is tempted to say that the poetry of the period fails, not because it was so much like prose—an age of prose and reason—but because it was so little like prose; because it could not incorporate into its being the prosaic; that is, the conflicting elements which are usually accommodated in prose.

The Beggar's Opera may be cited as a parallel case to the *Modest Proposal*. Gay found in the Newgate pastoral, which Swift proposed to him as a subject, means to absorb low materials, and means to develop a structure of ironies which parallels the earlier triumphs of the metaphysical poets. Empson shows how the play is at once a parody of the pastoral and a parody of the heroic, and how the resulting ironies reciprocate with each other. It is difficult to give examples short of quoting large sections of Empson's analysis. But his final paragraph may indicate how complex the make-up of the play is.

"For the final meaning of this play, whose glory it is to give itself so wholeheartedly to vulgarisation, I can only list a few approaches to its irony. 'I feel quite grateful to these fools; they make me feel sure I am right because they are so obviously wrong' (in this hopeful form satire is widely used to 'keep people going' after loss of faith); 'having got so far towards sympathy with the undermen, *non ragioniam di lor*, lest we come down to the *ultima ratio*'

(Voltaire not talking politics to his valet); 'one can see how impossible both the thieves and the politicians are if one compares them to heroes' (the polite literary assumption; the pose of detachment); 'low as these men are, the old heroes were like them, and one may well feel the stronger for them; life was never dignified, and is still spirited.' (The good spirits of Fielding making a Homeric parody of a village scuffle.) 'The old heroes were much more like the modern thief than the modern aristocrat; the present order of society is based on an inversion of real values' (Pope sometimes made rather fussy local satire out of this); 'this is always likely to happen; everything spiritual and valuable has a gross and revolting parody, very similar to it, with the same name; only unremitting effort can distinguish between them' (Swift); 'this always happens; no human distinction between high and low can be accepted for a moment; Christ on earth found no fit company but the thieves' (none of them accepted the full weight of the anarchy of this, but none of them forgot it; perhaps the mere easiness of Gay makes one feel it in him most easily). It is a fine thing that the play is still popular, however stupidly it is enjoyed."

Consideration of some of the detail of the play will indicate more clearly still its relation to the poetry of wit. Here are some of the lines from the play with Empson's comments:

——"That Jemmy Twitcher should peach me I own surprised me. 'Tis a plain proof that the world is all alike, and that even our gang can no more trust one another than other people; therefore, I beg you, gentlemen, to look well to yourselves, for, in all probability, you may live some months longer."

"And no more; take care because you are in danger" is the plain sense; but the turn of the phrase suggests "You may live as long as several months, so it is worth taking trouble. If you were dying soon like me you might be at peace." It is by these faint double meanings that he gets genuine dignity out of his ironical and genteel calm.

An odd trick is used to drive this home; as most literature uses the idea of our eventual death as a sort of frame or test for its conception of happiness, so this play uses hanging.

"Lucy. How happy am I, if you say this from your heart! For I love thee so, that I could sooner bear to see thee hanged than in the arms of another."

It is true enough, but she means merely "dead" by *hanged;* no other form of death occurs to her.

"Mrs. P. Away, hussy. Hang your husband, and be dutiful." *Hang* here has its real sense crossed with the light use in swearing—"don't trouble about him; he's a nuisance; be dutiful to your parents."

"Polly. And will absence change your love?

Mach. If you doubt it, let me stay—and be hanged."

"Whatever happens" or even "and be hanged to you," but he really would be hanged.

At its best the literature of the early eighteenth century shows the structure of early seventeenth-century poetry, but constricted and narrowed in scope.

It may seem rather remarkable that the *Modest Proposal* and *The Beggar's Opera* have been chosen here to represent the highest achievement of the first half of the eighteenth century, for they both have a large satiric element, and the traditional view holds that satire, by its very nature, lies outside the realm of great poetry. Indeed, the relative failure of neoclassic poetry has long been put down to the neoclassic poets' preoccupation with satire.

This Romantic criticism of neoclassic poetry deserves a little further commentary. Satire is not in itself inimical to the poetic impulse, though most formal satires, one may grant, fail to achieve the qualities of the greatest poetry. Perhaps one may best consider the matter in this way. We have already argued that particular scenes, words, or situations are not in themselves poetic or unpoetic; and by saying this, we may have seemed to remove altogether the possibility of setting up a distinction between satire and the other forms of poetry. Certainly we shall have removed the basis on which satire has been distinguished from the other forms in the past. But one may still make the distinction on the basis of the poet's attitude.

It is possible to isolate, on the one hand, an attitude of almost pure approval or sympathy, and, on the other, one of almost complete disapproval (the negative or satiric). The extremes, of course, are never realized in absolute purity; but we can point to a simple and affectionate love poem as tending to mark one limit, and to a simple and direct satire as marking the other. Now it is apparent that an attitude of almost any complexity will involve a mixture of these basic attitudes, whether it be in love poetry, or religious poetry, or tragedy. If this is true, the highest type of satire will hardly be recognizable as such. It will merge imperceptibly into some form like tragedy, for example. Seen in these terms, the Elizabethan period, no less than the eighteenth century, turns out to be a period in which the satiric element was very great though we shall have to look for examples to such works as *Hamlet, Timon of Athens,* and *Lear* rather than to the formal satires of Hall and Marston.

The prime mistake of the neoclassic period, then, was not that it gave vent to the satiric impulse but rather that it segregated it from other impulses, leaving its tragedy too noble and too easily didactic; or, on the other hand, when it attempted to stir the heartstrings, too sentimental. Neoclassic love poetry is too exclusively love poetry; neoclassic satire, too narrowly satiric.

The apparent exceptions test and corroborate the rule. The "Portrait of Atticus," we have said, is better than most of the portraits of *The Dunciad* because there Pope's judgment is most mixed and his attitude least simple. And to turn back to Dryden for a moment, Dryden's greatest sustained poem, in some respects, is his *Hind and the Panther;*

for his earlier allegiance to the Anglican Church and a continuing sympathy with, and understanding of, its position, make his satire complex and rich.

In general, the terms used commonly in the textbooks to describe neoclassic poetry need a thorough overhauling. The poetry of the Age of Reason is not, as we have seen, "intellectual." Its "perfection of form" is valid aesthetically only in so far as we subscribe to the limitations of form which the poets of the period accepted. If we mean by *form* the arrangement of the various elements of the poem in order to further the poet's total intention, then Keats's "Ode to Autumn" has perfection of form quite as much as does Pope's *Rape of the Lock;* and so, for that matter, does Donne's "Nocturnal on St. Lucy's Day." So also with terms like "propriety," "correctness," and "finish."

We have spoken thus far primarily of poets like Pope, Swift, and Gay. The so-called pre-Romantic poets require some further attention, though in speaking of Thomson we have anticipated a number of things which must be said of them. It is perfectly valid to consider them as "pre-Romantics," and the textbooks have doubtless been right in emphasizing the Romantic qualities to be found in them. But the textbooks have insisted rather too much on the metaphor of these poets "struggling to burst the fetters of neoclassicism." There is, in fact, a great deal of continuity in the poetry of the century.

The pre-Romantic poets, hardly less than Pope, are descriptive and didactic. There is little change in the structure of their poetry, though the descriptive and didactic matter is changed: rural landscapes for London ballrooms; didactic accounts of wool-raising, hunting, cane-growing, for the didactic *Moral Essays.*

It is true that the pre-Romantics tended more and more to write in Milton's blank verse or Milton's octosyllabic couplet than in the heroic couplet of Pope. But Milton, after all, even from a neoclassic point of view, had quite as good a title to classicism as did Pope. And Pope himself

had already got deep into Milton's debt in using such de-
vices as personification, classic allusions, and the magnifi-
cently general epithet.   Many an eighteenth-century poet
who might have been embarrassed somewhat at the charge
of romanticism preferred to follow what he conceived to be
Milton's classic practice rather than Pope's.

It is a little more to the point to notice what the imitators
of Milton in the eighteenth century preferred not to imitate
in his poetry.   For example, such daring and illogical state-
ments as

> The Sun to me is dark
> And silent as the Moon,
> When she deserts the night
> Hid in her vacant interlunar cave.

Samson speaks these magnificent lines in his blindness; but
logically the sun is no more "silent" than when he had his
eyesight.   The metaphor is justified, but it cannot be justi-
fied by eighteenth-century critical theory.   Milton's imi-
tators, for the most part, left such irrationalities alone; and
this is one of the reasons why their imitations are so much
less exciting than their original.   (Empson, in his *English
Pastoral Poetry*, has pointed out a great many such items
in examining Bentley's edition of *Paradise Lost*.)   They also
preferred to let alone Milton's continual and energetic word
play:

> . . . but still his strength conceal'd,
> Which *tempted* our *attempt,* and wrought our fall.

> Thither full fraught with mischievous revenge,
> *Accurst,* and in *a cursed* hour he hies.

> On the bare outside of this World, that seem'd
> *Firm* land imbosom'd without *Firmament* . . . [italics
> mine].

Such devices were presumably too Elizabethan—too close
to the pun—to attract an age given over to abstract pro-
priety.

A realization of the basic continuity of eighteenth-century poetry will explain many matters which most historians of English literature tend to obscure: for instance, why Collins and Gray, two poets who make consistent use of the Romantic materials—Gothic, Celtic, and Norse stories, and the scenery of country graveyards, for example—are justly regarded as two of the most "classic" of the English poets; or why a poet like Young could be a satirist in the manner of Pope and at the same time a member of the Graveyard School.

What it is important to see is that the changes introduced by the forerunners of Romanticism did little to reinvigorate metaphor or to make verse more flexible and varied ("rough"). The pre-Romantics do tend, as the century advances, toward more "wildness" (though they stop far short of the wildness of a Sandburg or a Whitman). They become bolder in their emphasis on the emotions, avowing themselves frankly to be enthusiasts. Most of all, they go to an extreme in insisting on the intrinsic poetic quality of certain classes of objects. But these tendencies lead them still farther away from the structure of Elizabethan poetry.

With many of the pre-Romantics, it is almost sufficient merely to point to the new poetic objects—owls, ivy, ruined towers, and yew trees. Indeed, some of their poems may be considered as little more than display cases filled with collections of such objects tied loosely together with appropriate interjections:

> See yonder Hallow'd Fane! the pious Work
> Of Names once fam'd, now dubious or forgot,
> And buried 'midst the Wreck of Things which were:
> There lie interr'd the more illustrious Dead.
> The Wind is up: Hark! how it howls! Methinks
> Till now, I never heard a Sound so dreary:
> Doors creak, and Windows clap, and Night's foul Bird
> Rook'd in the Spire screams loud. . . .

Perhaps never before or since have poetic terms become clichés so rapidly; and this is a measure of the weight of the dependence placed upon them in securing the poetic effect.

In such poetry there is the very minimum of metaphor. We can describe the process by which the metaphor was sloughed off as follows: The neoclassic poets had tended to use poetic materials in order to decorate or dignify the subject in question. The pre-Romantic poets (with a change, of course, in the kind of objects considered poetic) were often content merely to point to the objects themselves.

Robert Burns will illustrate the extreme to which emphasis on the materials of poetry had been pushed by the end of the century. For Burns's popularity represents, in large measure, an interest in local color and picturesque primitivism—interests not foreign to our own civilization. And Burns himself was not unwilling to play up to this interest. His frequent apologies for his ignorance and unconventionality fall somewhere between honest naïveté and knowing irony. Burns is never either the simple peasant on the one hand, nor on the other, the craftsman who is ironically attacking the reigning conventions. There is a certain self-consciousness about his work that is perhaps not to be completely detached from shrewdness. It is an impurity which injures some of his more serious work. The strongest element in Burns is to be found in his efforts to absorb the conventionally unpoetic into poetry. But the attempt is not made in his more serious poetry; it is limited to the satires and to the lighter verse: for example, "The Jolly Beggars," "To a Louse," or "Tam O'Shanter."

If this praise of Burns as a satirist and writer of light verse seems willfully perverse in view of Burns's reputation as a simple, artless poet, the poet of the heart, one must simply call for inspection of the poems in question. Ironically, for those who insist on "nature," it was not the romantic plowman who restored liberty to the imagination, but the cockney Blake. Blake represents, as Burns does not,

the return to the daring of Elizabethan metaphor, to the
use of serious irony, to a bold willingness to risk obscurity,
and even to something very close to metaphysical wit.

Blake's metaphor is vigorous. In "London," a sigh is
made to "run in tears down palace walls"; "the youthful
harlot's curse" blasts "the new-born infant's ear"; in "The
Mental Traveler" shrieks can be caught "in cups of gold";
in "The Scoffers" the grains of sand, blown back into the
scoffers' eyes, become, in turn, "gems" shining in the light
of truth, and then sands along the Red Sea shore over
which the Chosen People are to pass. The metaphor is
made to define and carry the idea; it represents a fusion of
image and idea, and is thus a successful attempt to break
through the deadening influence of Hobbes. In its kind it
stands almost alone in its period.

One further comment on Blake's wit. Consider the fol-
lowing lines from "London":

> How the chimney-sweeper's cry
> Every blackening church appalls. . .

The blackening of the church walls by the soot becomes a
sign of the church's sin in failing to protest against the un-
Christian exploitation of children as chimney sweepers,
the soot of the sweeps' trade besmirching the churches
themselves. But Blake goes further and states it as if the
cry of the child had the effect of a curse, and there is a
suggestion that the church is blackened at the cry as well
as appalled. Moreover, by the word *appalled*, Blake sug-
gests that the cry throws a pall over the church; the church
is dead. The poets of the early seventeenth century would
have had no trouble in recognizing this as a witty com-
parison, brilliantly and successfully executed. Blake is a
metaphysical poet. But the elements which make him such
a poet appeared rarely in the poetry of his period and never
elsewhere in a form so extreme. He remains an isolated
and exceptional figure.

With the flowering of the Romantic tendencies early in

the nineteenth century there were signs of more radical changes. There was a reconsideration of poetic diction and an attempt to found it on a broader base and to incorporate the unpoetic. Metaphor became somewhat more vigorous and daring. The metaphysical poets were read and elicited some praise even though no poems were modeled upon them. Coleridge, as we have seen, even provided a new charter for the imagination. But the belief that poetry inhered in certain materials persisted. Most of all, the poets distrusted the intellect.

The key to the problem lies in the new cult of simplicity. As we have said in an earlier chapter, the neoclassic poets, too, had desired to be simple. But they had wished to be simple in order to be logically clear. They had even wished to be "natural," but their naturalness consisted in an approximation to the inevitable and, since this was the eighteenth century, the *logical* order of the world.

Romantic simplicity, on the other hand, was something quite different from logical clarity. The emphasis had shifted from the logical perspicuity of the poetry to the emotional lucidity of the poet. The Romantic poet distrusted the intellect as inimical to emotion and destructive of spontaneity.

Wordsworth will illustrate. His distrust of the intellect and the subleties of wit rarely allows him to make use of indirection in his poetry. It is no accident, therefore, that many of his best poems are long. His finest effects—as in "Michael"—are usually the result of the use of a cumulative process rather than the use of a few, carefully selected dramatic symbols.

We have already quoted Yeats's account of Wordsworth's characteristic limitation as an artist—that he lacks dramatic quality, and because he lacks this, is often flat and heavy. "This," Yeats goes on to say, "increases his popularity with the better kind of journalists and politicians who have written books." Quite so. For a Wordsworth who was consciously dramatic, a Wordsworth behind the mask, might puzzle such readers—might have puzzled himself.

One of the most striking evidences of the inaccuracy of the traditional account of English poetry is seen in the ease with which Shelley and Keats are paired. I do not mean to say that critics have not always been aware of differences of method and effect between the two poets; I have in mind differences of poetic caliber. The traditional historian hardly sees Shelley as a very unsatisfactory poet greatly inferior to Keats. A more considered view must surely hold him so.

Shelley is not merely guilty of poor craftsmanship—slovenly riming, loosely decorative and sometimes too gaudy metaphor. Consideration of the two poets on the basis of tone and attitude will reveal more important differences. Keats is rarely sentimental, Shelley frequently so. Keats is too much the artist to risk Shelley's sometimes embarrassing declarations—"I die, I faint, I fail," or "I fall upon the thorns of life! I bleed!" Keats, even in his apprentice stage, attempts to give his lyricism a restraining form; he maintains his objectivity as in "To Autumn"; he attempts a qualifying self-irony as in the "Ode to a Nightingale."

There is surely no attempt to turn Keats into a Donne, or, for that matter, into a Shakespeare or Milton, if one observes that his most mature poetry can be brought under the general principles of symbolist-metaphysical poetry. And if Shelley, measured by these principles, comes off rather badly, the issue may be more important than some readers will at first be willing to allow. For the charges of sentimentality, lack of proportion, confusion of abstract generalization with symbol, and confusion of propaganda with imaginative insight are not charges to be dismissed lightly.

Does it add any clarification to say with one of the popular histories of English poetry that Keats "worships beauty for beauty's sake, with none of the secondary moral intentions of . . . Shelley"? Cannot the essential distinction between them be stated somewhat as follows: Shelley tends to make a point, to state a dogma, decking it with the beautiful and the ethereal. When his poetry fails, it fails through oversimplification or cloying floweriness. Keats, on the other hand, explores a particular experience—not as a favorite generalization to be beautified—but as an object to be explored in its full ramifications. Even the abstract statement, "Beauty is Truth, Truth Beauty, that is all/Ye know on earth," cannot be removed from the poem without violence. It is defined and given meaning only in terms of the context, and is taken legitimately only as a statement elicited by the preceding lines of the poem, and as one element in the whole experience. It is not intended to be a generalization which can march out of the poem and take its place alongside the scientific and practical generalizations of the workaday world.

Both Keats and Coleridge, indeed, are separated from their contemporaries by a reluctance to force didacticism. They respect the complexity of experience too much to violate it by oversimplification; the concrete, too much to indulge in easy abstractions. They think through their images. Instead of the formula employed by Shelley in his "Ode to a Skylark"—lush imagery followed by the abstract

> Our sweetest songs are those that tell
> of saddest thought . . .

Keats gives us the "Ode to a Nightingale." Instead of Wordsworth's rather flat generalization

> The eye—it cannot choose but see;
> We cannot bid the ear be still;
> Our bodies feel, where'er they be,
> Against or with our will.
>
> Nor less I deem that there are Powers
> Which of themselves our minds impress;
> That we can feed this mind of ours
> In a wise passiveness . . .

Coleridge, finding adequate symbols for the theme, gives us the "Rime of the Ancient Mariner," and the mariner achieves in his experience a dramatic contact with those Powers. But what a difference between the *experience* which Wordsworth's lines abstract and summarize and that which Coleridge's symbolist poem transmits. The comparison is unfair to Wordsworth because it measures one of his inferior poems against Coleridge's best poem; but it may throw light on Wordsworth's typical method and may indicate why Coleridge's great poem so far exceeds the triviality of its apparent subject.

Victorian poetry hardly calls for extended comment here. The points to be made against it on the basis already set forth are perfectly obvious, and have been made often—have been made even by people who would not accept an application of the same critical principles to the Romantic poets. The motive here is not to add anything to the indictment, but merely to relate the poetry of the Victorians to the foregoing pattern.

Victorian poetry does offer occasion for a convenient summary; for, if poetry since the Restoration has been characterized by a confusion between imaginative and scientific organization, the Victorian period will furnish an illustration of this confusion in its final and most extreme form. Poetry is left impaled on one of the two horns of the dilemma: poetry with a message, the "philosophy" of Tennyson and Browning—the attempt to substitute poetry for religion; or, on the other hand, pure poetry, art for art's sake.

With the progress of science in the nineteenth century, the later developments of science became harder and harder to reconcile with established values. The poet felt strongly the pressure upon himself to present solutions or at least inspirational messages. Life was too real and too earnest for him to tolerate what he had come to feel was a mere playing with ideas and images. Poetry tended to become, more or less consciously, a substitute for religion.

(One may also observe the converse: religion is charged with being merely "poetry," i.e., fairy tales, charming or malignant; or religion tries to purge itself of poetry altogether and become ethical philosophy.)

But the tendency to pure poetry or escapist poetry (and later, to some forms of imagist poetry) was also intensified by the increasing prestige of science. That prestige in the field of general statement discouraged poets from making statements of their own (as Mr. Max Eastman thinks that it should); or, the emphasis on scientific statement having deprived them of the particular and the ungeneralized, the poets retire into the realm of pure poetry. The dissociation of sensibility is complete.

The two tendencies are sometimes found in combination. One of Tennyson's weaker poems, "The Palace of Art," will illustrate, though their combination, as Tennyson attempted it here, is far from constituting a reunification of sensibility. In the poem, the soul is permitted to inhabit her pleasure house for several years before her selfishness is made to turn her joy into bitterness. But the reader, one should not forget, is allowed to indulge himself in the beauties also. The poet describes the details of the palace with loving enjoyment, and the reader is expected to find them beautiful too. It is in this inventory of the palace that the reader is expected to find the imagery, the description, the concrete, and the poetic. Poet and reader having tarried awhile in the Ivory Tower, the edifying moral is appended and didacticism is complied with.

The poem furnishes a crude example of the structure to be found in more subtle form in poem after poem of the period. Tennyson, and the other Victorian poets, have, of course, a stronger side. What it is important to observe is this: that Tennyson's characteristic fault, the dull and sometimes pompous didacticism of "Locksley Hall," on the one hand, and the incredible sentimentality of "Blush it through the East," on the other, are two defects which are really aspects of the same misconception of poetry. They are defects of which a poet like Marvell—whatever Marvell's faults are—could not have been guilty.

Browning may be thought to have fared somewhat better. And it is true that Browning attempts to come to terms with the unpoetic. He was consequently considered by his contemporaries to be sometimes fantastic and obscure. Indeed, there have lately been some attempts to use Browning as a sort of critical steppingstone to Donne. But the metaphysical elements in Browning are really very superficial. It is true that Browning avoids the extreme instances of Tennyson's faults. But Browning, where he breaks the Victorian conventions most, is least willing to be serious. A somewhat wider range of tone and a more vigorous dramatic sense are, thus, nullified by a lowering of the emotional tension. As F. R. Leavis has well put the matter, Browning's poetry "belongs to the world he lives in, and he lives happily in the Victorian world with no sense of disharmony. But is this altogether by reason of qualities that should recommend a poet? There are kinds of strength a poet is best without. And it is too plain that Browning would have been less robust if he had been more sensitive and intelligent."

Other nineteenth-century figures, some of them highly interesting, must be passed over. One would like to comment on Gerard Hopkins and Emily Dickinson as poets who transcended Victorianism, pointing out that their poetry, significantly, is characterized by the use of vigorous metaphor, the incorporation of the difficult and unpoetic, and the use of dramatic shifts of tone. (One notices too that they incur from conventional readers the charge of obscurity.) It would also be interesting to discuss the reasons for the appearance of pre-Raphaelitism as an anti-scientific movement and the reasons for its failure; or, the success of Matthew Arnold within certain rather narrow limits, and the necessity of those limits for his success; or, the Victorian restriction of wit to the *vers de société* of poets like Praed. But the treatment of such problems as these has been implied by the foregoing discussion.

The breakup of Victorianism and the break with the Victorians made by modern poets have already been treated in earlier chapters. William Butler Yeats in particular has been given special examination. But there is another modern English poet, Thomas Hardy, whom we have not mentioned, whose beginnings, like those of Yeats, go far back into the Victorian period. A comment on Hardy's relations to Victorianism and to the metaphysicals may properly bring these notes to an end.

We have interpreted Yeats's interest in "magic," Rosicrucianism, and all those modes of thought which deal, not with the scientific intellect but with the intellect expressing itself in symbols, as an attempt to transcend the limitations placed upon the imagination by Thomas Hobbes. We have claimed that his later poetry approximates the structure of the poets who wrote before Hobbes's influence had made itself felt.

Thomas Hardy is in some respects an even better test case than Yeats. Hardy had no conscious connection with the school of Donne. He attempted no radical re-estimates of the poetry of the past. For him, Shelley and Keats, apparently equally, were still "those matchless singers." But one may find in his work the structure of metaphysical poetry.

His characteristic fault, for example, is their fault—the heterogeneous yoked together rather than united. Victorian poetic diction, dialect words from Dorsetshire, Latinisms, coinages of the poet, often jangle together. And what is true of the diction is true of other aspects of his poetry. But on occasion Hardy does manage to fuse his material into a unity which serves his ironical contemplation of human circumstance. Like the seventeenth-century poets, he makes frequent use of the paradox.

His successful blending of opposites is perhaps most

clearly illustrated by such a poem as "The Convergence of
the Twain (Lines on the loss of the Titanic)." The great
ship and the iceberg, in man's purposes so utterly dissoci-
ated, are ironically meant for each other in the larger pur-
poses of fate.

> Alien they seemed to be:
> No mortal eye could see
> The intimate welding of their later history,

> Or sign that they were bent
> By paths coincident
> On being anon twin halves of one august event,

> Till the Spinner of the Years
> Said "Now!" And each one hears,
> And consummation comes, and jars two hemispheres.

The structure of the poem with its ironical contrasts—

> Over the mirrors meant
> To glass the opulent
> The sea-worm crawls—grotesque, slimed, dumb, indif-
> ferent—

serves to corroborate the dramatic tension set forth in the
poem. And the fable, the "intimate welding" of the ship
and the iceberg, is in itself a parable of fusion, the welding
of the opposed, which is the ground plan of the poem.
Hardy is successful, and the last line of the poem is true,
not only for the poet's particular fable, but for the internal
structure of the poem. Consummation does come, and
jars the reader himself with the charm and surprise of great
poetry.

This sketch of a new history of English poetry since the
Renaissance may well be regarded as an impertinence.
Some of the judgments are trite; others, heretical. More-
over, its brevity allows no room for saving qualifications or
convincing illustrations. It is frankly a sketch, but it may
serve to suggest the general theory of the history of English
poetry implied by the practice of the modern poets.

At the worst, at least this much may be said in its defense: the orthodox histories of English poetry do not offer a valid alternative. They will have to be rewritten—if not as expansion of the sketch just given, at least with more consistency than they now possess, and with emphasis on a more vital conception of the nature of poetry than that which now underlies them.

A SELECTED BIBLIOGRAPHY

OF MODERN CRITICISM

Blackmur, R. P. *The Double Agent.* New York, Arrow Editions, 1935.

Burke, Kenneth. *Counterstatement.* New York, Harcourt, Brace, 1931.

Eastman, Max. *The Literary Mind.* New York, Scribner's, 1931.

Eliot, T. S. *Selected Essays.* New York, Harcourt, Brace, 1932.

—— *The Use of Poetry.* Harvard University Press, 1933.

Empson, William. *Seven Types of Ambiguity.* London, Chatto and Windus, 1930.

—— *English Pastoral Poetry.* New York, Norton, 1938.

Housman, A. E. *The Name and Nature of Poetry.* Cambridge University Press, 1933.

Leavis, F. R. *New Bearings in English Poetry.* London, Chatto and Windus, 1932.

Lucas, F. L. *The Decline and Fall of the Romantic Ideal.* New York, Macmillan, 1937.

Matthiessen, F. O. *The Achievement of T. S. Eliot.* Boston and New York, Houghton Mifflin, 1935.

Ransom, John Crowe. *The World's Body.* New York, Scribner's, 1938.

Richards, I. A. *The Principles of Literary Criticism.* New York, Harcourt, Brace, 1925.

—— *Science and Poetry.* 2nd ed. London, Kegan Paul, 1935.

—— *Coleridge on Imagination.* New York, Harcourt, Brace, 1935.

Sparrow, John. *Sense and Poetry.* New Haven, Yale University Press, 1934.

Tate, Allen. *Reactionary Essays.* New York, Scribner's, 1936.

Yeats, W. B. *Autobiographies.* New York, Macmillan, 1926.

—— *Essays.* New York, Macmillan, 1924.

—— *A Vision.* New York, Macmillan, 1938.

—— *Wheels and Butterflies.* New York, Macmillan, 1934.

INDEX

J